Mass Media Between the Wars

Mass Media
Between the Wars

*PERCEPTIONS OF
CULTURAL TENSION, 1918-1941*

Edited by **Catherine L. Covert**
and **John D. Stevens**

Syracuse University Press 1984

Library of Congress Cataloging in Publication Data
Main entry under title:

Mass media between the wars, 1918-1941.

      Bibliography: p.
      Includes index.
      1. Mass media—United States—History—20th century—
Addresses, essays, lectures, 2. United States—Popular
culture—Addresses, essays, lectures. I. Covert,
Catherine L. II. Stevens, John D.
P92.U5M285 1984   302.2'34'0973   83-20329
ISBN 0-8156-2037-0

Manufactured in the United States of America

Contents

Contributors

JAMES BOYLAN is head of the journalism studies program at the University of Massachusetts, Amherst. Editor of the *Columbia Journalism Review* from 1961 to 1969 and 1976 to 1979, he edited an anthology from the *New York World* in 1973. His study on the election of 1946 is forthcoming. He holds a Ph.D. in history from Columbia University.

CATHERINE L. COVERT was professor of public communications at Syracuse University until her death in 1983. Past head of the History Division of the Association for Education in Journalism and Mass Communications, she earned a doctorate in history from Syracuse. She published on many aspects of culture, professionalism, and mass media.

MARK FACKLER is an associate professor in the Department of Speech-Communication, University of Minnesota, Minneapolis. He received a Ph.D. in communications from the University of Illinois in 1982. He has contributed to *Journalism Quarterly, Journal of Communication,* and is co-author of *Media Ethics: Cases and Moral Reasoning* (1982).

SALLY F. GRIFFITH is a Ph.D. candidate in history at The Johns Hopkins University. Her chapter was written during her tenure as a predoctoral fellow at the Smithsonian Institution. It forms a part of her doctoral dissertation on William Allen White's editorship of the *Emporia Gazette,* 1895-1930.

MICHELLE HERWALD was assistant professor at Chatham College in Pittsburgh, Pennsylvania. She received her Ph.D. in cultural history at the University of Michigan and has taught at Oregon and Mt. Holyoke College. She is the author of a forthcoming book, a cultural analysis of *Amazing Stories,* the first science fiction magazine. Under a grant from the National Endowment for the Humanities she is currently working on a study of popular culture during World War II.

MICHAEL KIRKHORN is associate professor of journalism at the Univerity of Kentucky. He was a Nieman Fellow at Harvard University, and he received a Ph.D. in public communication from the Union Graduate School in 1978. His professional affiliations have included the *Milwaukee Journal* and the *Chicago Tribune,* and his articles have been published in a number of national magazines. He is currently studying journalistic habits and rituals.

MARION MARZOLF is associate professor of communication at the University of Michigan where she received a Ph.D. in American studies. Her history of women in American journalism, *Up from the Footnote,* has received a national research award. She has published widely on the immigrant press, and is currently working on a study of the American journalist and the new journalism of the 1890s.

JAMES E. MURPHY taught journalism and mass communications at Southern Illinois University, Carbondale, before his death in 1983. He received a Ph.D. in mass communications from the University of Iowa. Formerly a member of the Marquette University faculty, he also published in the history of Native American publications.

JOAN SHELLEY RUBIN, who received a Ph.D. from Yale University, is assistant professor of history and American studies at the State University of New York, Brockport. She is the author of *Constance Rourke and American Culture* (1980) and is at work on a study of the dissemination of elite culture in modern America.

MICHAEL SCHUDSON is associate professor in the department of sociology and communication at the University of California, San Diego. He is the author of *Discovering the News* (1978) and the forthcoming *Advertising in American Culture.* He received a Ph.D. from Harvard and taught at the University of Chicago.

RICHARD A. SCHWARZLOSE teaches at the Medill School of Journalism, Northwestern University. He has contributed to various journals on subjects in communication history, ethics, teaching, and press-government relations. His bibliographic essay on newspapers appears in the third volume of the *Handbook of American Popular Culture* (1981), and his dissertation, *The American Wire Services, A Study of Their Development as a Social Institution,* has been reprinted by Arno Press. He received a Ph.D. in communications from the University of Illinois.

JOHN D. STEVENS is professor of communication at the University of Michigan and former head of the History Division of the Association for Education in Journalism and Mass Communications. His most recent books are *Communciation History* (1980), and *Shaping the First Amendment* (1982). He received a doctorate in mass communication from the University of Wisconsin.

WARREN SUSMAN is professor of history and director of the Center for Cultural Studies at Rutgers University. A former vice-president of the American Historical Association, he has written widely on the period between the two wars. He edited *Culture and Commitment* (1973) and contributed the influential essay, "'Personality' and Twentieth Century Culture," to *New Directions in Intellectual History* (1979).

JENNIFER TEBBE is associate professor of political science and American studies at Massachusetts College of Pharmacy and Applied Health Sciences in Boston. She received a Ph.D. in American studies from Case Western Reserve University. Her publications include "Print and American Culture" in the 1981 bibliography issue of *American Quarterly*. She is working on a study of the history of television advertising in America.

Preface

> "No," he added, "I shall not resort to clichés, I will not say that at eighty-three I have become sated. Only those who have never lived say that." He threw back his head, laughing, and in the same movement raised his hands, saying it was mere pretense to believe oneself immune to surprise. . . . Only a deep sense of insecurity would force a man to suffer such a foolish loss as that of his innate capacity to be amazed. . . . Death conquers only those who are not surprised by it; life as well.
>
> Carlos Fuentes, *Distant Relations* (1982)

In September of 1913 a small American magazine, *Poetry and Drama,* published a manifesto issued by the Committee of the Futurist Movement in Milan. Celebrating what it called the new "wireless imagination," the manifesto seemed to explode from the page. Indeed its author, the young Italian F. T. Marinetti, was gaining a name among artists as a "genius" of the modern spirit. A complete renewal of the human sensibility, he declared, had taken place with the stunning new technology of communication.

The telegraph, the phonograph, the film, and the big daily paper had joined to produce a new modern consciousness. Life would now be suffused with passion, art, and idealism. There would be a horror of the old, a love of the unforeseen.

Marinetti himself would wind up ignominiously in the future he invoked, an artist turned Fascist demagogue. But his lyrical outburst of 1913 was prophetic for his American readers. Mass communications would indeed be increasingly linked to a new kind of consciousness, specifically in the 1920s and the 1930s. And his relish for the unforeseen, the unexpected, would provide a key concept in understanding both process and period.

The essays to this book take from Marinetti's version two elements. First they see in his "wireless imagination" a symbol of a new kind of interaction between consciousness and culture increasingly evident to people of that period and increasingly important to us as historians now. It is a major purpose of this book to point up the importance of the 1920s and the 1930s as a period in which people exhibited what our keynote essayist, Warren Susman, calls a "cultural concern" for the relationship between communication and their experience. The thoughtful among them became increasingly conscious of communication—both personal and mass communication—as a factor in shaping lives and as fundamental concern for individuals. There was also, says Susman, an ironic sense that amid burgeoning mass communications people were, in fact, *not* communicating as they wished to. With the awareness came a search for ways to resolve the dilemma.

Secondly, the essayists in this book appropriate Marinetti's emphasis on the unforeseen, using it as a probe. They pay close attention to what people of the 1920s and 1930s see as "unexpected" and to how they react. People dealing with what seems to them unprecedented are people off balance. They may love it, as Marinetti asserted, or they may fight, flee, contain, or deny, but they must cope in some way. There is no steady state. They are not frozen in historical postures. The dynamics of their situation—the action and the feeling—come sharply into focus.

The disconcerting close-up of the new movies is an example. Early viewers saw on the screen an appalling, gigantic face which came swimming into view, as one man said, "without any arms or legs!" People simply had no experience with huge, disembodied faces. Their shock can highlight the normal context in which moving faces had been seen. It can point up the discontinuity between those old human conditions for encounter and the new dehumanized context — telephone, phonograph, wireless, film — in which they were increasingly embedded by World War I.

The years after World War I with their ostentatious courtship of "normalcy" would seem offhand to be bad candidates for a study of the abnormal. And yet as such a period strongly endorses one value, there may appear a fascination with it hidden underside, its anti-value. Subsequently, the anti-value materializes openly and full force. Such a paradox operated between 1918 and 1941. Despite relief at the end of war and its disruptions, those who stayed home in America as well as the expatriate adventurers seemed restless and searching. Almost 400,000 readers crowded the New York Public Library in 1921. Such masses were seeking something, said one librarian, "an emancipation of the intellectual life . . . a broadening of the spiritual life . . . perhaps a new religion." At the other end of the cultural scale a favorite *avant-garde* style among artists and writers was the surrealist, the juxtaposition of the disconnected and the inapposite, to achieve through shock and surprise some fugitive meaning unavailable any other way.

For some the search for meaning evaporated, leaving only the cultivation of shock for its own sake, the "delicious *frisson*" invoked by Edmund Wilson for the intelligentsia, the "thrill killing" set forth by the tabloids for the plebeians. For still others, there was a retreat into irony or disillusion. But by the 1930s the unexpected no longer needed to be courted; neither could it be avoided or suppressed. Depression, dictatorship, war—the antithesis of normalcy had arrived.

In 1929, the crucial hinge year between the two decades, Walter Lippmann blamed the whole sensibility on the mass media. "Novelties crowd the consciousness of modern man," he asserted, "the press, the radio, the moving picture, have enormously multiplied the number of unseen events and strange people and queer doings with which he has to be concerned. . . . [He] finds it increasingly difficult to believe that through it all there is order, permanence, and connecting principle."

The sense of enforced concern with queer doings was sometimes precipitated by media content, sometimes by their form. And from the contrast between what Americans of the 1920s and 1930s had historically *expected* and what they in fact *found,* as reflected in mass media, the essayists in this volume illumine contrasts between old and new assumptions. They get a better fix on value tensions of the age.

What was considered "news," for example, provides a prime clue to hidden assumptions. From what was reported as unexpected, one can deduce what had been expected, valued, taken for granted. Indeed, the ideal news story of the period was a small expeditionary force, organized to fare past the edges of the normal and to bring back whatever would upset the settled perceptions of the group. Every astonishing headline, newscast, or newsreel implied an affronted norm.

Take the news stories between 1910 and 1925 pointing with dismay to the "invasion of privacy" committed by radio. The idea that anyone should expect privacy in talking over the radio seems ridiculous to us, trapped as we are in our idea that radio means broadcasting to all in range. Pondering these early stories, one finally sees they report an affront to the old assumption born of late nineteenth-century experience that the new radio would be a telephone without wires, that it ought therefore to connect two people for private talk, and that "listening in" was unethical if not a crime. From this one can further postulate larger assumptions about rights and threats to privacy, in increasingly compelling concern as the century advanced. Thus the idea of the unexpected in media content pointed out hitherto unnoticed cultural assumptions.

Sometimes media form did the same thing, providing an especially helpful diagnostic device in that it changed so strikingly through these two decades. Old and new cultural preoccupations were reflected in the contrast between old and new expressive patterns, indeed, appearing at every cultural level. In high culture there was formal innovation in literature, drama, and the arts. Such innovation was paralleled in the popular media. New form voiced new values, put shape to beliefs in conflict.

Out of growing tension over free expression as well as rationalization of industry and commerce came new forms of radio and film. Out of sharpening cultural conflict between the sensual and the material matured journalistic styles of sensationalism and objectivity. Out of the accelerating tempo of commercial lives came the pre-shrunk opinions of *Time* magazine; out of self-conscious urbanism, *The New Yorker;* out of the mounting power of corporate industrialism, *Fortune;* out of the increasing acceptability of the reproduced visual image, *Life.* To such probing of the relationship between culture and mass communications in the period between the wars this book devotes its three sections. Essays in the first section pursue the theme of connection, illustrating first the idea that historic media forms connect the past to the present when they are read now as symbolic texts to attitudes in past culture. Secondly, they debate ways in which the mass media connected the individual to the culture — and individuals to each other — within their own historic period.

Essayists in the second section focus more intensively on relating media form and content to the ways they were experienced by people of the period. Individuals hoped for great things from innovation in technology and form. They had ventured into new ways of communicating with euphoria. Yet media often seemed to frustrate expectations. While philosophers and sociologists debated, media consumers grew disillusioned; media professionals dropped out. Essays in this section frequently convey a sense of individuals alienated, hopes betrayed.

In the third section, essayists perceive human attempts to transcend alienation and frustration amid the media machines. These essayists discern a certain resurgence of individual creativity, choice and responsibility. They suggest that all professionals did not succumb to rigidities of media form or content, that all consumers were not battered into submission by technology or professional expertise. In this final section comes the suggestion of resilience, of the search for mastery by professionals and consumers, individuals and groups.

These are the themes and questions addressed by this book,

themes and questions which arose in this unsettled period and which have since remained to trouble the peace of those concerned about communication and culture in this century.

When John D. Stevens and I first discussed the idea on which this book is based, we determined to bring together two kinds of historians to discuss it: those on faculties of schools in mass communication and those based in academic departments of history. The two groups typically present their work to different meetings and publish in different journals. We wanted a blend of older and younger scholars. What we got was a rich mix, not only of ages and historical perspectives, but of subjects, disciplines, and methods.

Another feature of this book is the particularly comprehensive bibliography on history, culture, and communications prepared by Jennifer Tebbe, of the Massachusetts College of Pharmacy, Boston, Massachusetts.

Thanks to a grant from the Howard R. Marsh Center for the Study of Journalistic Performance at the Department of Communication, University of Michigan, the men and women represented in this volume came together to debate their ideas in an Ann Arbor conference under Stevens' leadership on October 30 and 31, 1981. Acknowledgment is made to the S. I. Newhouse School of Public Communications at Syracuse University which has made posssible a semester's leave enabling me to complete the process of editing their work. Special thanks go to these insightful critics, David Hollinger, Terry Hynes, Wiliam Porter, and Howard Segal, and Marion Marzolf, and to Maxwell McCombs for good counsel on both conference and publication. We are grateful to the Syracuse University Communications Research Center for editorial support and to Lynne E. Manuel for creative attention to preparation of the manuscript. We thank especially the Syracuse Univerity Press for the care and immagination devoted to seeing this book through production.

Extensively revised after the conference, the essayists' contributions range across newspaper, magazine, radio, and film. They treat a variety of media functions — information, entertainment, advertising, public relations. Shaped principally by a cultural studies approach, they draw also on sociology, anthropology, political science, literature, and philosophy. Individual essays are influenced by histories of sensibility, of professsionalism, of technology.

Nonetheless the most notable combination comes in juxtaposing the views of the academic historians, on the one hand, with those of historians in communication schools, on the other. Although academic historians in this century have broadened their classic concern for political history through waves of attention to social, cultural, and intellectual experience, they seldom have viewed the mass media as more than evidentiary sources — to document dates and events or to denounce as "distorting" more complex phenomena. Until the recent emergence of a history which has ranged more adventurously across social and cultural levels, with a companion focus on the ways both elite and common folk communicated, the mass media have been transparent to such historians' gaze. To them the media have appeared a means of viewing history, not fit historical subjects in themselves.

Historians in schools of mass communication traditionally focused on personal and institutional histories, isolated from almost all more general historical process except the political, and from almost all media process except that of print journalism. Only within the last half century has a connection been forged between media and social history; only in the last few years has significant attention attached to electronic as well as print communications and to the technological, economic, and industrial implications of both. Media process as emblematic of cultural or intellectual process is still fresh territory for media historians too.

On this little-trod ground, both groups meet. In these essays their perspectives merge or clash. Their intent is not to produce definite answers, but to define larger questions, questions increasingly relevant now amid another revolution in communication.

Carlos Fuentes says that if you chase the past out the window, it will come back through the front door again, wearing the strangest disguises. It is good to understand the past for its own sake. And if it does nonetheless appear again, perhaps that understanding can help us penetrate the disguise.

Wellfleet, Massachussetts   Catherine L. Covert

Summer 1983

Communication and Culture
Keynote Essay

Warren Susman

Any essay which discusses, however informally, the history of mass communication must of necessity take note of the significance of form. And thus the form of one's discourse itself comes to be a significant matter.

The ideal essay, of course, would be formulated to include a few carefully chosen texts — preferably anthropological. The text would be followed by several significant caveats, as prelude to a series of assertions — bold ones, of course — that in a speculative essay may stand free of ordinary proof or demonstration. And of course one should finish with a peroration, one sufficiently eloquent so that one's readers would fail to recall the author's many errors in the course of the essay itself. Texts, caveats, assertions, peroration: certainly enough formal apparatus to satisfy the most devout historian of culture and communications.

My texts (anthropological):

> Communication constitutes the core of culture and indeed of life itself.
>
> Edward T. Hall (1966)

> Culture communicates; the complex interconnectedness of cultural events itself conveys information to those who participate in those events. . . . We must know a lot about the cultural context, the setting of the stage, before we can even begin to decode the message.
>
> Edmund Leach (1976)

My caveats:

Too many of us who study mass communications have tried to decode the messages we have discovered without sufficient awareness of a larger cultural context. That "complex interconnectedness" of which the distinguished British social anthropologist speaks should alert us to the difficulties we face and the risks we run when we isolate aspects of the larger, more general communicative process that in fundamental ways is culture itself. Our work, for practics fact — for indeed we are all aware that media somehow affect the general culture while at the same time the general culture shapes the media — we will miss the crucial issue of *relationships,* perhaps the most essential of all cultural questions. We have often become insistent on thinking in too rigid and awkward causal terms; we ought rather to be thinking "ecologically," in terms of a total interacting environment. The environment of communications should be our central concern. And if we can remember Leach's fundamental statement "culture communicates," we will begin to know better what we mean when we write about communication.

All my other caveats follow from this approach. My second caveat warns against any kind of technological determinism. The acceptance of any technological innovation obviously depends on the nature of the culture into which any proposed innovation is introduced. Even more significantly, the *form* such innovation takes is culturally shaped. When we speak of the impact of the automobile on American society, for example, we do not mean simply a technological achievement but a particular form of that engineering accomplishment. Henry Ford's genius lay not only in his mastery of the technique of mass production. Rather we can attribute to him a real cultural revolution as well: the "invention" in some real sense of the "form" this automobile would take. For it was Ford who created the idea of the Family Car, owned, operated, repaired by the family head, used by the family primarily for leisure purposes. Ford did not invent the automobile or even the significant new engineering details. But he transformed the invention from the plaything of the well-to-do to the necessity of every family. He took a technological innovation and created a special cultural form from it.

Culture also shaped the motion picture, even though its inventors had a limited vision of the nature and function of film. At the very outset of the creation of film as form in France, two very different propositions for cultural form seemed to compete: the brothers Lumière concentrated on brief films of everyday life, using the motion picture camera to record and document; George Melies (present when the Lumière brothers showed their first films in 1895) concentrated his efforts on the world of illusion made possible by the use of trick photography. Further, the significant form of film best known today can be said to have been created by D. W. Griffith for American middle-class audiences with his *Birth of a Nation* (1915). This development occurred more than ten years after the "birth" of a film industry, and it was to be the cultural form in which American films have made their great impact ever since. My point is not simply to spotlight significant creators of cultural forms. Rather, study indicates that only after a fuller comprehension of the cultural context in which each creator worked, the cultural context in which such work was accepted, can we begin to understand. I stress the ecological approach.

Third, we must pay careful attention to the problems raised by form *and* content and the precise relationship between them. We must not speak abstractly about technologies but rather see them concretely within the culture; so too we must avoid abstract discussions of formal matters and issues of content. Here we run into several problems. We begin with the almost inevitable separation of cultural products: high, popular, folk, for example. Or at least, since the days of Van Wyck Brooks, highbrow and lowbrow. This leads us to assume that popular culture is radically different from high culture. And so it in fact may be. But my ecological vision forces me to think again; there must be some relationship, if not in form then in content (issues, problems, themes) or if not in content perhaps in form ("advanced" literature's fascination for the "forms" of modern art, the film, etc. as formal literary devices). Do popular cultural matters operate by "formula" and high cultural by "conventions?" And how different are they? Or, better, how do these cultural products relate, how do they or can they coexist?

These questions suggest a series of other problems. One of the more difficult problems is the precise relationship between form and content, especially in the popular culture provided by the media. New technological developments too often seem to signal radical cultural transformation. A Whig theory of change results, generally: not only is the cultural and social order transformed, but those transformations "modernize" and improve life. In fact, given a culture that pre-exists and has consequences (recall "culture communicates") there is no reason to assume either the necessity of overwhelming change or that in fact what is basic to that culture has changed. Certain formal elements may change without any deeper social or even psychological changes.

Even more startling, we have many examples that specifically reveal that the most radical change in form may still retain the most traditional content. For example, D. W. Griffith is in fact an *avant-garde* artist. His methods of editing, his brilliant and complex use of a variety of

shots to special effect, all suggest a master modernist, an innovator creating new possibilities for motion pictures readily recognized by critics and
students alike. So advanced were some of his techniques that audiences
were sometimes puzzled and confused (witness *Intolerance,* 1916). Yet for
all of his formal radicalism there is nothing very radical or even new about
the basic content of his films, the story line, his ideas about women,
masculinity, family, virtue. Here he remains a mid-nineteenth century
Victorian. An even better example would be conservative content of the
radio soap operas of the 1930s. Soaps were the source of countless jokes.
And yet, the formal method of the lowly soaps has exceptional aspects.
Time is stretched out almost endlesslessly. Several weeks of program can in
fact be only a few minutes in the "life" of those in the story itself. Such a
radical readjustment of formal temporal order has significant consequences for the listener. A form is created that in some ways appears radically
different from the supposed real-life content. Thus changes in media may
effect changes in both form and content or in one or the other or in the
relationship between them. The matter is far from simple in this world of
relationships.

There remains at least one final problem in relation to this caveat:
When analysts attempt to read the message of the soaps in the response of
the audience, to what, in fact, is the audience reacting? Are they reacting to
both form *and* content? One or the other? The form of the soap may be
considered at least as important or even more important than the content:
the ritual of repeated programs daily, the ritual closing and ending, even
the ritual placement of the commercials might have communications
consequences. The ritual itself might indeed be the message. I know this
kind of analysis offends those who believe the pill is more important than
the ritual of taking it, but I am one of those who will continue to wonder
what the role of instructions ("take every three hours") plays in the efficacy
of the pill-taking. Even the very act of listening or seeing has cultural
consequences, if only because the cultural setting itself proposes a meaning
to these acts.

Fourth, the ecological model should alert us to the dangers of
complete surrender to the media or to a new technological innovation as a
characteristic cultural response. Too many critics of contemporary culture
audiences give way before every new technology and are easily manipulated by powerful media. Complex cultures, however, rarely operate this
way; moreover, there is often resistance to both new technologies and to
what the media propose. This resistance is a cultural fact of profound
significance too little explored. Too little interested in the holdouts and
their achievements, cultural historians, like military historians, are too

COMMUNICATION AND CULTURE

often interested in the victors and what they have won. Further, when this factor is analyzed along with the modifications required because of existing cultural patterns, a very different story often surfaces from the one historians of communciation like to tell.

My fifth caveat is perhaps an unnecessary warning, implicit in those that have gone before. Since culture shapes experience, it obviously shapes the way we will respond to new technologies and new media; it will shape the anticipations we have of them and of the world in which we live. Thus, in the interwar period there were expectations built into the complex culture we are discussing. Culture offers us ways to anticipate; and it gives us methods of coping with the unanticipated, and the unexpected. We must pay careful attention to the expected and unexpected, and to the ways the culture provides for dealing with both.

In the New York World's Fair of 1939-40, communications played a crucial role in visualizing the future. Yet the Fair itself refused to recognize the beginnings of a second World War, surely something of consequences for a World of Tomorrow. Furthermore, with all the enthusiasm for human use of new technology, the Fair's experts were often mistaken; they were trapped too clearly in their own world. Norman Bel Geddes, whose Furturama for General Motors was the hit exhibition of the Fair, projected the new cities and the new world demanded by the automobile, General Motors' main product, but he failed to consider anywhere near the number of filling stations such a volume of cars would require. The point is that anticipation is cultural, as are the ways in which we cope with the unexpected. Imagination in real ways, and therefore the imaginary, are shaped by culture.

My last caveat: always remember that an investigator is a product of the culture he or she is investigating. When we think about communication or culture, we are participants in a discussion and a debate which has been characteristic of this culture for a long time. One reason we talk so persistently about the impact of media is because talking and thinking about the media and technology have become cultural characteristics. In a sense, we are hardly able *not* to think and talk about the media. And we engage in this enterprise with a particular set of questions and a special language provided for us from the start. Not only do the media help shape the way we think about the media, but thinking about the media helps shape the way the media operate. There is a complex relationship between the way the media are used and the way we think about those uses.

The time has come for some assertions. I have already suggested the first: from at least the middle of the nineteenth century, there occurred what historians have called a "communication revolution." By this is generally meant a fundamental change in the way goods, services, people, and ideas are put in motion over space by the application of new forms of steam, electricity, and machines. Those who have studied this revolution have been concerned primarily with its economic and social consequences. At least as important were fundamental changes in the way of thinking about the world. Of course, the very conception of time and space was transformed. But along with this change came different ways of thinking about man and society. While these are generally known, these changes have been too seldom analyzed as a foundation of the way we think about culture and communications today.

My assertion: by the 1920s there had developed a way of thinking about society, culture and communications that was to have significant consequences for communication itself. Late nineteenth and early twentieth century American thinkers worried about community, haunted by the fear that the new urban, industrial world of mass communications would destroy real community. Thus, thinkers often began with a definition of community. For Josiah Royce, America's leading Idealist thinker, the human self knows himself through a process of interpretation, what others tell him about himself, what he sees in others about himself. Community, therefore, is essential if there is to be any self knowledge, and any real community is in fact a community of interpretation. He defines the community in terms of communication.

George Herbert Mead, the American pragmatist at the University of Chicago, defined society as a series of social acts. A social act itself, he said, is a communicative process. And the sociologist Charles H. Cooley at the University of Michigan defined society in *Social Organization* (1909) as a mental complex held together by communications.

At the new University of Chicago, established in the 1890s, philosophers, sociologists, and educators showed exceptional concern for the problem of communication. Park, Small, Burgess, Thomas, Dewey, Mead, and their students not only studied the role of the media and of communication in the ghetto and the neighborhood, but they also expressed deep concern over the disappearance of face-to-face communication previously thought to make the family, the group, the community possible. This concern often represented a real fear of modern civilization.

Many social theorists pragmatically began to see mass communication as an answer to the problem of the disappearance of face-to-face communication. These theorists argued that instruments of communication might help create their own communities based on electronic communications themselves and no longer on geography or on any kind of contiguity. Could the new community be forged from the instruments of the new communicators? The most sanguine glimpsed enormous possibility here.

At the start of the interwar period, thinkers were examining both the great potential and the terrible price those possibilities might entail. Edward Sapir captured these tendencies in his article on Communications for the *Encyclopedia of Social Sciences* (1930). He wrote that the increase in the sheer radius of communication, the lessening of the importance of geography, can be had only at some cost. Communication cannot be kept "within desirable bounds." It tends to cheapen literary and artistic values.

> All effects which demand a certain intimacy of understanding tend to become difficult and are therefore avoided. It is a question of whether the obvious increase of overt communication is not being constantly corrected . . . by the creation of new obstacles to communication. The fear of being too easily understood may, in many cases, be more aptly defined as the fear of being understood by too many — so many, indeed, as to endanger the psychological reality of the image of the enlarged self confronting the not-self.

At the same time Sapir spoke with enthusiasm of the new communications making the whole world the "psychological equivalent of a primitive tribe."

For those of you who hear premature echoes of Marshall McLuhan in these analyses you are quite within reason. The philosophers and sociologists at Chicago, in fact, helped train Harold Innis, Canada's great historian of communications, who, in turn, helped train Marshall McLuhan. When the University of Chicago was founded, the coming of Marshall McLuhan seemed almost inevitable in the logic of ecological cultural history. The debate over the role of communications exploded most fittingly in the media in the 1880s and 1890s and found a specific center in Chicago, that hub of communications. This discussion is an important aspect of the story of communications.

The period 1920-40, an era when the study of communication emerges as a field in its own right, holds a special place in this history. By 1928 I. A. Richards, the literary critic, is able to offer one of the first definitions of communications as a discrete aspect of the human experience: "Communication takes place when one mind so acts upon its environment that another mind is influenced, and in that other mind an experience occurs which is like the experience of the first mind, and is caused in part by the experience."

By the 1920s there is a sharpening and a focusing on the issue of culture and communication. Significant doubts flourish amid significant hopes. But all agree that there was a new world and that communication in large part had helped make it.

Perhaps a literary reference will make my assertion even more dramatically clear. In 1919 Sherwood Anderson published a volume of short stories about a small middle-western town, Winesburg, Ohio, which he called "a book of grotesques." Each of these stories deals with some psychological transformation in the life of one or another residents of Winesburg, which Anderson explains from a nearly sociological perspective:

> In the last fifty years a vast change has taken place in the lives of our people. A revolution has in fact taken place. The coming industrialism, attended by all the roar and rattle of affairs, the shrill cries of millions of new voices that have come among us from overseas, the going and coming of trains, the growth of cities, the building of the interurban car lines that weave in and out of towns and past farmhouses, and now in these later days the coming of the automobiles has worked a tremendous change in the lives and in the habits of thought of our people of Mid-America. Books, badly imagined and written though they may be in the hurry of our times, are in every household, magazines circulate by the millions of copies, newspapers are everywhere. In our day a farmer standing by the stove in the store in his village has his mind filled to overflowing with the words of other men. The newspapers and the magazines have pumped him full. Much of the old brutal ignorance that had in it also a kind of beautiful childlike innocence is gone forever. The farmer by the stove is brother to the men of the cities, and if you listen you will find him talking as glibly and as senselessly as the best city man of us all.

In the world before such changes, Anderson tells us, men did not need words in books and magazines and newspapers. By implication, one might assume, they did not need motion pictures and radios. For they had God, not in a book, but in their hearts. Now "Godliness," the title of the story from which this passage comes, is problematic.

The genius of *Winesburg, Ohio* is its formulation of what became a brilliant and central paradox. Here in the age of easy and mass communication of press, movies, radio, automobile, telegraph, telephone, photograph; here in an age when it appears everyone can know what everyone else knows, everyone can know what everyone else thinks; here no real, private, human communication is possible. I think it not insignificant that the hero in Anderson's book, George Willard, is a newspaperman and that the hotel he lives in, run by his Mother, is next to the railroad which will take him out of town forever in the final story. The telegraph, as well as the newspaper, is featured in several stories. One of Anderson's characters, a telegraph operator, becomes a poet in the story in which he figures. Yet, it is ironic that the citizens of Winesburg are totally unable to communicate with one another. "The communion between George Willard," Anderson tells us, "and his Mother was outwardly a formal thing without meaning." Anderson even uses the word "communion," attaching a religious signifi- cance to genuine communciation. This newspaper man, however, is a creature of forms without significance (is that the world of mass communications?).

This theme — the fundamental problem of public versus private communication, and the suggestion that one makes the other impossible — dominates aspects of the culture and is crucial to any understanding of it in the twentiety century. It lay at the heart of many questions that have been defined basically as sociological and psychological. The problem itself was definitively presented in the period under review. No more brilliant example can be found than in one of the greatest literary achieve- ments of the period. Very early in Robert Musil's *The Man Without Qualities* (1930) the Austrian novelist offers a discussion of a possible place where one might spend one's life, or at least, a place where it would be smart to stay. Musil's analysis represents an ideal toward which Americans strive while at the same time indicates the price that might have to be paid:

> For some time now such a social *idée fixe* has been a kind of super-American city where everyone rushes about, or stands still, with a stopwatch in his hand. Air and earth form an ant-hill, veined by channels of traffic, rising storey upon storey. Overhead trains, overground trains, underground trains, pneumatic express mails carrying consignments of human beings, chains of motor vehicles all racing along horizontally, express lifts vertically pumping crowds from one traffic level to another ... At the junctions one leaps from one means of transport to another, is instantly sucked in and snatched away by the rhythm of it, which makes a syncope, a pause, a little gap of twenty seconds between two roaring outbursts of speed, and in these intervals in the general rhythm one hastily exchanges a few words with others. Questions and answers click into each other like cogs of a machine. Each person has nothing but quite definite tasks. The various professions are concentrated at definite places. One eats while in motion. Amusements are concentrated in other parts of the city. And elsewhere again are the towers to which one returns and finds wife, family, gramophone, and soul. Tension and relaxation, activ- ity and love are meticulously kept separate in time and are weighted out according to formulae arrived at in extensive laboratory work. If during any of these activities one runs up against a difficulty, one simply drops the whole thing; for one will find another thing or perhaps, later on, a better way, or someone else will find the way that one has missed. It does not matter in the least, but nothing wastes so much communal energy as the presumption that one is called upon not to let go of a definite personal aim. In a community with energies constantly flowing through it, every

road leads to a good goal, if one does not spend too much time hesitating and thinking it over. The targets are set up at a short distance, but life is short too, and in this way one gets a maximum of achievement out of it. And man needs no more for his happiness; for what one achieves is what moulds the spirit, whereas what one wants, without fulfilment, only warps it. So far as happiness is concerned it matters very little what one wants; the main thing is that one should get it. Besides, zoology makes it clear that a sum of reduced individuals may very well form a totality of genius.

What I intend to suggest here in my use of this pasage from Musil, as well as in my caveats, is a simple and obvious but often overlooked fact: various technologies come into the culture adjusted in terms of a form and function shaped significantly by that culture itself.

The early masters of cinema in the United States developed an ability to deal with huge crowds, "Crowd Splendor" Vachel Lindsay called it in his superb *The Art of the Motion Picture*, 1915 and 1922. To this development the genius of D. W. Griffith added the important close-up, that unique concentration on the human face quite unavailable in a real world but only possible because of the camera. These two images became crucial to film: the mass on the one hand and the individual on the other. Montage allowed a juxtaposition of such images. Could we argue that this was a formal aesthetic response to an intellectual issue? Any examination of the rest of the culture (and culture does communciate) reveals a fundamental and deep-seated anxiety about the problem of the individual in a mass society. Film enabled a demonstration and probing of that problem iconographically. In addition, films from the start (again of course they are "motion" pictures but is any particular kind of motion implied? Early films confined motion to the frame) dealt with and were exemplars of mobility in space.

To many Americans movement in space was the equivalent of social mobility itself. But for a long time Americans had a special fondness for vast panoramas of space, movement in space. In my view, many of the Luminist paintings from the nineteenth century now attracting so much critical attention used their vaunted light to heighten a sense of vast and endless space. And if we discover, too, that such special spaces, such an opportunity to move in space was somehow joined ideologically with ideas of freedom or social movement as well, then all the more reason to examine film as an inheritor of that tradition. It is difficult to think of film using the special technological capabilities unique to it without such movement over space and even over time: the chase is fundamental — automobile, train, Indians, men in armies, men on foot pursuing other men, men pursuing women. Further, the film adopted and made iconologically its own the traditional story of a journey (as old at least as Homer). Film often made it myth as well in our Westerns. These films technically yield to iconographic demonstration of our fundamental cultural problems and concerns.

One more iconographic assertion: one of the characteristics of modern American culture has been the conversion of methods of communication into icons; objects of everyday life become of iconographic significance in the modern world; none are more useful, it would seem, than those out of the realm of communications. This is especially the case with visual media, but it operates in the world of sound and print as well. Fast moving trains suggest something beyond the image, as does the roar of engines and the toot of whistles on radio. Leo Marx and others have shown how often the locomotive was the "machine in the garden," and at least since 1876 and the writing of Tolstoy's *Anna Karenina,* that same locomotive has had powerful significance as it chugged through the landscape of modern literature, and in Anna's case was the instrument of her death. In more recent times Watty Piper has used the train to provide a moral example for children in the famous *Little Engine That Could.* By the late 1930s and early 1940s so pervasive were the instruments of modern communication in our literature that they served as something more than symbol or metaphor in a series of what have become classic American short stories: Delmore Schwartz's "In Dreams Begin Responsibilities" (motion pictures); John Cheever's "The Enormous Radio"; Lionel Trilling's "Of This Time, Of That Place" (photography).

Even the telephone found itself adopted for popular cultural use, often the iconographic image of the inability to communicate. Irving Berlin's song has its singer "all alone by the telephone." In film both Luise Rainer's great telephone scene (for which she won an Academy Award) in *The Great Ziegfeld* and Shirley Booth's memorable call to her mother in *Come Back, Little Sheba* link the telephonic act with disappointment and even tragedy. And in *Sorry Wrong Number* and *Dial M for Murder* the telephone becomes an object of terror and even murder. Even in the bright Broadway musical comedy *Bye Bye Birdie,* the kids we see as the Second Act begins are all busily talking on the phone without seeming to communicate. The phone company keeps advertising, "Reach out and touch someone," but the iconography of popular culture often suggests the inability in fact to do that very thing or perhaps a danger in trying. (I should add parenthetically that when I call my mother she invariably asks immediately, "What's the matter?" She cannot quite believe that anyone would use the phone except to deliver bad news.) Thus the culture takes an attitude, if I may be permitted a strange turn of phrase, toward the devices of communication which becomes clear as a message when we see these used iconograpically in cultural works.

Frank Capra's *It Happened One Night* captures this tension brilliantly. This fine and funny movie is a classic and very much a part of the world in which it was made and in which it triumphed in 1934. I know of no other film so compellingly dependent upon communications icons to establish virtually every scene.

A brief review of the initial location of each part of the screenplay may be of assistance:

Part I opens in a yacht carefully anchored amid many other yachts. The first part ends with the sending of telegrams, but more of that later.

The setting of Part II and the series of shots that establish the action in the first instances of the meeting of our hero and heroine are so important that I quote directly from Robert Riskin's screenplay:

> The RAILROAD STATION of an active terminal in Miami fades in. The view moves down to the entrance gate to the trains, passengers hurrying through it; then picks out two men, obviously detectives, who have their eyes peeled on everyone passing through. Then the view affords a glimpse of ELLIE, who standing watching the detectives. This scene wiping off, we see an AIR TRANSPORT, with several detectives stand around in a watchful pose. This scene wiping off, the front of a WESTERN UNION OFFICE comes into view. Several people walk in and out. At the side of the door, two detectives are on the lookout.
>
> This scene also wipes off, revealing the WAITING ROOM of a BUS STATION. Over the ticket window there is a sign reading "BUY BUS TICKETS HERE," and a line forms in front of it. Here too there are two detectives.

Part III begins in a telegraph office before moving to a bus station where we hear (barely) an announcer calling bus departures over a public address system.

Part IV opens at night on a road where the bus has been forced to stop by a wash-out on the road ahead. This leads to the first night at Duke's Auto Camp, an institution created by the communications revolution, and suggests a new life style to which the wealthy heroine, Ellie Andrews is completely unaccustomed. This is an important aspect of the film, rich in comedy but also suggestive of how much life has been transformed by new methods of communication, in this case the automobile.

Part V finds us in the sky and most specifically in the cockpit of an airplane.

While Part VI begins in a newspaper office with a flood of telegrams, it culminates with "That Night" that "It Happened": a pastoral in a cow pasture, removed from the world of mechanical communications.

The road (and this leads to the famous hitch-hiking scene) is the setting for the beginning of Part VII.

Part VIII is the only part in the script that fails to begin with some aspect of the devices of communication. We are in Andrews' office, occupied by our heroine's father.

The last part, IX, also might appear to be an exception since it opens on the lawn of the Andrews estate. We shall soon discover that lawn is a launching pad for airplanes, autogyro, and finally the wedding car.

Our leading characters are identified iconographically. We meet Ellie Andrews on her father's yacht, an immediate vision of wealth. We meet Peter Warne in a phone booth in a station. He is drunken, arrogant, unpleasant, and his phone booth setting somehow enhances these qualities as his fellow drunken reporters hover in and around, urging him to resign from his paper. As I have suggested, virtually no known means of communication is left unexploited icongraphically in the film: telegrams, radios, police calls, newspapers and newspaper headlines, newsreel cameras and camera men, photographs, telephones (generally leading to misunderstanding), police cars and motorcycles, typewriters. There is every kind of car from Model T to limousine. Indeed, the famous hitch-hiking scene is almost an excuse to review every car and truck on the American road in the early 1930s. The iconography is extended to the newer institutions housing the devices of communications: stations, auto-court, diners, the whole range. This situation includes demands for a new life style, not only in the camp but in the diner, and most especially on the road itself (the hitch-hiking lesson as an example.)

The hero is a newspaperman, a familiar figure in many American films, bent on "getting a story." In the end, he is less interested in the story than in the girl herself: characteristic American tale, but one that tells us something about attitudes toward the press and toward public communications as well.

It Happened One Night is a story about communications. It exemplifies in a nearly archetypal twentieth century American way the inability of individuals to communicate privately in the world of such awesome, constant, universal public communication. Adrift in a world of communication where every private act (especially of the rich and famous) is public property, our hero and heroine can communicate only when they leave that world totally. In one wonderful moment, when these two leave the road at night, they climb over the barbed wire (a product of industrial America that cuts off communication) into a haystack. There in little light and confined space, a natural world of cantaloupe and carrot, they can find out who they are and be at last themselves in face-to-face communion.

The very next scene — it is morning and light and the vast road beckons — the hitch-hiking scene dramatically counterposes the image of the human body against the image of speeding machines, the automobiles. The first human contact with a third party who picks them up, steals their belongings and leaves them behind. Finally, dependence on mechanical means of communication leads to misunderstanding and almost to an act of destruction. Ellie is preparing to marry her playboy lover of the airplane and autogyro. There is, of course, a happy Capra ending. Peter and Ellie elope in a jalopy and in the famous last scene they are back in the auto-court. This time we *see* nothing; we learn what we can learn from our ears. As on their initial stay at the auto-camp, the unmarried couple erect a blanket on a line between them. They call it the "walls of Jericho." Thus, at the film's end, the marriage assured, we hear the bugle sound, pulling down, we suppose, those walls — an act surely of communication but an act not of the twentieth century but rather of some Biblical or mythical time. *It Happened One Night* expresses several fundamental myths of modern American culture.

I am proposing that Americans think of their culture as one of communication; their social theory and their basic cultural works often reflect these basic concerns. We delight in works about newspapers, television, radio, the theater, the railroad, the automobile, the airplane, and we worry about our inability to communicate privately.

Peroration: I want to finish the quotation from Robert Musil's *The Man Without Qualities,* cited earlier. It deals in a special way with the situation in the United States. Will you remember as you read that *It Happened One Night* might be called a travel-fantasy (we have many travel-fantasies in the interwar period, perhaps, best of all, the brilliant film version of *The Wizard of Oz*) and recall (when you read Musil's reference to "cow-eyed gaze" that so enraptured the Greeks) that our crucial moment in the film occurs in a cow pasture.

> It is by no means certain that things must turn out this way, but such imaginings are among the travel-fantasies that mirror our awareness of the unresting motion in which we are borne along. These fantasies are superficial, uneasy and short. God only knows how things are really going to turn out. One might think that we have the beginning on our hands at every instant and therefore ought to be making a plan for us all. If we don't like the high-speed thing, all right, then let's have something else! Something, for instance, in slow motion, in a gauzily billowing, sea-sluggishly mysterious happiness and with that deep cow-eyed gaze

that long ago so enraptured the Greeks. But that is far from being the way of it: we are in the hands of the thing. We travel in it day and night, and do everything else in it too: shaving, eating, making love, reading books, carying out our professional duties, as though the four walls were stand-ing still; and the uncanny thing about it is merely that the walls are travelling without our noticing it, throwing their rails out ahead like long, gropingly curving antennae, without our knowing where it is all going. And for all that, we like if possible to think of ourselves as being part of the forces controlling the train of events. That is a very vague role to play, and it sometimes happens, when one looks out of the window after a longish interval, that one sees the scene has changed. What is flying past flies past because it can't be otherwise, but for all our resignation we become more and more aware of an unpleasant feeling that we may have overshot our destination or have got on to the wrong line. And one day one suddenly has a wild craving: Get out! Jump clear! It is nostalgic yearning to be brought to a standstill, to cease evolving, to get stuck, to turn back to a point that lies before the wrong fork. And in the good old days when there was still such a place as Imperial Austria, one could leave the train of events, get into an ordinary train on an ordinary railway-line, and travel back home.

It is characteristic to read the period 1920-40 in terms of dramatic tensions that informed the culture. Certainly this is a serious and signifi-cant way to read a culture, since complex cultures are often the products of "things" — ideas, structures, classes, life styles — held in tension rather than the exemplum of one tendency, one dominant vision. The same Americans who have dreamed about new methods of communication and who continue to delight in even further possibilities have at the same time created a culture in which significant works use these very devices as icons against themselves. Americans want the world, that land of Oz, and yet are anxious to get home again, wanting that magic and exciting world of constant motion and yet wanting to yell, "Get Off, Jump!" to all who will listen.

The world of modern communications has other dangers. We know it creates stereotypes; we know that it repeats "facts" until often lies become true in the constant retelling. Years ago I did a study of the American expatriates in France. As I began to interview Americans who lived in France between the wars, I soon discovered that they often knew less about their lives than I did from reading other sources. I came to realize that what they now called their own memory was in fact a recollec-tion of what had appeared in the media about the American expatriates. They had read all the autobiographies of others, all the many articles, seen some of the shows and movies, taken in the various journalistic accounts.

They remembered being places when I knew from indisputable sources that they had not. I was both too young and too stupid to see what I really had uncovered: the nature and function of a myth that had been created by the media, so powerful a myth that even bright people (or perhaps especially bright and imaginative people who after all had shared in at least a spiritual sense the mythic expatriate experience or perhaps the expatriate travel-fantasy) believed it true for themselves.

I must offer my own confession about the myth-making power of the media. In my researches I read three English-language daily newspapers published in Paris from 1919 until 1939. I spent eight to ten hours a day with these newspapers for almost a six-month period. It had its consequences. Months after I would remind my wife of things we had done or seen: "Remember . . .?" "No," she would gently chide, "You just read about that. We really weren't there." This happened more than once. I have always regretted that I somehow did not persuade my wife to read all the papers with me. Would she, too, have "remembered" and could we have remained on a travel-fantasy of our own?

We live in a world of modern communication with whatever consequences that may exact for culture. We also live, however, in a world and in a culture where constant discussion of the media and their role, of communications and their consequences for good and evil, is a fundamental aspect of culture as environment. Those of us who study this world must constantly be aware of both, and of the profound interrelationship between the two.

Mass Media Between the Wars

Section I
Connection

Another phenomenon implying a special sensitivity to "division" is the postwar popularity . . . of the famous injunction on the title page of Forster's *Howard's End,* which was published four years before the war: "Only connect." To become enthusiastic about connecting it is first necessary to perceive things as regrettably disjoined if not actively opposed and polarized.

Paul Fussell, *The Great War and Modern Memory* (1975)

Essays in this group explore the theme of connection—first, the idea that the historic content and form of mass media connect us to our past by serving as a text which can be read as symbolic of past culture; second, the idea that mass communications connected people within that past, bearing messages back and forth between people and their culture, between individuals and groups.

The authors deal with specific situations, but these test cases cast light on larger questions about relationships between media and human experience.

Pursuing the idea of media as text to past attitudes and preoccupations, Joan Shelley Rubin sees scripts of one radio program in the 1930s, the "Swift Hour," as revealing a tension between nineteenth and twentieth-century ideas about literature and the arts. John Stevens reads the small town newspapers of the 1920s as representative forms expressing the conflict between the old and cherished myth of the noble agrarian calling and the encroaching values of the urban culture.

Michelle Herwald sees purveyors of the distinctive science fiction of the period as consciously attempting to usher readers into the technological future, acclimatizing them to the unexpected. Despite the raucous reputation of the urban tabloids, James E. Murphy finds, they served a valuable social function, teaching waves of new immigrants to the city how to behave in acceptable fashion and helping them to make sense of their bewildering new surroundings.

In this section's final essay, Michael Schudson assails the conclusion that cigarette advertising caused the spread of cigarette smoking among women in the 1920s, suggesting that advertising functioned instead more conservatively to legitimate their smoking after they had already begun.

These studies imply more general questions: How did communications shape lives? Enable individuals to adjust or resist their surroundings? Express or shape tensions between old values and those emerging as the century advanced? What assumptions have been made about the power of media to promote change or to support traditional values in American lives, assumptions that history may or may not confirm?

1 Swift's Premium Ham

William Lyon Phelps and The Redefinition of Culture

Joan Shelley Rubin

During the 1934-35 radio season, retired Yale professor William Lyon Phelps, for over forty years a popularizer of literature in the classroom and the lecture hall, exchanged the podium for the studio microphone. Appearing on the Swift Hour variety show, he brought to the air waves the "charm, personality, and love of life" which, in the narrator's words, had made him an "inspiration" to "millions."[1] Phelps reviewed books, Broadway plays, and noted items of literary interest; he dispensed advice about daily living, and occasionally delivered commercials. Yet Phelps did more than launch best-sellers and promote bacon and butter in an appealing manner. Rather, his Swift Hour performances, like his earlier activities, entailed a redefinition of the nature and role of the cultured person, one which retained traditional esteem for culture while aligning it with the needs and values of modern America.

This essay explores the tensions contained in that redefinition by treating the Swift Hour as a text, on the assumption that a radio broadcast, like a novel or a film, can be explicated to reveal the attitudes and preoccupations of the culture which produced it. By addressing directly both the form and content of the programs, it departs from other writings on radio which have talked around such matters; even J. Fred MacDonald's *Don't Touch That Dial* (1979) and Arthur Frank Wertheim's *Radio Comedy* (1979), for example, which so valuably move the study of radio beyond legal, political, and institutional history to an exploration of programming, contain strikingly few quotations of what was actually said on the air.[2] Its intent is therefore not to be comprehensive, nor to claim that Phelps was intrinsically important to the development of the medium, but rather to provide a model for an approach to radio broadcasts as cultural documents and to point the way to further examination of comparable programs as a basis for generalization.

In 1930, Joy Elmer Morgan, editor of the *Journal of the National Education Association* and chairman of the National Committee on Education by Radio, proclaimed radio "the most powerful stimulus that has ever come to the human mind." Summarizing the dreams that educators had attached to the medium throughout the preceding decade, Morgan argued that radio's particular strength lay in its capacity to improve the "quality of thinking among the masses" by exposing millions of people to the finest intellects civilization had produced. Broadcasting's benefits, in Morgan's view, consisted of more than the elevation of individual taste; it promised to engender a unified culture devoted to "intelligent living."

"Who can estimate the motivating and inspiring force of some future occasion," Morgan asked, "when the entire race will listen to one of its brilliant scientists as he explains some great truth? A world language is as [certain as] tomorrow's sun. It will be the language of the best radio programs."[3] Four years later, against the backdrop of what he saw as worsening cultural as well as economic depression, Morgan emphasized even more strongly the desirability of a "national culture" and called, in the vocabulary of the New Deal, for "planning" and government regulation to achieve the "enlightenment" radio could foster.[4]

Yet the prospects for the united, harmonious, critically astute audience Morgan envisioned were rapidly fading even as he wrote. Proposals for legislation and Presidential commissions on radio policy notwithstanding, educational radio was, by the mid-1930s, doomed to defeat by its arch-enemy: commercial broadcasting. Whereas colleges and universities held licenses for seventy-two stations by the end of 1922, by 1933 most had either given up completely, gone part-time, or begun to accept advertising in order to survive. Experiments in broadcasting to public schools, numerous in the early 1920s, had fizzled out by the end of the decade. The problem, as Morgan and others understood it, was that businessmen had assumed control of radio. Large chain-owned stations had either forced educational institutions off the air or enticed them to sell time for commercial uses.[5] Networks were willing to retain only those educational programs which did not "bore" listeners too much. Under such conditions, observers complained, the creative possibilities of radio could never be realized. "Do you imagine for a moment," asked the critic James Rorty in the *Nation* for March 9, 1932, "that education can permanently function as an appendage of toothpaste-and-cigarette-sponsored jazz and vaudeville?" A similarly disillusioned writer announced in the *Forum*, "Now we know definitely what we have got in radio — just another disintegrating toy. Just another medium — like the newspapers, the magazines, the billboards, and the mail box — for advertisers to use in pestering us." A few years later, in an article entitled "I'm Signing Off," an anonymous announcer declared in the same magazine, "I am sickened when I am obliged to ballyhoo Schubert and cheer him on as if he were a famous quarterback doing a broken field run."

What was worse, the radio audience was actually collaborating with commercial interests by shunning whatever educational programs remained, in favor of comedies or soap operas. By 1939, when the sociologist Paul F. Lazarsfeld tabulated the preferences of Buffalo residents, he concluded that while the average middle- or upper-income listener played the radio slightly more than twenty hours a week, and the average working-class listener approximately 23.5 hours a week, the first group tuned into "serious broadcasts" an average of 12.4 minutes a week, and the second group only 6.7 minutes.[7] Among listeners with incomes between $2-5,000 (that is, middle-class listeners), the most popular program in 1937-38, according to one nationwide survey, was Major Bowes, an amateur hour with audience balloting featuring everything from hog calling to musical try-outs.[8] Lazarsfeld reported that, contrary to popular expectation, as one moved down the scale of what he termed "cultural levels," based on either income or education, the amount of serious listening declined.[9] Despite radio's theoretical potential for cultural transformation, Lazarsfeld's data indicated only the tenacity of radio as a vehicle for amusement and escape. Lazarsfeld's and Harry Field's later study, *The People Look at Radio* (1946), even noted that most listeners did not object to advertisements. In those circumstances the authors proposed only that the broadcaster keep radio "slightly above what the masses want. In this way, he may contribute to a systematic rise in the general cultural level without defeating the educational goal by driving the audience away."[10]

Yet Lazarsfeld's conclusions about classroom and discussion programs, disheartening as they were for visionaries like Morgan, did not apply to certain other kinds of informational formats on the air in the 1930s: the advice program concerned with food or health or gardening, the variety hour containing literary talks and historical drama, the book review by a well-known personality, the quiz show. Far from alienating the audience, the performers on such programs enjoyed a popularity and influence rarely accorded the participants in radio roundtables or public affairs presentations or lectures; for example, when a sample of 745 high school students replied to the question "What are the programs from which you can learn something?," 28.6 percent mentioned quizzes and 5.1 percent singled out "popularized information," as against .7 percent for "straight education."[11] Lazarsfeld's remark in Radio and the Printed Page (1940) that educators "obviously feel" that a "how to get along" program, or a "quiz contest" is "beneath their dignity" overlooked the fact that by that time several scholars and critics, in addition to more practically-oriented home economists and dentists, had become radio stars — on the audience's terms.[12] John Erskine, professor of English at Columbia and the originator of the "great books" curriculum there, not only appeared on broadcasts from time to time but advocated that educators learn "how to speak over the air" and to devise new, entertaining forms for presenting their subject matter. Erskine's Columbia protégé, the critic Clifton Fadiman, was a "regular" on the "Information, Please!" quiz program beginning in 1938. Alexander Woollcott, an accomplished reviewer, ran a weekly book and opinion program off and on from 1929 to 1940. Finally, there was William Lyon Phelps, Lampson Professor of English at Yale, whose Swift Hour broadcasts, because they have been preserved in the Library of Congress, are an invaluable resource for exploring this well-populated middle region of early radio, a terrain located between Amos 'n' Andy and the American School of the Air, between Morgan's ideals and Rorty's despair.

"Billy" Phelps, as he was universally called, was, by the time of his radio appearances, the nation's best-known popularizer of literature. Born in New Haven, Connecticut, in 1865, he graduated from Yale in 1887, completed a Ph.D. from Harvard four years later, and in 1892 embarked on a forty-one-year career as a member of the Yale faculty. Although Phelps had followed nineteenth-century scholarly convention in his dissertation *The Beginnings of the English Romantic Movement,* he rebelled against Yale's emphasis on a classical curriculum by offering courses on the modern novel and modern drama. His later reputation as a conservative and a moralist has overshadowed his early stance as a innovator and iconoclast: he introduced his students to Ibsen and Tolstoy, gave as much attention to Browning as to Shakespeare, and later welcomed the poetic experiments of Amy Lowell and the satire of Sinclair Lewis. But he became more famous as a public speaker and book reviewer than as an original scholar. Beginning in 1895, he ventured outside academia to address women's clubs, Chautauqua gatherings, and lecture series on literary topics. In addition, he wrote frequently for magazines: his column "As I Like It" ran monthly in *Scribner's* from 1922 to 1936; he was a frequent contributor to the *Ladies' Home Journal* and the *Delineator;* the *Rotarian* began carrying his book reviews in 1933. His writings and speeches, often collected and published as books, typically interlaced background on the authors under discussion with Phelps's own reminiscences of literary figures, accounts of his European travels, or observations about life and letters. That chatty approach, coupled with Phelps's cheery outlook, passion for sports, and hospitable attitude toward almost anything between covers (Oswald Garrison Villard called him "The most easily pleased book reviewer in America"[13]) antagonized the *avant-garde:* for example, the *American Mercury* writer John Bakeless dismissed him as a "book-booster" and a buffoon.[14] Yet it is a great mistake not to treat him seriously, for with the reading public he earned what one journalist, Joseph J. Reilly, called "a peculiarly personal triumph."

"Hundreds of people who have never heard him lecture (although he has lectured in every state of the Union) but whose acquaintance is based on books and articles," Reilly noted in 1938, "have come to regard him as nothing less than an intimate personal friend."[15] By the early 1920s, his performances on the lecture circuit drew up to two thousand people.[16] His wide acceptance as guide and authority prompted Edward Bok, the editor of the *Ladies' Home Journal,* to introduce a sketch of Phelps in 1925 with the caption, "Nobody has ever said it until Billy Phelps says it."[17]

Upon his retirement from Yale, Phelps extended his following to include the radio audience. In 1933, a former student persuaded him to deliver programs on "good reading" and "courage," after which he gave thirteen more talks. It was during the next year's season, however, that he became an established voice on the air. On Saturday evenings at eight o'clock, listeners who tuned into the NBC network could hear Phelps teamed with Sigmund Romberg, the conductor and composer of such operettas as *The Student Prince* and the star of the newly created Swift Hour, broadcasting over station WEAF, New York. By December, 1934, the success of the venture merited an item in *Newsweek:* "More than 16 percent of America's radio sets were dialed" to the show, which "led the field of six new hour programs in the race for popularity" and lagged "only two points behind the older program of Armour," Swift's competitor.[18] Both the form and the substance of the broadcast, which was billed as "an hour of melody, drama (or anecdote), and song," illuminate the premises that governed Phelps's role as a tastemaker of the airwaves.

The Swift Hour characteristically opened with the announcement that the program featured the music of Romberg, followed by a few bars of theme song. Next came the initial introduction of Phelps, first formally — as "Professor William Lyon Phelps" — and second, as if to humanize and demystify him, by way of some complimentary, descriptive phrase preceding his nickname: "the genial, informative Billy Phelps of Yale," "the friendly and engaging Billy Phelps of Yale," "the beloved," "the ever-popular," etc.[19]

Such designations, which always incorporated a reference to Yale, carried a double message: they certified Phelps as a representative of the

best education America had to offer while at the same time suggesting that
he was just a "regular guy" akin to the average listener. Bakeless sarcasti-
cally noticed the first of those appeals when he wrote that "the Phelpsian
outpourings . . . spout from a pundit of a famous university, and are
therefore fondly believed to be the final dictum of infallible literary taste in
circulating libraries and women's clubs from Eastport, Keokuk, and
Dubuque, to San Pedro and Walla Walla." Reilly highlighted the second
attribute when he cited the story that Phelps responded to the question
"Which would you rather do, discover a beautiful poem or see Yale defeat
Harvard on the gridiron?" with the answer "I never smashed my hat over a
beautiful poem."[20]

Subsequent exchanges typicall called upon the "Professor," who
responded with a brief comment either hinting at his topic for the evening
or revealing that he was indeed unintimidating: "If I were now given the
opportunity to spend every day for the next five hundred years with an
invariable program of work every morning, golf every afternoon, and
social entertainment every evening," he declared on one broadcast, "I
should accept with alacrity." His next comment built on the disarming
image of a golfing educator by implying that the culture he purveyed was
compatible with amusement, and that he and his listeners were, regardless
of his professionial stature, sharing an experience of mutual pleasure: "I
know we're going to have a most entertaining hour together." In effect, his
remark gave his audience credit for the ability to provide him with exactly
the socializing he had just been praising. His style of delivery reinforced the
sense that he was meeting his listeners as friends: his tone was conversational rather than dramatic or pedagogical, his upper-class accent moder-
ated by a sprightly pace and medium pitch.

Having thus established a mood of both cultivation and informal-
ity, the Swift Hour quickly proceeded to its first musical selection, generally a Romberg arrangement of a familiar classic such as *The Merry
Widow*. Although the order of presentation varied somewhat, the next
segment was most often a commercial, the content of which strikingly
paralleled the message of Phelps's portions of the program.

Stressing Swift and Company's fifty-year record of "service,"
"responsibility," "quality," "dependability," and "fairness," attributes
which implied stability and selflessness in a time of economic distress, the
advertisements also portrayed the company as a mentor and upholder of
standards. The Swift Hour, one commercial proclaimed, was designed to
"entertain you and help you in the selection of fine foods for your table"
including such food "classics" of New England as lard.[21] Another stated
that Swift was engaged in balancing new methods of preparing products

against venerable old ways, a juggling act one can see Phelps performing in his literary observations, which often included references to the classics and recommendations of contemporary fiction.[22] In fact, Phelps identified himself with his sponsor to the extent that he supplanted the announcer on at least one commercial, hailing not books but "foods distinguished by their excellence" and extending "on behalf of Mr. Romberg, myself, and the entire cast heartiest congratulations" on the occasion of the company's jubilee.[23] Such advertisements were repudiations of the image of American businessmen as "boobs" and Babbitts; they suggested instead that culture and business were both parts of the same enterprise. Sponsor, professor, and musical performers alike, it seemed, were interested in improving taste in both senses of the word, a purpose which ostensibly differentiated the program from the frivolous "Major Bowes" and thereby enhanced its educational appeal.

The affinity between selling ham and selling culture eased the transition from one to the other when, following another interlude of Romberg arrangements, the announcer called on Phelps for his weekly commentary. For five minutes, Phelps spoke about books, the theater, or his philosophy of life, bringing to the topic his characteristic blend of fact, opinion, and personal anecdote. For example, discussing new books, plays, and movies on February 23, 1935, he touted Thornton Wilder's *Heaven's My Destination* and thanked Wilder for writing short books, flipped abruptly to a story concerning James Hilton and dubbed him a worthy replacement for Hardy and Conrad, quickly described Pearl Buck's life, identified the "greatest biography" of the season, moved on to the theater and issued decisive verdicts on current performances, and pronounced the film *David Copperfield* "the best picture I ever saw" — made from "the best novel in the English language." His March 16, 1935, address on "Youth," which reflected a more liberal attitude than his Menckenite critics accorded him, moved from his personal approval of youthful idealism to references to Ibsen, Homer, the Egyptians, and a young Yale graduate.

This amalgamation of wide-ranging, superficial allusions, absolute pronouncements, and comments on everyday life transmitted the message that underlay not only Phelps's segment of the program but the Swift Hour as a whole: culture was accessible to, and comprehensible by, the average listener. One could enter the ranks of "cultured" individuals without formal education or even great effort. The effect of Phelps's juxtaposition of gossip, homily, and criticism was to humanize art and to place it on the same level as everyday experience.

Phelps's strategy is even clearer in his March 23, 1935, talk entitled

"The Art of Living Together," which linked Turgenev and Hawthorne with Phelps's observations about marriage. When, for example, Phelps cited Turgenev's remark that he would give all his art "if there were one woman who cared whether he came home to dinner," he tacitly assured the audience that their activities were as valuable as a great writer's. (He was especially complimenting women who, in light of the emphasis on food selection and household management in the program's commercials, were assumed to comprise the majority of Swift Hour listeners.[24]) After describing the contribution of Hawthorne's wife to her husband's success and announcing in passing that Hawthorne was "the greatest literary artist in American history," he moved on to a general discussion of marriage: that it could be a blissful state for "many people, rich, and poor, educated and uneducated," that it was "a success within the reach of the average man." The fact that a critic and professor even assessed such institutions as marriage while handing down judgments about writing implied a lack of distance between books and life and suggested that the two were interchangeable. Therefore, when Phelps told the audience that they could succeed in marriage regardless of education or social position, they might readily conclude that, by the same token, lack of schooling was no barrier to culture. If books were important for the way they illuminated everyday experience, the reverse, Phelps was intimating, might be true as well — that one's experience was sufficient to allow one to comprehend literature.

On another broadcast, Phelps made that understanding explicit, in terms that reveal a good deal about his values. After prescribing a rule for happiness ("take nothing for granted"), he asserted that the greatest books — the Bible and Shakespeare — were still the "best sellers," a statement that at once accepted the legitimacy of commercial measures of culture and calmed fears that materialism had destroyed artistic standards. Phelps went on to declare: "The entire intellectual wealth of mankind is within reach of every humble person. You've got a mind. Why not cultivate it? Not every person can become a personage, but every person can become a personality."[25] Such a remark corroborates Warren Susman's observation that a concern with "personality," as opposed to "character," seems a feature of twentieth-century America.[26] Phelps, as a model personality himself, owed much of his popularity, one might argue, to the strength of this preoccupation. In any case, that shift in vision, if one accepts Susman's hypothesis, dictated a parallel shift in the aim of reading. Its object, Phelps seemed to suggest, was not primarily to fulfill a moral duty, or to train mental powers in order to instill self-discipline, or to contribute to the possibility of social progress by fostering new ideas, or even so much to develop individual abilities. It was instead to make oneself more interesting. That goal was entirely compatible with, and could potentially enhance, the pursuit of profit; the interesting person could, in theory, be more likely to achieve success in business. But it was a less formidable task to prevent oneself from "boring others" than to carry the responsibility of safeguarding civilization by reading the classics. In fact, Phelps told his audience that culture was more than accessible; it could be fun. The avowed purpose of the Swift Hour, as the announcer declared, was to "offer fine music and discriminating comment for your enjoyment," just as Swift and Company offered "the opportunity to increase your enjoyment at table." Phelps provided "enjoyment" of culture rather than edification; he purveyed a taste for great books, as pleasurable, as attainable, and as commonplace as a Sunday dinner of Swift's "premium ham."

The medium of radio itself fostered the conclusion that culture was both accessible and that, to quote a phrase of Randolph Bourne's, it "could be imbibed." Radio brought Phelps's Yale classroom to Peoria, allowing members of the audience, however untutored, the sense that they were receiving an Ivy League education, with all the distinction and authority such an education conferred. Phelps was well aware of that appeal and made the most of it. For example, he commented at the beginning of his broadcast for February 9, 1935: "When I come to these weekly Swift reunions I feel as if I were attending a class reunion with many of my former pupils" who, he observed, "don't seem a day older than last time." Phelps not only turned his listeners into honorary Yalies; by mentioning their appearance, he compensated for the loss of face-to-face contact that radio necessarily entailed. Similarly, Phelps's habit of ending the broadcast with the comment "Now I must take my train to New Haven" enlarged the audience's opportunity to feel that they had secured entrance to an exclusive educational institution: by reminding listeners that Phelps had emerged from, and was returning to, an elitist university and by playing on their knowledge of Yale's location, his sign-off both emphasized the connection between culture prestige and made the audience privileged "insiders."

Phelps's countless Chautauqua and women's clubs presentations no doubt furnished something of the same sense of access, but radio could create the effect more strongly because, paradoxically perhaps, it could operate more personally. Hadley Cantril and Gordon W. Allport noticed this difference between broadcasting and the lecture hall in their study, *The Psychology of Radio,* which appeared while Phelps's Swift Hour talks were in progress. Although the absence of visual cues interposed greater distance between listener and speaker, radio permitted the audience a more "individualistic" response, since there was no way to observe, or necessity to comply with, the reactions of others.[27]

"Billy Phelps of Yale," the announcer on the January 5, 1935, broadcast declared, was "this program's personal don," as if Phelps stood ready to guide each listener through his lesson. To sit alone in your living room and hear Phelps's voice was to be able to fantasize all the more easily that he was speaking directly to you, that he took a special interest in what you read and thought, and that the fact that you had never set foot in a college did not make you any less his Yale student. Phelps's tone and stance epitomized what Cantril and Allport identified as the chief explanation for radio's popularity: its capacity to enable the listener "to participate with a feeling of personal involvement in the events of the outside world from which he would otherwise be excluded."[28]

The form of Phelps's talks, moreover, underscored his message about culture. Phelps's work as a whole seems to draw on an unvarying stock of "one-liners," which he enunciated in print as well as on the air: "If the whole world played golf and tennis we might not have had the world war"; Jesus was "the most interesting person in history"; "the most fascinating thing about life is mystery."[29] The constraints of limited time and an unseen, undifferentiated audience, however, dictated that he rely even more on aphorisms and concise pronouncements. On an early 1935 broadcast, for example, Phelps delivered his list of "best books" of the preceding year so rapidly that no listener could easily take notes on individual titles. Similarly, his theater reviews were often single, isolated sentences: "I think the best new play of the season is *Merrily We Roll Along.*[30]

Such lists and epigrams did not pretend to provide literary analysis or to teach the audience to arrive at its own critical judgments. Their function was instead to create in the listener the sense that she or he was "in the know" about the arts. The pace of Phelps's Swift Hour segments suggested that the attainment of culture was a matter of acquiring inside information. Phelps's gossipy anecdotes — "Years later I was talking with AE, whose real name is . . ." — worked the same way. It was not as important to read books as to know about them, an activity which would not take much time away from business. Radio abetted that conclusion by dispensing with print altogether; it amounted to a statement that new technology had made the traditional method of becoming cultured obsolete. Although Phelps's ostensible purpose was to encourage reading, radio by its very nature could subvert that goal.[31]

The context of Phelps's talks — the variety hour format — elaborated on the same point: a bit of opera, a dramatic sketch, a snippet of musical history added up to a cultural education. In the case of the Swift Hour, Romberg used his talents as a composer to make the classics readily available: on one broadcast, for example, he presented a rendition of *Ave Maria* reworded in order to make it fit into the plot of an operetta based on Schubert's life, after which he offered the original version. That is, he translated Schubert's song into contemporary idiom and then eased the audience into the real thing. Other features of the show made for similarly effortless swallowing. Both before and after Phelps's longer talk, the announcer frequently called on him to make brief comments about the program's musical portions. On one broadcast, Phelps prepared the audience for an excerpt from *La Boheme* by depicting the colorful atmosphere of the Latin Quarter and then declaring that the orchestra would play "under Mr. Romberg's baton and with my own personal blessing." On another, he introduced Hungarian selections by romantically describing gypsies and their special instruments.

Sometimes Phelps simply supplied enthusiasm, of which he had an unlimited fund: "Mr. Romberg, I love all good music, but when I visit you I can't wait to hear what you've just composed."[32] In each case, however, Phelps acted as a mediator between the audience and the music, lending his professional stamp of approval to the program's definition of culture while engaging the imagination, good will, and confidence of the listener. One reminiscence of Phelps recorded the effectiveness of such mediation by quoting a "workman" who said that "he didn't know music, or know how to read one note from another, yet . . . Professor Phelps, through a radio program, had brought him an understanding of music, such as he had never had before."[33]

The juxtaposition of the musical selections themselves likewise removed culture from a rarefied atmosphere and made the classics go down easy: on the February 9, 1935, show, for example, the orchestra played the overture to *Die Fledermaus* and Romberg's *Like a Star in the Night* in quick succession, and gave as much time to the *Swift Anniversary March* as to the selection from Wagner which preceded it, as if all those pieces were of the same quality and significance. Finally, the Swift Hour regularly devoted fifteen minutes of the program's second half hour to a sketch — sometimes a love story, sometimes a mystery, sometimes an episode from musical history — which served as a vehicle for the performance of more music. Without exception, these dramas featured exotic settings (Japan, post war Paris, New Orleans in pirate days, Ireland, a London theatre, Strauss's Vienna), reflecting what Warren Susman has characterized as the American fascination in the 1930s with the definition of culture in the anthropological sense of a "way of life."[34] But the Swift

Hour dramas, by functioning as excuses for excerpts from Haydn or Wagner or Romberg himself, also made a statement about culture in the more limited sense of "high culture": like Phelps's mediating role and the program's sequence of musical numbers, they presented the classics as both serious and entertaining, esoteric and comprehensible.

This mixed message suggests that Phelps's Swift Hour broadcasts were a product of the convergence of longstanding assumptions about the importance of culture and the unexpected expansion of a prosperous middle class in modern America. Nineteenth-century Americans had linked refinement with social prestige: the phrase "the best men," which, as John G. Sproat has noted, described the liberal ideal of political and economic leadership, encompassed familiarity with, and reverence for, books and the arts.[35] Even if the electorate rejected such leaders at the polls, many Americans, in Richard Hofstadter's words, "also felt a certain respectful and wistful regard"[36] for their authority in cultural matters. Some businessmen at least partly endorsed liberal education and saw the pursuit of learning as "higher" than the accumulation of wealth.[37]

This equation of culture with respectability and laudable distance from business values persisted to some extent in the twentieth century: hence the consumers of the 1920s, according to Ellis Hawley, sought through "cultural products" such as book clubs a "sense of upward movement into more refined social circles."[38] Music and art, the Lynds observed in *Middletown,* seemed "to serve in part as a symbol that one belong[ed] to the privileged segment of the community."[39] But, the late nineteenth century also saw the patron of the arts superseded by the practical self-made man who enjoyed status as well as wealth, without ever passing through Harvard or even the public library.

In the widening prosperity of the 1920s, it was increasingly clear that success might have nothing to do with culture. In some quarters, education was no longer the passport to a position mere money could not confer; far from tempering and transcending commercialism, culture was often subordinated to it — when it was even considered. At the same moment Middletown mothers were insisting, as their own mothers had, that their daughters take music lessons to acquire social grace and standing, Sinclair Lewis was depicting Chum Frink intent on convincing Babbitt and his cronies in the Boosters Club that an orchestra would be good for the pocketbook: "'I don't care a rap for all this long-haired music. . . . But that isn't the point. Culture has become as necessary an adornment and advertisement for a city today as pavements. . . . The thing to do then, as a live bunch of go-getters, is to capitalize Culture; to go right out and grab it.'"[40] Frink's pitch was bad enough, a representative of the older outlook might have commented; worse was the fact that some of his hearers no doubt remained unpersuaded that an orchestra had any utility at all.

Phelps addressed the question of the place and meaning of culture not so much by resolving it as by playing both sides. His approach, which was perfected by the 1920s, was just as pertinent to Depression as to prosperity, and could meet a range of needs. Despite his early interest in modernism, his typical public pronouncements provided the comforting sense that time-honored standards still applied, an affirmation which could be especially appealing in the psychological and economic upheaval of the 1930s. To the housewife anxious because her husband's business was floundering, he announced that she might obtain, more easily than ever, the knowledge of the arts that had traditionally signified success. To the executive who held on to his money but retained an uneasy feeling that, without education, his triumph was incomplete, Phelps gave assurances that refinement was a matter of tuning in next week. Yet his message could also satisfy those who questioned the relevance of culture to commerce; it left ample room for the conclusion that "business civilization" was civilization enough. In fact, what Phelps offered on the Swift Hour may best be summarized not as education but as appreciation. To appreciate culture was to understand that it was good for you, to pay homage to the heritage of Western civilization, to acknowledge long-established aesthetic judgments, to make a limited commitment of time and energy to the improvement of personality — and then to get down to business or to consume the latest household appliances. It was an activity entirely suited to a society that associated culture with certain desirable qualities and therefore cared to define it, yet had increasingly strong positive associations with materialism as well.[41]

Moreover, Phelps's posture — at once self-confident and self-effacing implies particular tensions about the proper role of the expert. In general, radio enhanced the prominence of figures, Phelps among them, who, as Cantril and Allport pointed out, made pronouncements about "what to eat, what to read, what to buy, what exercise to take, what to think of the music we hear, and how to treat our colds." ("Over the air," they added, "the distinction between the expert and the advertiser is often intentionally vague," a strategy reflected in the Swift Hour commercials.[42]) But high visibility was, in the case of book reviewers at least, accompanied by a high degree of ambivalence about the assertion of authority, as if the experts sensed that they might antagonize an audience fresh from triumphs in the more important world of the marketplace. In a 1931 article for *Publishers Weekly* entitled "Fatal to Review: How Does One Review Books Over the Air?" Harry Salpeter argued that the best radio reviewers adopted a "politely deferential conversation technique," gently wooing an audience which, Salpeter implied, was in no mood to defer to them. The ideal radio critic, according to Salpeter, was a "glittering dragon fly" rather than a "mole," a performer who emphasized his own personality and that of the author rather than a scholar who stressed the content of the book. Phelps, of course, was a model exponent of such an approach, but Salpeter's article is a reminder that he was not unique; Alexander Woollcott, Salpeter noted, was a master of the same style, and Salpeter himself followed it on the air.[43] Yet their success came at the expense of the critic's traditional role; the dragon fly's flight was away from aesthetic and moral judgments toward the safer ground of entertainment and information. Although recent scholars have stressed increased reliance on expertise as a characteristic of modern American culture, Phelps's compliance with the dictum that actually reviewing a book was "fatal" to the work and the critic alike suggests a more complex pattern than the idea of deference implies.[44]

In the case of the Swift Hour, however, even Phelps's refutation, as the show's announcer put it, of the "current superstition that college professors are dreary fellows"[45] was not enough to prevent what amounted to that deadly twist of the dial, as if the tensions within the program could not be held in balance indefinitely. When the new season began in the fall of 1935, Phelps was no longer the Swift Hour's "personal don." Although because he went on to subsequent ventures in broadcasting it would be wrong automatically to assume that he was a casualty of unfavorable audience response, the format the *Swift Hour* adopted after Phelps's departure seems to symbolize a resolution of the conflict inherent in his role — a resolution in favor of listeners who did not require guidance or even care much for the arts. On the September 10, 1935, program Deems Taylor, himself a well-known cultural authority, has replaced Phelps as the *Swift Hour's* co-host, but he serves only as a guest at "Rommie's" "informal party" in the studio. The songs begin, punctuated by the jokes and laughter and applause of the chorus, members of which are introduced as "Mr. Romberg's young people." Gone is the Yale classroom; now the audience is attending a gay New York social event with a carefree bunch of kids.

In view of that transformation, Phelps's stint as Swift's "premium ham" appears as a way station in the development of American radio. A far cry from Morgan's fantasy of elevating the race by exposing listeners to instruction from the nation's most brilliant teachers, it was still a long distance from a concept of programming which relegated most educational functions to a separate network. Taken together with Phelps's wider activities as lecturer and writer, his broadcasts also suggest that radio was only one reflection of a reassessment of culture for the "average person" in the 1920s and '30s; the same struggles and tensions surfaced, one may speculate, in libraries and museums, in magazines and book clubs, in women's organizations and adult education courses. The glare of the historian's spotlight on the *avant-garde* has obscured such institutions, yet in their development and in the career of such figures as Phelps lie the bases for a greater understanding of the nature and quality of American life in our century.[46]

Notes

1. Oct. 17, 1934. Tapes of this and the other broadcasts cited below are available without restriction in the bequest of Sigmund Romberg, Library of Congress Motion Picture, Broadcasting, and Recorded Sound Division, Washington, D.C. One broadcast is unfortunately fragmentary and undated.

2. The standard institutional study is Erik Barnouw, *A Tower in Babel* (New York: Oxford University Press, 1961), and *The Golden Web* (New York: Oxford University Press, 1968), the first two of his three volumes on the history of broadcasting. See also Gleason Archer's classic *History of Radio To 1926* (New York: American Historical Society, 1938); David Holbrook Culbert, *News for Everyman: Radio and Foreign Affairs in Thirties America* (Westport, Ct.: Greenwood Press, 1976); and Philip T. Rosen, *The Modern Stentors: Radio Broadcasters and the Federal Government, 1920-1934* (Westport, Ct.: Greenwood Press, 1980). In addition to the volumes by MacDonald (Chicago: Nelson-Hall, 1979) and Wertheim (New York: Oxford University Press, 1979), see for provocative new essays, which nevertheless slight textual analysis, the in-depth issue on radio. *Journal of Popular Culture* (Fall 1978).

3. Joy Elmer Morgan, "Radio and Education," in Martin Codel, ed., *Radio and Its Future* (New York: Harper and Brothers, 1950), pp. 71-72.

4. Joy Elmer Morgan, "A National Culture — By-Product or Objective of National Planning?" in Tracy F. Tyler, ed., *Radio as a Cultural Agency* (Washington: The National Committee on Education by Radio, 1934), pp. 26-31.

5. Barnouw, *A Tower in Babel*, pp. 97-98, 173-75, 272-75.

6. James Rorty, "Free Air: A Strictly Imaginary Educational Broadcast," Nation, 9 March 1932, p. 281; Jack Woodford, "Radio — A Blessing or a Curse?," *Forum* 81 (March 1929): 169; "I'm Signing Off," *Forum* 87 (February 1932): 113.

7. Paul F. Lazarsfeld, *Radio and the Printed Page* (New York: Duell, Sloan and Pearce, 1940), pp. 31, 35.

8. *Ibid.*, pp. 16-24.

9. *Ibid.*, p. 21.

10. Paul F. Lazarsfeld and Harry Field, *The People Look at Radio* (Chapel Hill: The University of North Carolina Press, 1946), p. 73.

11. Lazarsfeld, *Radio and the Printed Page*, p. 54.

12. *Ibid.*, p. 93.

13. *Newsweek*, 17 April 1939, p. 44.

14. John Bakeless, "William Lyon Phelps, Book-Booster," *American Mercury* 36 (November 1935): 266-72.

15. Joseph J. Reilly, " 'Billy' Phelps of Yale," *Commonweal*, 28 January 1938, pp. 277-78.

16. See a letter from Phelps to Mr. Pratt of Houghton Mifflin Company, March 20, 1922 in the Phelps Collection, Houghton Library, Harvard University, Cambridge, Massachusetts.

17. *Ladies' Home Journal* 42 (Feburary 1925): 18. For more biographical information on Phelps, in addition to the sources cited herein, see William Lyon Phelps, *Autobiography with Letters* (New York: Oxford University Press, 1939); Lucius Beebe, "Billy Phelps of Yale," *Reader's Digest* 34 (February 1939): 29-33; Sinclair Lewis, "William Lyon Phelps," *Saturday Review*, 1 April 1939, pp. 3-4; Edgar Johnson, "Brother Cheeryble," *New Republic*, 17 May 1939, pp. 53-54; Henry Seidel Canby, "William Lyon Phelps," *Saturday Review*, 4 September 1943, p. 12; Frederick A. Pottle, "Phelps, William Lyon," *Dictionary of American Biography: Supplement Three: 1941-45* (New York: Charles Scribner's Sons, 1973), pp. 601-03; and Phelps's obituary in the *New York Times*, 22 August 1943, p. 37. The bulk of Phelps's papers are at the Beinecke Rare Book and Manuscript Library, Yale University, New Haven, Connecticut.

18. *Newsweek*, 1 December 1934, p. 28.

19. 9 February 1935; 16 February 1935; 27 October 1934; 16 March 1935.

20. Bakeless, "William Lyon Phelps, Book Booster," *American Mercury* 36 (November 1935): 268; Reilly, "'Billy' Phelps of Yale," *Commonweal*, 28 January 1938, p. 377.

21. 2 February 1935.

22. 9 February 1935.

23. This is from the undated broadcast.

24. This conclusion would be consistent with the findings of Hadley Cantril and Gordon W. Allport that more women than men expressed a preference for literary programs on the air. See Cantril and Allport, *The Psychology of Radio* (New York: Harper & Brothers, 1935), p. 268.

25. 27 October 1934.

26. Warren Susman, "'Personality' and the Making of Twentieth-Century Culture," in John Higham and Paul K. Conkin, eds., *New Directions in American Intellectual History* (Baltimore: The Johns Hopkins University Press, 1979), pp. 212-26.

27. Cantril and Allport, *The Psychology of Radio*, p. 13.

28. *Ibid.*, p. 260.

29. 27 October 1934; 13 April 1935; 5 January 1935.

30. 23 February 1935.

31. One of Lazarsfeld's studies noted that the greatest number of listeners reporting follow-up reading after radio broadcasts were those already prepared by education or habit to read. Phelps did spur some reading, or at least book-buying — Lazarsfeld quoted one bookseller who said she wanted to "wring his neck" for causing runs on the market — and one suspects that those who carried out his recommendations belonged to the group Lazarsfeld identified as most likely to follow up: "prolific readers of less education." Nevertheless Lazarsfeld's data indicated that the majority of listeners, regardless of education, reported no reading as a result of a radio broadcast. *Radio and the Printed Page*, pp. 299, 308.

32. 15 January 1935; 16 February 1935; 27 October 1934.

33. Florence Holladay Barber, *Fellow of Infinite Jest* (New Haven: Payne and Lane Printers, 1939), p. 158.

34. Warren Susman, ed., *Culture and Commitment: 1929-45* (New York: George Braziller, 1973), pp. 1-24.

35. John G. Sproat, *"The Best Men": Liberal Reformers in the Gilded Age* (New York: Oxford University Press, 1968), p. 150.

36. Richard Hofstadter, *Anti-Intellectualism in American Life* (New York: Vintage Books, 1966), p. 244.

37. *Ibid.*, pp. 248-60.

38. Ellis Hawley, *The Great War and the Search for a Modern Order* (New York: St. Martin's Press, 1969), p. 166.

39. Robert and Helen Merrill Lynd, *Middletown* (New York: Harcourt, Brace & World, 1956), pp. 247-48.

40. Sinclair Lewis, *Babbitt* (1922; New York: Signet, 1961), p. 212.

41. For overviews of the culture of the 1920s and '30s, see, in addition to the Hawley and Susman volumes cited above, William E. Leuchtenburg *The Perils of Prosperity* (Chicago: University of Chicago Press, 1958); Roderick Nash, *The Nervous Generation* (Chicago: Rand McNally, 1970); Warren Susman, "The Thirties," in Stanley Coben and Lorman Ratner, eds., *The Development of an American Culture* (Englewood Cliffs, N.J.: Prentice-Hall, 1970); and Richard H. Pells, *Radical Visions and American Dreams* (New York: Harper and Row, 1973).

42. Cantril and Allport, *The Psychology of Radio*, p. 23.

43. Harry Salpeter, "Fatal to Review: How Does One Review Books Over the Air?," *Publisher's Weekly*, 16 May 1931, pp. 2417-19.

44. See, for example, Robert Wiebe, *The Search for Order* (New York: Hill and Wang, 1967); Philip Rieff, *The Triumph of the Therapeutic: Uses of Faith After Freud* (New York: Harper and Row, 1966); Thomas L. Haskell, *The Emergence of Professional Social Science* (Urbana: University of Illinois Press, 1977); and especially Christopher Lasch, *Haven in a Heartless World* (New York: Basic Books, 1977), and *The Culture of Narcissism* (New York: Norton, 1978).

45. 5 January 1935.

46. There is, for example, no adequate scholarly study of Phelps, Henry Seidel Canby, Dorothy Canfield Fisher, Clifton Fadiman, John Erskine, or Amy Loveman — all critics who shaped popular literary taste in the 1920s and '30s. By contrast, Frederick Hoffman's *The Twenties* (New York: Viking, 1955); Alfred Kazin's *On Native Grounds* (Garden City, N.Y.: Doubleday Anchor Books, 1956); Malcolm Cowley's *Exile's Return* (New York: Viking, 1951), *A Second Flowering* (New York: Viking, 1973), and *The Dream of the Golden Mountains* (New York: Viking, 1980); Daniel Aaron's *Writers on the Left* (New York: Harcourt, Brace & World, 1961); and numerous individual biographies and critical treatments of Pound, Eliot, Hemingway, Fitzgerald, Lewis, Wolfe, Dos Passos, and the advocates of "proletarian literature" provide abundant discussion of the *avant-garde*.

2 Small Town Editors and the "Modernized" Agrarian Myth

John D. Stevens

Rural spokesmen always have blamed the cities for their economic woes. Greenbackers, Populists and Grangers screamed about financial exploitation, and so did the farmers of the 1920s, dismayed at finding themselves in a decade of hard times while much of the nation enjoyed prosperity. But they vented their anger in ways that went beyond economics; they cast their attacks in "good versus evil" moralistic terms.

In short, they returned to the Agrarian Myth. In trying to defend what was left of that myth — the belief that there is a peculiar nobility which accrues to those who work the soil — rural editors and their allies betrayed its inherent weakness. They learned that the fruits of modernity, which they wanted so much, came saturated with urban values; they could not have one without the other.

There is nothing peculiarly American about the Agrarian Myth, a theme that can be traced from Graeco-Roman times in the mythology of many nations.[1] Its essence is that because agriculture provides the food, clothing and raw materials for society, it is not just another way to make a living; it is a way of life, a noble calling. Agrarian values are virtuous and patriotic, those of the city evil and avaracious.

Agrarianism has had few more articulate champions than John Taylor of Caroline, a rich planter who served in both the Virginia and national legislatures and who produced a stream of books, letters and pamphlets in the decades following the American Revolution. Like many who came after him, he saw the trend toward factories at the expense of agriculture not only as a crime but as a sin:

> At an awful day of judgment, the discrimination of the good from the wicked, is not made by the criterion of sects or dogmas, but by one which constitutes the daily employment and the great end of agricul-

21

ture. The judge upon this occasion has by anticipation pronounced, that
to feed the hungry, clothe the naked, and give drink to the thirsty, are the
passports of future happiness; and the divine intelligence which selected
an agricultural state as a paradise for its first favourites, has there again
prescribed the agricultural virtues as the means for the admission of their
posterity into heaven.[2]

Attempts to explain the 1920s in terms of the rural-urban conflict
overlook the merging of interests in that same decade. National media,
national brands, chain stores, and improved roads were among the forces
reducing the essential differences. Small town editors sometimes praised
these trends and at other times denounced them. Their ambiguity is not
surprising; it was an ambiguous decade. The more manifestly ridiculous
the Agrarian Myth became, the more strongly its champions defended it.
People do not give up their myths easily.

Make no mistake about it: the provincials were in command of
public life in America. That is precisely what outraged Sinclair Lewis, H.
L. Mencken, and the expatriate intellectuals. The villagers were tough
political in-fighters, not above retaining legislative majorities by ignoring
constitutional mandates to reapportion themselves. They wanted to legis-
late the states and the nation back into the kind of prewar Eden they
thought they remembered, where Fundamentalist religion was secure,
where smart-aleck intellectuals knew their place, and where traditional
values of decency, thrift, neighborliness, family, patriotism, and American
superiority were unquestioned.

The provincials opposed the League of Nations for the same
reasons they stood so resolutely against immigration, the fear that contacts
with "foreigners" would dilute the manifest superiority of American
values. If speakers at Ku Klux Klan rallies were sometimes too bombastic
for their tastes, they recognized the oratorical style from their Fundamentalist churches and much of the content from their Rotary Club speakers.
The clash centered on Prohibition, an attempt by non-metropolitan,
white, middle-class Protestants to impose their moral values on the rest of
the nation. For fourteen years they succeeded.[3]

Certainly not all who lived in the hinterlands shared all these
values, any more than all who lived in cities objected to all of them. The Ku
Klux Klan thrived in many cities, where by no means everyone favored
unrestricted immigration, joining the League, or permitting legalized
booze. Attitudes toward Prohibition varied from neighborhood to neighborhood within the same cities, based largely on ethnicity.

It is easy to make too much of the fact that the 1920 Census
disclosed that for the first time a majority of Americans lived in "urban"

places. "Urban" meant towns of 2,500, almost exactly the size of Sauk Center, Minnesota, the model for Sinclair Lewis's Gopher Prairie. Towns many times that large — the Zeniths, if you will — were still rural in outlook. In terms of that distinction, relatively few Americans lived in real "cities."[4]

George F. Babbitt, like most of Zenith's civic leaders, was a product of smaller villages. Lewis underlined the similarity in this brief scene:

> Chum Frink had recently been on a lecture tour among the small towns, and he chuckled "Awful good to get back to civilization! I certainly been seeing some hick towns! I mean — Course the folks there are the best on earth, but gee whiz, those Main Street burgs are slow, and you fellows can't hardly appreciate what it means to be here with a bunch of live ones!"
>
> "You bet!" exulted Orville Jones. "They're the best folks on earth, those small-town folks, but oh, mama! What conversation! Why, say, they can't talk about anything but the weather and the nee-oo Ford, by heckalorum!"
>
> "That's right. They all talk about just the same things," said Eddie Swanson.
>
> "Don't they though! They just say the same thing over and over," said Vergil Gunch.[5]

The towns, both large and small, had their newspapers, although by the end of World War I, the trends toward chain ownership, consolidation, and one-newspaper towns were well under way. Villages that once had supported at least two papers, one for each political party, now had one. There were 14,000 weeklies, most of them published in small towns and trying to serve both the town readers and the nearby farmers. Many published news and features prepared and sent from distant cities, and the smallest still ran "patent insides," pages printed afar and shipped in, ready for the local editors to add material on the reverse sides.

Farm Economic Plight

During the preceding quarter-century of prosperity, American farmers had gone deeply into debt to plant more acreage, to use more workers, and to buy more expensive equipment. In the wake of World War I, they faced glutted markets. Between 1919 and 1921, corn dropped from $1.56 to 57¢, wheat from $2.14 to $1.19, and cotton from 29.6¢ to 12.3¢. The Secretary of Agriculture said farmers were selling at bankruptcy levels. The price of farm Irmer institutes under the auspices of the county

agents or the American Farm Bureau. Many of them, especially the young
and ambitious, put down their plows and headed for the cities. A New
England farmer was quoted in 1923: "This old farming community is like
the fish pond with the game fish all fished out; all we've got left now is the
bullheads and the suckers." More than a million southern blacks, mostly
from the rural areas, joined the exodus to the industrial cities of the north.[7]

The rural newspapers and the farm magazines complained about
the unfairness of all this, of course, but they found they had unaccustomed
company. Businessmen and industrialists said again and again that the
nation could not be truly prosperous if the farmers were not. "Businessmen
are just as interested in the development of the farm as the farmer himself,"
a Louisiana newspaper observed in 1928.[8] But there was a crucial difference in emphasis. They sang the praises of the farmer, not because they
thought he was noble, but because he was just another businessman,
increasingly concerned with efficient production and "scientific farming."
On a cruder level, of course, they also needed him as a consumer. The more
they stressed the interdependence of all *businesses,* the less ground it left
the agrarians to think of themselves in a "calling." The news accounts of
meetings of the Rotary Clubs and the Farm Bureaus sounded more and
more alike.

Farm leaders were grateful for this unexpected support from both
business and labor, but apparently they did not recognize that it undermined the basic premise of the Agrarian Myth. As one historian noted:

> Thus, the first doctrine of agrarianism was being transformed,
> however slowly, from a moral into an economic creed. Actually, it would
> be more accurate to say that there was a shift in emphasis. . . . Perhaps of
> more significance for the future, however, was the growing tendency . . .
> to look upon all industries as interdependent. . . . This point of view
> became widespread among farmers in the 1920s, serving as an argument
> for government aid to agriculture.[9]

Under the circumstances, rural editors had to soft-pedal direct
attacks on the economic system and upon factories. Villages were going all
out to attract factories, many offering free land, buildings and tax incen-
tives. The editor of a Michigan weekly wrote in 1922 that his town "ought
to be planning and pushing" to draw new plants. Two years later, he
painted the competition to attract factories as a life-or-death matter. The
town must again show the kind of spirit it had displayed in raising $40,000
to keep a plant from moving to Grand Rapids.[10] Papers in other towns
echoed these sentiments. Many, like Gopher Prairie, had sad experiences.
Its Commercial Club outfitted the town band in new uniforms, hired a

semi-pro pitcher for its baseball team, and installed street lights. The net result, however, was "one small shy factory which planned to make wooden automobile-wheels," which went belly-up within a year.

The rural spokesmen shifted to moral arguments. People in the cities did not *really* work. Unions, with their attempts to limit hours and to get wages so high that they forced up prices everyone else had to pay, were the proof of that. Strikes were anathema to the farmers. "If the farmer had shown his dislike for the pay he was getting and had quit, he would have been like the union workers who struck, and by so doing, put all kinds of business on the kibosch, besides running in debt for the food he needed for his family," wrote one weekly editor.[11]

City dwellers were pleasure-mad, their wives and children spoiled. They did not even know their neighbors or care about them. The liquor question provided a perfect focus for all this moral hostility. Al Smith was a non-Protestant, wet representative of the most notorious of all city political machines, Tammany Hall. His "East Side, West Side" theme song roused few kindly thoughts in the towns and villages.[12] While it no doubt would have come as a terrible shock to the agrarian radicals of a few decades earlier, the small towns in rural areas became the center of rock-ribbed political conservatism in the period between the World Wars.

Acceptance of Credit Buying

Before Gopher Prairie could hitch its wagon to modernism, it had to shuck some traditional values, one of the most fundamental of which was thrift. Farmers traditionally had gone to local banks for loans to buy seed, land, and equipment, but these were short-term and clearly work-related. In the 1920s came a new kind of credit buying, first of automobiles and then of other consumer goods. Many of these loans furthered not work, but pleasure; to compound the heresy, the money came from afar.

By 1920 ads in the newspapers offered new Fords for as little as one-third down. By 1926 three of four new cars were purchased on credit, and half the families in America had cars; the proportion was about the same in cities and in the country. Three times as many automobiles were registered at the end of the decade as at the beginning. Since local banks were not geared to handle such business, the automobile manufacturers set up their own finance firms. The loans generally were made for up to 16 months. Fewer than 1 in 100 lost the car for failing to meet the payments.[13] "We'd rather do without clothes than give up the car," a working-class mother of nine in Middletown told the Lynds.[14]

Credit buying was the key to developing a consumer society. The traditional Protestant ethos stressed salvation through self-denial. The prudent man husbanded his resources, both material and spiritual, to call upon that proverbial rainy day. Exponents of the new religion, such as the therapists and the advertising agencies, stressed the importance of using — "investing" if you will — one's resources. They were not scarce; they would multiply with use.[15]

The advertisements sought not only to call attention to available goods but to create a demand for those goods. As David Potter would suggest, advertising's most powerful effects are "not upon the economics of our distribution system; they are upon the values of our society." Certainly advertisements affirmed the rites of consumerism, generated as they had to be from a matrix of social acceptability.[16]

Some editors viewed with suspicion the mania for cars and the attendant credit buying. "People are spending their time in riding about the country in autos for pleasure when they ought to be working," wrote one.[17]

There were occasional — very occasional — warnings in the press about reckless credit purchases. For example, the Caro (Michigan) weekly complained: "The easy plan of purchasing automobiles has a tendency to lure many a man into investing more than good business judgment will warrant." If the craze for buying cars on time did not end soon, the editor warned, there was "grave danger of business suicide."[18]

The family that found Jehovah did not strike them dead for going into debt and that they really could meet monthly car payments was often ready for more credit buying. By the middle of the decade, ads for furniture, appliance, jewelry, and clothing stores usually mentioned "easy terms." A Minnesota editor complained about young people who went into debt in order to start out married life with all the things it had taken their parents a lifetime to accumulate: "One thing is certain and that is that those who work for what they get and add to their equipment gradually as they can add the extras will get the most enjoyment out of them."[19]

Such occasional lectures on thrift were drowned out in the ads in the newspapers, the magazines, the farm journals, and on the radio that chorused "Buy! Buy! Buy!"

Buy At Home

Best of all, buy from the hometown merchants. There probably were more editorials on that topic than any other during the decade. The themes, reinforced in full-page ads with twenty to twenty-five local business signatories, were the same: "the local businessman knows you and wants your continuing business"; "keep the money at home"; and "city stores are not really cheaper."

An editor tried to distinguish "rural businessmen" from "city profiteers": "You may be in a quandary as to how the city merchants can be cutting the price 25 percent while the country merchant does not follow suit. To begin with, the city prices are 25 percent higher to start with than the average country clothier."[20]

Every survey showed the opposite. City stores, especially the spreading chain stores, did offer lower prices. In any case, this advice had no noticable effect. A university survey of an Ohio county seat in 1927 found almost no loyalty to local merchants. Residents shopped wherever it was cheapest.[21] Probably the newspaper editor and his wife did the same.

The editors faced a dilemma when offered advertising by mail-order firms and merchants in other towns. How could they, in good conscience, accept such ads while urging readers to shop at home? Most of them ran the ads, although a few boasted in editorials of their refusal to do so. A book written for rural editors in 1928 said any editor who refused such "foreign" advertising was "no businessman."[22] In 1920s parlance, that was a harsh condemnation.

Of course, it was hard to tell by then who were "home merchants." By 1925, there were 22,000 grocery stores owned by the chains, many of them in small towns. Drug, variety, and dry goods stores were also parts of chains. Branch banks were spreading, too, a trend protested by one weekly: "We all know what it has meant to small towns to have chain stores with headquarters in some big city substituted for the home-owned institution, where the owner is directly dependent upon the local public." Although the editor did not acknowledge it, one thing it meant was more advertising. *Editor & Publisher,* the weekly trade magazine for newspapers, hailed the trend to chain stores, precisely because they did buy more ads than local retailers.[23]

Urbanized Content

America's best-known small town editor, William Allen White, concluded that by 1923 journalism had become more a business than a profession. He admitted that his Emporia (Kansas) *Gazette* was a part of the national distribution system, more attuned to serving the needs of advertisers than readers.[24] Whether this was new or not, White thought it was.

If editorial content was primarily something to wrap around the ads, then it made sense to run the cheapest and least controversial content, available from ready-print and boilerplate syndicates, located in distant cities. They would send either specified pages preprinted (innocuous copy with national ads already in place) or parts of pages, ready to be cast into type. Larger newspapers bought individual features — serialized fiction, comics, crossword puzzles and columns — and reset them on their own Linotypes.[25]

How much of this material did weeklies run? A 1920 survey of Missouri weeklies found 40 percent of editorial space devoted to syndicated material, and a survey two years later of Connecticut weeklies found nearly half.[26]

Local content tended to be *very* local and personal. ("Little Eleanor Butler accidentally fell against a hot stove Thursday and burned one hand.") Sociologist Robert E. Park defined news as organized gossip and in 1925 called local news "the very stuff that democracy is made of."[27]

Such personal news, focused on almost exclusively, also kept the editor out of trouble. When a journalism professor asked a Kansas editor why he almost never published anything about local controversies, he was told: "A newspaper that is bound to have all the news can turn a peaceable town into a bedlam. People like my policy."[28]

While there were editors who cared about more than profits, it was possible by the 1920s for a rural editor to make a comfortable living. Figures are hard to come by, but even in 1920 New York country editors reported an annual income of $2,000, double that for public school teachers. A Mississippi editor told a conference of editors in 1925 that after he deducted his salary of $300 a week, his weekly still netted $8,000. Much of that, of course, came from job printing.[29]

Movie Advertisements

Although most of the movies that played in the Rosebud Movie Palaces of the small towns were escapist and innocuous, the ads for them certainly stood out in the otherwise gray pages of the weekly newspapers. Ads featured scantily clad girls and racy copy, such as, "Lovemaking and heartbreaking as it is practiced by the fast-stepping young of today"; "Jazz Mad — A bubbling Toast to Youth — The dregs bitter with remorse — Daring — Exotic"; "Slaves of pleasure, lost in the spell of Broadway's lights and laughter. Driven by the lash of unfulfilled desires — on and on — dancing, loving, thirsting for new sensations — beyond the law —

beyond virtue — into the abyss."[30] Editors apparently did not worry about the ill effects of such advertising or such films on their readers.

Movie theaters in even the most conservative rural areas showed "documentaries" about venereal disease, prostitution and drug addiction. Perhaps because there were separate showings for men and women, accompanied by lectures by "experts," editors endorsed them as well as carrying their suggestive ads. The sex films had such titles as *The Port of Missing Girls, Which Way Are You Headed?* and *Are You Fit To Marry?* One editor praised such a film for presenting "plain, earnest and helpful" information about the venereal disease "menace," while another wrote: "It is gratifying to know that at last our false modesty is being set aside and the young people are being taught the true value of sex cleanliness."[31] Drug films included *The Devil's Needle* and *Human Wreckage,* the last written and presented by the widow of Wallace Reid, a Hollywood actor who died of drugs.

Many of these films were "quickies," produced on small budgets to capitalize on news events; however, even major studios produced some. Playing as they did, one or two days on a special performance basis, in each town, the films showed for many years.[32]

Rural Defensiveness

Whether they called him rube, bumpkin, or hick, the big city and national media — to say nothing of the vaudeville comedians — made their country cousin the butt of their humor. Those in the rural areas did not suffer this in silence. They found the jibes particularly galling at a time when they were on the outside of the national feast, looking in.

In answer to such critics, a small California daily listed some great men who grew up in hamlets and concluded, "A hick town is a place where a boy has an excellent opportunity to lay the foundation of future greatness." The comedians who got cheap laughs at the expense of the small town, wrote a Minnesota editor, were to be pitied because they never had known the friendliness and neighborliness of such places. "Give us the small town every day," he wrote.[33]

In 1921, *Country Gentleman* magazine commissioned a series by leading illustrations to show "what the farmer really looks like." As for verbal portraits, H. L. Mencken and some of his writers in *The American Mercury* were the arch-villains. Mencken and his ilk were not intelligent, wrote a Maine daily, "they are simply sex-obsessed, believing that to be outspoken to the degree of outlawry is all that is required to make one a genius."[34]

College boys, many of them refugees from small towns them-selves, might snicker at the articles, but they went down hard with their elders. In 1928, Marquis Childs, not yet the nationally syndicated colum-nist, wrote a piece for Mencken which accused small towns not only of being sinful but of taking a sniggering pride in their pathetic attempts to be naughty. Childs labeled it "a pleasurable sense of wrongdoing, the chal-lenging stimulation of having accepted a dare of long standing."[35]

The attitude toward big city critics was summarized in a 1920 cartoon. A "Huck Finn"-type office boy was saying to his editor:

> The big city papers kin poke fun at us for tellin' 'bout Paul Jones' new chicken coop — but, by Hek! We never fall fer no guff 'bout Mrs. Algernon Morganbilt's pomperanian [sic] pup "Piffle" havin' the pip and a lotta other items like that, witch them city papers print, do we boss? The editor's simple response was "Nope."[36]

Many editorials in the small town papers decried immorality. As often as the editors could, they identified immoral trends with the city, but sometimes they acknowledged problems, even in their corner of the world. For example, a weekly deplored "romantic boobs intent on squeezing their cuties" while driving: "There's too confounded much of this sort of things hereabouts. Old-fashioned ideas of decency used to limit hugging, kissing, and other demonstrations of adolescent romance to the privacy of the front parlor."[37]

The small town editors often combined their attacks on evils of the cities with praise for their own way of life. "By and large the man who succeeds in one place will succeed in another, and he will have a pleasanter, more normal life in the tall timber," said a northern Michigan weekly.[38] The abandonment of Eden theme frequently recurred. The Carmi (Illinois) Tribune-Star wrote that "in every city we find men of mature years, heads of families who would give anything to get back to the sanity and purity of country life — but they cannot." A Michigan weekly was sure that the ill-advised prodigals would return from the cities, buy some land and "settle down to lives of contentment and happiness." A small California daily warned the "juvenile army of longers after life and excitement" that they eventually would "give anything to get back to the simple pleasures and real friends of the small town."[39]

Seldom was the hostility toward the city spelled out so openly as in this comment from an Arkansas weekly: "The city yap will soon be breezing out to see his country cousins with the expectation of having the time of his life. Our small village stuff tickles him, while his funny city ways are duck soup for us, for he's as green in our town as we are in his. City life can't be so difficult if he gets by."[40]

The rural forces sought to define "deviance" in order to unify their own bonds. Kai T. Erikson would suggest that a society, by agreeing on what violates norms, spells out exactly what it finds acceptable. There has been little agreement from society to society or even in the same society over time; thus deviancy is a conferred quality, not an inherent one. These decisions are dramatized in trials, but the reaffirmation would have little real strength without reporting, since it is through the news accounts that most of the society participates vicariously in the reaffirmation.[41]

As Justice Felix Frankfurther would later say, "Justice must satisfy the appearance of justice."[42] The public and the trial participants must have faith in the symbols and rituals as well as the outcome. Certainly the newspapers of the 1920s carried much news and editorial comment on behavior defined as "deviant," both the type that came before the courts and that which did not.

Divorce, for example, received much more attention. Although the divorce rate did not really soar in that decade (rather it increased at roughly the same rate as in preceding decades), there were far more stories of divorce, many of them detailed. These included not only the nationally reported cases such as that of Peaches Browning or of the Charlie Chaplins, but also local cases. The Charlevoix (Michigan) *Courier,* for example, devoted more than a column of its front page in 1925 to detailed testimony from the divorce trial in a nearby city. A congressman's secretary testified that his wife had admitted to a string of infidelities.[43] Perhaps the editors were helping society define what was "deviant" in order to defend marriage, which they saw as an embattled institution.

While all societies punished such heinous crimes as murder and rape, there is little agreement on lesser offenses. Rural judges went lightly on poachers but were hell on trespassers; city courts dealt lightly with "victimless" crimes but sometimes cracked down on speeders or jaywalkers. On no social question of the 1920s was the difference in rural and urban attitudes so clearly differentiated as on Prohibition.

Enforcement of Prohibition

Small town editors were unanimous, or nearly so, on Prohibition.[44] Joseph R. Gusfield labeled it a "symbolic crusade" and defined Prohibition as a "battle in the struggle for status between two divergent styles of life. It marked the public affirmation of the abstemious, ascetic questions of American Protestantism. In this sense, it was an act of ceremonial deference toward the old middle-class culture. If the law was often disobeyed and not enforced, the respectability of its adherents was honored in the breach."[45]

Under local option laws, the rural areas had largely voted themselves dry before the enactment of the Volstead Act. The real question was whether a national law could force Prohibition on the cities. There were similar moves to outlaw or tighten laws against adultery, boxing, gambling, drug use and homosexuality, but none of those struck such a deep chord as Prohibition. Norman H. Clark would describe Prohibition as a long-term effort to defend the ideal of American nuclear family.[46]

Rural editors never tired of painting horror pictures of the old days of the saloon. Decades of temperance activity had won many adherents in these areas, long before there were any state or federal bans. Editors kept reassuring their readers that there was no chance of repeal or even modification of Prohibition. Big city papers championed the "destructive liquor interests," a downstate Illinois weekly wrote in 1923, but "clear thinking" rural editors who had "no selfish motive in thus enlisting on the side of the right" would see the Prohibition's continuation. Rural votes had enacted it, said the editor, and rural votes would defend it.[47]

When a weekly in western Michigan published a ballot in the spring of 1926, the editor found that his dry editorials were in accord with his community. Three-fourths of the 224 respondents urged "strong enforcement," while only eight favored repeal.[48]

Prohibition was fine, wrote one weekly, even if it did "make hypocrites and lawbreakers out of a great many respectable citizens who occasionally take a drink."[49] Probably many editors "wrote dry but drank wet"; still, most insisted that their areas were dryer — and better — places than they had been before the law.

The well-behaved crowds at the 1925 county fair were contrasted by a Michigan weekly with the rowdy ones in the days before Prohibition. Gone were the "beery smells" and the bawdy talk. "Never again the old licensed liquor saloon," said the editor. To modify the law by permitting beer, wrote a Wisconsin paper, would signal a flagging in the enthusiasm for enforcement and would serve as a first step to total repeal.[50]

Another indication of how strongly those in farm states felt came when the administrators in two South Dakota colleges, Dakota Wesleyan and Northern State, forbid their student debaters from taking the affirmative side in debates on the national topic, the revision of the Volstead Act. Even debating the topic, said the college officials, encouraged illegal activity.[51]

Although the Grange was largely a social order by the 1920s, it was foursquare for Prohibition, as the minutes of the state and national meetings made clear. Often the resolutions identified the Wet forces with the wicked city. For example, the 1923 Michigan Grange meeting resolution supporting stronger enforcement for Prohibition, included this remark: "Our democracy is positively menaced by the raids of the lawless emanating from our great centers of population."

An Alabama newspaper noted that all those arrested in a recent raid on Texas Guinnan's New York speakeasy had foreign names. Most were "alien in thought and act" and lacked the "lifelong training in American ideals." The best solution, said the editor was "wholesale deportations."[52]

Editors often pointed out that the loudest calls for repeal came from the immigrant groups in big cities. Their "foreign" drinking habits were just one more irritant to editors in small towns, who almost unanimously wanted immigration cut off, or at least drastically reduced. (Congress did just that in the acts of 1921 and 1924.[53]) "Alien people in an alien land who do not assimilate our ideas but try to promote hotbeds of violence and Bolshevism" should not only be kept out but deported if they were already here, wrote a Grange paper,[54] and those sentiments were echoed across the land.

Editors implicitly distinguished "old immigration" from "new immigration." A weekly in Minnesota that regularly carried ads for touring Swedish-language entertainments, wanted the gates closed and the undesirables shipped out before the nation was "stocked with criminals, insane and other kinds of people whom other countries want to get rid of." A small daily in a predominately German county of Wisconsin decried the "overwhelming proportion of undesirables" among recent arrivals and feared they would swamp American institutions.[55]

There were suggestions that the immigrants be steered onto the vacant farms, but one editor scoffed: "Those immigrants are going straight to Ford's and other factories where big wages are paid."[56] Had the Italians, Poles, Russians, Greeks, and others tried to move into rural areas, they would not have been greeted warmly. Although most ruralites had almost no contact with such people, they feared anyone who was different. They damned them for huddling together in the city ghettos, and they damned them for any plan to move into the countryside.

Some hostility was thinly veiled anti-semitism. Such feelings were on the rise in the 1920s, as the long lists of incidents published each year in the yearbooks of the American Jewish Committee attested. Nonetheless, it was not fashionable to publish in newspapers (aside from special cases such as Henry Ford's Dearborn *Independent*) virulently anti-semitic remarks; instead the editors focused on events which embraced the concept without labeling it. One example will suffice, the Loeb-Leopold trial of 1924. The two defendants were rich Jews from Chicago, and the crime, the thrill killing of a youth, clearly heinous.

After decrying Chicago as the "prolific mother of crime and criminal ideas," the Hastings (Michigan) *Banner* added: "If these perverts were to be tried in Hastings or in any place where decent standards of life are maintained by the majority, there can be no question . . . they would get the limit of the law." A northern Wisconsin daily urged the judge to act courageously to restore "some of the old country respect for the law into the present generation." A Georgia weekly which seldom ran editorials devoted two columns of its front page to its outrage about the failure to execute "those two Chicago degenerates."[57] There were similar outcries against Sacco and Vanzetti. Although not from Chicago or New York, they were "foreigners" who lived in the East and espoused radical ideas.

Conclusions

The United States was changing in fundamental ways in the 1920s. The changes not only alarmed but confused those in the rural areas. Those who lived in the Gopher Prairies, and even those who had moved to the Zeniths, had always known their "enemies" were the big cities and their institutions. But with the spread of automobiles, roads, chain stores, mass media, and manufacturing plants, the traditional lines were blurred. Editors could no longer lash out at the cities without, at the same time, assailing their own towns.

Finding themselves and their values under attack, the agrarians attempted to recast the struggle in moralistic terms. They invoked the rhetoric, but not really the spirit, of the Agrarian Myth. They cast about for what was truly distinctive about rural life and values, and they found there was not much left. As Kirschner wrote of the agrarian, "Once he began to enjoy this tender embrace with the new society, he could no longer really attack it with quite the same unqualified conviction."[58] The agrarian had been co-opted, and he had been a willing partner in the process.

The keynote speaker at the 1929 convention of the Washington State Farm Bureau drew cheers when he invoked an even older myth, that of Hercules' inability to subdue the smaller Antaeus. Each time Hercules hurled Antaeus down, he picked up strength from his mother, the Earth. Hercules won only when he held Antaeus aloft. The speaker told the audience, largely wheat growers, that they were also engaged in a mighty struggle against powerful monopolistic interests. "Your only hope is to keep close to the soil," he told them. "Stay by your mother, the earth, and from her draw the strength which will enable you to hold your own against the modern Hercules."[59]

Even a half century later politicians could win applause by invoking the Agrarian Myth, just as some Southern demagogues would invoke "bloody shirt" oratory; however, by 1930 agrarians no more expected the tide to turn in favor of their values than the Southerners expected a reversal of the outcome of the Civil War. Nostalgia served as a patina on the past, especially for those who had never known the earlier era first-hand. (Thoreau has more appeal for those trapped in a big city than for those who are trying, perhaps like Thoreau, with little success, to eke a living out of a field of beans.)

It is important to remember that there were people who took the Agrarian Myth seriously, who did believe that theirs was a true calling. As James B. Shideler would point out, it is unfortunate that the defeat of this idealism was so total. "Much that was good in American country life was lost and much that was trashy and life-diminishing and hazardous won out."[60]

The mass media certainly contributed to the outcome. People across the nation, in the cities and in the country, were listening to the same radio programs, responding to the same advertising appeals, watching the same motion pictures, and to an increasing degree, reading the same words in their newspapers and magazines. But it is simplistic to suggest that the mass media caused the merging of rural and urban interests. As always, the media were symptoms as well as precursors of change.

So, by the time the stock market crash of 1929 punctuated the complex decade of the 1920s, what was left of the Agrarian Myth? Not much, really. Although they were reluctant to admit it, even to themselves, the provincials already had imbibed too freely of the forbidden fruit of materialism ever again to retreat to their rural Eden. Deep down, they had no desire to retreat.

Notes

1. Paul H. Johnstone, "Old Ideals Versus New Ideas in Farm Life," *USDA Yearbook*, 1940, pp. 111-170, summarizes the literature on the Agrarian Myth succinctly.

2. Quoted in Loren Baritz, *City on a Hill* (New York: John Wiley, 1964), p. 198.

3. Loren Baritz, ed., *The Culture of the Twenties* (Indianapolis: Bobbs-Merrill, 1970), pp. xv-lv.

4. Gopher Prairie is the locale for Sinclair Lewis, *Main Street* (New York: Harcourt, Brace & World, 1920); Zenith is the setting for his Babbitt (New York: Harcourt, Brace & World, 1922).

5. Lewis, *Babbitt*, pp. 117-118.

6. James C. Malin, *The United States and the World War* (Boston: Ginn & Com-

pany, 1930), pp. 228-229. See also the annual reports of the U.S. Secretary of Agriculture.

7. Theodore Saloutos and John D. Hicks, *Agricultural Discontent in the Middle West, 1930-1939* (Madison: University of Wisconsin Press, 1951); Grant McConnell, *The Decline of American Democracy* (New York: Atheneum, 1969). Quote from New York *Times*, 2 January 1923.

8. Baton Rouge *Morning Advocate*, 25 September 1928.

9. Clifford B. Anderson, "The Metamorphosis of American Agrarian Idealism in the 1920's and 1930's," *Agricultural History* 35 (October 1961): 182-188.

10. Hastings (Michigan) *Banner*, 1 February 1922 and 10 December 1924.

11. Manchester (Michigan) Enterprise, 1 July 1920.

12. Don S. Kirschner, *City and Country: Rural Responses to Urbanization in the 1920's* (Westport, Ct.: Greenwood Press, 1970), pp. 23-43; Edmund A. Moore, *A Catholic Runs for President* (New York: Ronald Press, 1956), pp. 41-108.

13. James J. Flink, *The Car Culture* (Cambridge: MIT Press, 1975), p. 148; J. A. Estey, "Financing the Sale of Automobiles," *Annals of American Association of Political and Social Sciences* 116 (November 1924): 44-49.

14. Robert S. and Helen M. Lynd, *Middletown* (New York: Harcourt, Brace & World, 1929); Mark S. Foster, "The Automobile and the City," *Michigan Quarterly Review* 20 (Fall 1980 Winter 1981): 459-471.

15. T. J. Jackson Lears, "From Salvation to Self-Realization: Advertising and the Therapeutic Roots of the Consumer Culture, 1880-1930," paper presented to American Historical Association, 1980.

16. David Potter, *People of Plenty* (Chicago: University of Chicago Press, 1954), p. 233. Some recent writers have disagreed with Potter, e.g., Lears, *No Place of Grace: Antimodernism and the Transformation of American Culture, 1880-1920* (New York: Pantheon, 1981). See also James Carey, "A Cultural Approach to Communication," *Journal of Communication* 2 (1975): 1-22.

17. Cedar Springs (Michigan) *Liberal*, 11 July 1923.

18. Caro (Michigan) *Tuscola County Advertiser*, 2 October 1925.

19. Anoka (Minnesota) *County Union*, 6 January 1926.

20. Fowlerville (Michigan) *Review*, 7 July 1920.

21. Perry P. Denune, *Business Research Bulletin* (Columbus: Ohio State University, 1927), p. 60.

22. Phil C. Bing, *The Country Weekly* (New York: Appleton, 1928), 281.

23. Hastings *Banner* 22 March 1927; *Editor & Publisher*, 22 March 1927.

24. *Autobiography of William Allen White* (New York: Macmillan, 1946), p. 626. See Griffith chapter in this volume.

25. John C. Sim, *The Grass Roots Press* (Ames: Iowa State University Press, 1969), p. 6; Edwin Emery and Michael Emery, *The Press and America*, 4th ed. (Englewood Cliffs, N.J.: Prentice-Hall, 1978), pp. 311-312.

26. Carl C. Taylor, "The Town Newspaper as a Town-Country Agency," *Proceedings* of Fourth American Country Life Association Convention (1921), pp. 36-46; Malcolm M. Willey, *The Country Newspaper* (Chapel Hill: University of North Carolina Press, 1926).

27. Newberry (Mich.) *News*, 6 May 1927; Robert E. Park, "The Natural History of the Newspaper," reprinted in Wilbur Schramm, ed., *Mass Communications* (Urbana: University of Illinois Press, 1949), p. 7-22.

28. Leon N. Flint, *The Conscience of the Newspaper* (New York: Appleton-Century, 1925), p. 75.

29. M. V. Atwood, "The Country Weekly's Future," *Quill* 9 (August 1921): pp. 8-9;

C.T. Reed, "Making 50 Per Cent Return on Country Newspaper Investment," *Journalism Bulletin* 36 (Columbia: University of Missouri, 1925), 72-73.

30. Ads for *Love 'Em and Leave 'Em*, Three Rivers (Michigan) *Commerical*, 14 March 1927; *Our Dancing Daughters*, Alpena *News*, 20 November 1928; *On With the Dance!*, Hastings *Banner*, 22 July 1920.

31. Hastings *Banner*, 18 March 1920; Ovid (Michigan) *Register-Union*, 4 November 1920.

32. Kathleen Karr, "The Long Square-Up: Exploitation Trends in Silent Film," *Journal of Popular Culture* 3 (Spring 1974): 107-128.

33. Alameda (California) *Times*, 26 March 1927; *Anoka County Union*, 11 August 1926.

34. Lewiston (Maine) *Evening Journal*, 18 August 1927.

35. Marquis Childs, "Midwestern Night's Entertainment," *American Mercury* 15 (October 1928): 174.

36. Ames (Iowa) *Daily Tribune*, 2 January 1920.

37. Manchester *Enterprise*, 5 April 1920.

38. *Osceola County Herald*, 12 October 1922.

39. Carmi (Illinois) *Tribune-Times*, 1 November 1923; Manchester *Enterprise*, 7 May 1920; Alameda *Times Star*, 10 January 1927. These themes were reiterated in full-page booster ads, e.g., Barron (Wisconsin) *Barron County Shield*, 11 August 1927.

40. Clinton (Arkansas) *Van Buren County Democrat*, 7 April 1 922.

41. Kai T. Erikson, *Wayward Puritans: A Study of Sociological Deviance* (New York: John Wiley, 1966), pp. 1-30. See also, John B. Brazil, "Murder Trials, Murder, and Twenties America," *American Quarterly* 33 (Summer 1981): 163-184.

42. *Offutt V. U.S.*, 348 U.S. 11, 14 (1954).

43. 1 January 1925.

44. Kirschner found this in the papers of Illinois and Iowa, and the author found the same in small town papers from coast to coast.

45. Joseph H. Gusfield, *Symbolic Crusade* (Urbana: University of Illinois Press, 1963), pp. 7-8. Even recent scholars who dispute Gusfield's conclusions credit him for drawing attention to the symbolic nature of Prohibition.

46. Norman H. Clark, *Deliver Us From Evil* (New York: Norton, 1976), p. 149.

47. Carmi *Tribune-Times*, 24 October 1923.

48. *Osceola County Herald*, 6 May 1926.

49. Newberry (Michigan) *News*, 18 October 1927.

50. Hastings *Banner*, 9 September 1925; *Barron County Shield*, 2 February 1928.

51. Boston *Globe*, 10 November 1926.

52. Mobile *Daily Resgister*, 6 August 1928.

53. See Marzolf chapter in this volume for discussion of immigration restriction.

54. *Michigan Patron*, 1 January 1921, p. 3.

55. Fosston (Minnesota) *Thirteen Towns*, 25 June 1926; Fond du Lac (Wisconsin) *Reporter*, 17 April 1922.

56. Manchester *Enterprise*, 2 August 1923.

57. Hastings *Banner*, 18 June 1924; Antigo (Wisconsin) *Daily Journal*, 11 August 1924; Decatur (Georgia) *New Era*, 13 September 1924.

58. Kirschner, *City and Country*, p. 255.

59. Colfax (Washington) *Gazette*, 18 January 1929.

60. James H. Shideler, "Flappers and Philosophers and Farmers: Rural-Urban Tensions of the Twenties," *Agricultural History* 47 (October 1973): 283-300.

3 Anticipating the Unexpected
Amazing Stories in the Interwar Years

Michelle Herwald

W hile "man has always lived in a technological age, insofar as his life and work have been bound up with his technology,"[1] the 1920s and 1930s earned the title "Machine Age" because of the accelerated pace of technological development and the increasing awareness of human dependence upon technology which they witnessed. According to Edwin E. Slosson, author of "Twentieth Century Science and Invention": "More has been added to the sum of human knowledge in most of the sciences during the first quarter of the twentieth century than in any whole century previous, and . . . all of the sciences have been more quickly and extensively applied to daily life than ever before."[2] Periodicals of the interwar years assessed the effects of this application of science to daily life. While marvelling at the new wonders of the scientific age, magazine articles of the period also questioned man's ability to understand and assimilate the changes which this scientific revolution wrought. They evaluated what this revolution was displacing, weighed the impact of this revolution upon human values, and wondered whether scientific advances were being matched by concomitant gains in knowledge of men and of social institutions.[3]

The debate over the meaning of the "Machine Age" which occurred in publications such as *World's Work, Outlook,* and the *New Republic* (where the mechanical environment was viewed "as a concrete social condition"[4]) contributed to the establishment of a new literary genre, science fiction (where the mechanical environment was presented symbolically).[5]

Busying itself "with the imaginative treatment of the . . . Machine Age,"[6] *Amazing Stories,* the first magazine to confine itself to science fiction, appeared in 1926.[7] From the start, the magazine identified science and its agent technology as key determinants of social change in the

39

interwar decades and published stories which focused on the social implications of technological development. Tending to emphasize the positive
implications of such development, *Amazing Stories* showered its readers
with the wonders of scientific possibilities and stressed ways in which
science had already introduced spectacular changes in American life. The
magazine contended, moreover, that the scientific age was just beginning.
Americans of the 1920s stood at "the threshold of a new and unprecedented era" of scientific progress.[8] Openly embracing both the nature and
the scope of the changes which this era would entail, the publication
encouraged its audience to welcome rather than fear technology. It published stories such as "Automaton" which portrayed a world populated by
mechanical men who were credited with lifting "struggling Humanity from
the tedium of ceaseless toil to a state of comparative ease and comfort."[9]

Assuming that resistance to social change is frequently rooted in
fear of the unknown, *Amazing Stories* attempted to make its readers
familiar with the contours of scientific development. Noting that science
was already introducing social change at a mind-boggling rate, the magazine presented itself as a means whereby its readers could keep abreast of
scientific advance and thus adapt to the rapid succession of social changes.

While they welcomed scientific advance as a source of social
change, the editors of *Amazing Stories* were nevertheless aware of the fact
that scientific advance could also create social tension. Tension of this sort
was revealed in the magazine primarily in two ways: (1) the gap between
science and the "average man" which was reflected in the "Discussions"
column, a letter to the editor section; and (2) fears expressed in the stories
that the scientific age would not be as positive as predicted.[10]

Science and the Average Man

Both editors and readers of *Amazing Stories* noted that, despite
living in a scientific age, only a small proportion of the population had
developed an appreciation of science or comprehension of its principles.
Why was the vast majority universed and disinterested in the scientific
world? Contributors to *Amazing Stories* attributed this apathy to the fact
that science had a very poor popular image. "To the average man [science
meant] a musty book sealed with seven seals."[11] The public viewed it as
"cold" and "dry." "Even in this scientific age," science was deemed a
"prohibitive subject"[12] which in the estimation of one reader spelled
"stodgy drudgery to the average human being."[13] In the mind of another
reader, who expressed his view in an editorial in the quarterly supplement

to the monthly magazine, science was "so complicated, so intricate" that only "technically trained scientific men" would be interested in it.[14] Restricting his reading to "familiar things that come easy," the average man, in the view of author/physician Miles Breuer, did not know or care anything about science.[15] The "small smattering of science" which the average man possesses was, according to author Frank Barclay, culled from "the Sunday Magazine sections of the newspapers and the tidbits of science to be found in the popular magazines."[16]

The editors of *Amazing Stories* set out to alter what they, their authors, and their readers believed to be the popular image of science. Editor Hugo Gernsback and his staff wanted to dispel what adherents of *Amazing Stories* perceived to be public distaste for science, dissolve apparent public disinterest in the scientific world, and render science comprehensible to a lay readership. One of the specific aims of the magazine, as articulated by reader Bertram Schumpf, was to "popularize" science, to "bring science to the masses" by rendering it fit for mass consumption.[17] This rendering was to be accomplished by showing people that science was, contrary to what they might believe, exciting, dynamic and comprehensible. Attempting to overcome popular prejudice against science, Gernsback turned to fiction, a medium which had already demonstrated its appeal to the non-scientist. Such readers of Gernsback's science fiction publications as C. A. Livingston and David Speaker appreciated this strategy. Livingston was confident that if science were "coupled with something that appeals to the average person's love for romance, excitement and the mystery of the unknown, in short, fiction," it would attract many followers.[18] Speaker reasoned that: "A total stranger to the world of science if not guided would probably never in the whole course of his life either willingly pick up a book treating . . . some scientific subject or show any desire to acquaint himself with some of the facts connected with the study. But let him once get engrossed in a 'Scientifiction' story from the pen of a skillful author and immediately his interest is awakened."[19]

By "mingling good science with good fiction," *Amazing Stories* sought not only to entertain its readers but to instruct them as well. Assuming the average man's distaste for science stemmed, in part, from his inability to understand it, the editors concluded that they must show the average man that science was within his grasp. This was to be accomplished by providing scientific data in what one reader termed "palatable form," serving "easily digested doses of science,"[20] which in the editors' words "need no special forcing . . . down the public's throat."[21] In other words, science was to be broken down to its simplest, most assimilable level.

Readers appreciated the way in which the "sugar coating" of the science in the stories helped to facilitate scientific learning. J. Roy Chapman praised *Amazing Stories* for making the acquisition of scientific knowledge "a pleasant and unconscious pastime."[22] Floyd Anderson commended the publication for "painlessly" educating the public.[23] Earle Brown asserted that the reader could *"not help* [emphasis added] getting a great deal of practical education out of it."[24] Douglass Benson claimed that because it offered "very good lessons in science in an easy, readable and interesting style,"[25] *Amazing Stories* was preferable to a scientific textbook.

Benson was one of several readers who favorably contrasted reading a good science fiction story with the tedium of prying scientific information from textbooks. Indeed, in the preface to the science questionnaire "What Do You Know?" the editors boasted about how frequently their readers "commented on the fact that there is more actual knowledge to be gained through reading [the] pages [of *Amazing Stories*] than from many a textbook." Describing the objective of their publication as supplying fiction "based on natural science so that the person who reads *Amazing Stories* will not feel that he is wasting his time on imaginary adventures and episodes, but . . . realize that he is studying science or perhaps imbibing" it, the editors asserted that the "kind of letters" which they received told them that they were succeeding in their efforts "in this direction."[26]

A number of readers' testimonies supported their contention. Catherine Moran thanked the authors for having sent her "to a surprising number of places where knowledge is stored—to archaeology, to geology, anthropology and embryology, to physics, to astronomy and optics."[27] Neil Tasker believed that science fiction taught him "more about Time, Space, Motion, Astronomy, the Fourth Dimension and countless other mysteries of the Universe" than any other source he could think of.[28] Others praised the magazine for rendering science comprehensible to them. One woman wrote that she was delighted to discover that the scientific explanations in the stories were "written as if [they] were meant to be understood by everybody."[29]

Despite these declarations, there were indications that the magazine was experiencing difficulty in achieving the objectives of its popularization campaign. The expectation that the average individual would develop an interest in science from reading *Amazing Stories* did not always materialize. Several readers revealed that they read the stories for their entertainment value, while ignoring their scientific dimensions. They complained that there were too many scientific explanations in the stories; and, moreover, that they were dry, uninteresting and unenjoyable. Conceding that it was all right to include scientific data in the stories so long "as it is kept on more or less 'popular' lines," one reader opposed suffocating mathematical dissertations.[30] Another suggested that when a story was filled with incomprehensible explanations, the average reader "skipped that part entirely."[31]

The editors were confident that science *could* be adapted to ordinary intelligence. But, despite every effort to make them simple, the lengthy scientific explanations which peppered the stories remained difficult for the non-scientist. And the feature "What Do You Know?" did not, as its preface promised, make it "possible for anyone to grasp the important facts." One reader remained convinced that "Mr. Average Reader wouldn't know any more about Newton's law of action and reaction," after he read the page that the questionnaire directed him to than before he began.[32] To the average person who tried to read *Amazing Stories* without some sort of scientific background, another reader observed, the magazine might as well have been written in Greek.[33]

Thus, contrary to its intention of reducing the gap between the average man and the scientist, *Amazing Stories'* educational efforts may have enforced the distance between the two. The inability to comprehend the science in the magazine created feelings of inferiority, anger and dejection on the part of a number of readers. Comprehension of the science in the magazine conversely produced pride and great satisfaction for others, who felt that it bespoke "a superior mentality."[34] At the same time that the editors marketed their product with the assurance that it could easily be understood by anyone, they also claimed to direct their wares to "a highly intelligent and appreciat[ive] audience."[35] Realizing that very few of his acquaintances could appreciate science fiction "because more than average intelligence is required to grasp the salient factor," Bryan Dunlavey feared that while "this requirement gratified" his ego, it nonetheless made him feel "uncomfortable—somehow undemocratic."[36]

The term "undemocratic" is an important one for it suggests that Dunlavey was aware that as society became more technological, it became, in turn, more complex and more exclusive. The dwindling number of people who understood the scientific world were in a position to make decisions for the majority of the population, those who were unversed in science and yet increasingly affected by it. The inability of this majority to participate effectively, if at all, in discussions of a scientific nature resulted in a kind of dependency of the unversed upon the versed.[37] Given the way in which science was pervading virtually every facet of American life in the twentieth century, the dependency upon the judgment and intentions of this scientific elite grew in significance in the postwar period. The efforts of the editors of *Amazing Stories* to broaden the ranks of that elite did little to reduce the capacity of this situation to generate social tension during the decades of the 1920s and 1930s.

Fears

Social tension also arose during this time period from the possibility that man would use technology neither wisely nor well. In spite of the fact that the publication promoted a very positive vision of scientific intentions, doubts remained.[38] These emanated primarily from three sources: (1) recognition that technology could be used for evil purposes as well as good; (2) recognition that technology greatly altered the ability of one individual to dominate many; and (3) recognition that technology could transcend human control. These doubts found expression in the stories in images of technological violence, a strain of violence developed under the auspices of technology which became the focus of scholars only in the aftermath of World War II.

By its very nature, technology could expand human capabilities. It extended senses, enhanced precision and compensated for weakness. In a technological age, physical strength proved to be of little importance. Weapons could turn an "unimposing fellow into the mightiest of killers."[39] Before modern technology, it required a good deal of physical effort to kill one individual; with modern technology the mere pressing of a button could kill thousands. Technology not only increased the range and improved the accuracy of violence, but it also altered its very character. Unlike violence which erupted unpredictably from uncontrollable rage and was totally irrational in nature, technological violence born in the rationality of its sponsor was methodical, planned, systematic, and impersonal.

The technological violence which appeared in the fiction of *Amazing Stories* and successor magazines in the interwar years can be divided into two distinct types: technological violence which was directed by man, and technological violence which was independent of human direction. The former technological violence was related to the capacity of technology to accelerate or amplify man's intent. The machine was neutral. Man decided whether it would be used for creative or destructive purposes. Placing an enormously increased potential for good or evil at man's disposal, technology magnified the power under an individual's control.[40] The power of the machine so increased the capacity of one man to direct another that it effected the transcendence of the technologically equipped over the unequipped. With a machine in tow, man became a superman, infinitely superior to others. Drunk with the power of the machine, he was infected by a technological vertigo which produced alienation. Thriving on what an analyst in 1928 called "an ecstasy of self extension in power,"[41] he was alienated in the Faustian as opposed to the Marxian sense (i.e., his alienation derived from being the manipulator of technology rather than its victim).[42]

Those who used technology this way seemed to adopt machine-like traits in a process which later scholarship would term "mechanomorphosis."[43] The perpetrator of technological violence appeared emotionally detached from his victims. His detachment stemmed not only from Faustian alienation, but also from the distance between attacker and victim which modern technology permitted. Technology killed "with such speed and distance that . . . cries of appeasement [or gestures of conciliation][54][44] were muted or not heard."[45] Viewing his victims as "objectified targets pinned in symbols to instrument boards," the "technologized killer" felt "no comradeship in death,"[46] no empathy for those he was about to annihilate.

Linking technological violence and the Great War, Lewis Mumford would observe in *Technics and Civilization* that: "the difference between the Athenians with their swords and shields fighting on the fields of Marathon, and the soldiers who faced each other with tanks, guns, flame-throwers and hand-grenades on the Western Front is the difference between the ritual of the dance and the routine of the slaughterhouse."[47] Observers of the period noted how "other wars had left their desolation, but The First World War was conspicuous in its spreading of desolation, with efficient and repetitious regularity."[48]

Science fiction stories confirmed the strong bond between technological violence and World War I in the popular psyche. Crediting the war with developing "the ultimate refinements in the destruction of human life,"[49] science fiction associated the war with engines of destruction, death-dealing devices and deadly gases.[50] Recalling how he and his science had killed thousands of his fellow men "in the last war," the scientist in a story of 1930 demonstrates how an atomic ray machine which his naive protege had envisioned being used for "a fuller life for the world" could also be used to kill.[51] Haunted by the technological destruction wrought by the war, science fictional characters were plagued by the likelihood that technology, or as one author termed it "diabolical inventiveness," would result in far worse devastation in future wars.[52]

In the first broad category of technologized violence appearing in science fiction in the interwar years, man predominated as the creator and director. In the second category, man was the target, its unfortunate, defenseless victim. His descent from the heights of Faustian manipulation to the depths of mechanical victimization began with increased dependence on machinery. In "Paradise and Iron," the story of a mysterious island run by automatic machinery, the population is described as being "so pampered by the machines," that they were not "quickly resourceful." "The people had become so accustomed to being waited on by machinery that they were helpless and [took] no initiative in personal matters."[53]

Human degeneracy told only half of the story of the emergence of the mastery of the machine over man. The other half was told by the traits attributed to the machine in stories of the interwar period. Consistently portrayed as devoid of any usual emotion, the machine *was* pictured as possessing "one emotional reaction," that is, if emotion is the appropriate term. It was obsessed by ambition, a "desire to increase its own efficiency."[54] At the core of this ambition was independence from human control. As man became more and more dependent upon the machine, the machine became more and more independent of man.[55] Ever assuming greater sophistication, the machine attained a level of complexity beyond the understanding of everyone but the highly specialized. The machine in "He Who Shrank" for example was described as "bewilderingly complicated, a maze of gears, wheels, switchboards, lights, levers, buttons, tubing and intricacies beyond . . . comprehension.[56] None of the people in "Paradise and Iron" understood how the machines worked. When a machine broke down, the people stood by helplessly until a repair machine arrived.

Like the repair machine in "Paradise and Iron," numerous machines in the stories of the period functioned automatically. Once set in motion they achieved "a somewhat autonomous life."[57] For the hero of "Paradise and Iron," the autonomy of the machine resulted in the "silly" but very revealing "tendency . . . of attributing personalities to machines as though they had minds of their own."[58] The tendency to anthropomorphize automatic machinery was quite common in the science fiction of the 1920s and 30s. Machines assumed both human consciousness and forms. The "Infinite Brain," a forerunner of the computer, exactly duplicated "the mechanical and electrical processes occurring in the human brain."[59] Robots which resembled man not only mentally, but physically as well, appeared regularly. Whatever the form, automatic machinery harbored malevolent intentions. Seeming "to spout everything indicative of complete destruction,"[60] it was described as a "menace to humanity,"[61] "sinister in appearance" and "foreboding" in its deliberate action."[62] "Entirely metallic,"[63] the machine was portrayed as threatening "the very foundations of civilization."[64]

Devoid of compassion for its creator, increasingly independent from his control, ascribed with direful intentions, the machine also appeared in many respects superior to man. So Professor Holtz, the creator of the "Automaton," found that "everything that is done by a human being can be done better and more efficiently by a machine!" After comparing man's clumsiness to the "efficiency of mechanical movement" and man's puny muscles to the power of the machine, the professor concluded that "there is practically no line of work that the machine does not now, or will not in the future, do better, faster and cheaper than man alone can do it."[65]

Merely tolerated as inferiors, men had to accommodate themselves to mechanical standards.[66] Perhaps the ultimate form of such accommodation was provided in the "The Sunken World" by Stanton Coblentz where "scores of grime-faced and sooty men" were clamped to the ground by iron vises and "fastened by long rods to the wheels above." All the while the rods moved with clock-like regularity up and down pulling the arms of the men with them and leading an astonished observer to exclaim, "It ain't the men that work the machines! It's the machines that work the men!" Bound to the machines as slaves, men served the machine's discretion.[67] When no longer useful, the men "were crushed and mangled by the very masters they had served." Their hearts and brains were gnashed by the steel jaws without causing the great wheels to cease to turn "or the leaves to clatter."[68]

The notion of the machine destroying its creator conjured up the image of Frankenstein, the manufactured monster whose imagery was given fresh emphasis in the influential play, *R.U.R.*, by Czechoslovakian Karel Capek. Depicting the ruthless extermination of the human race by robots, the imaginative contents of the drama, which opened in New York in 1922, figured prominently in the iconography of American science fiction of the interwar years. The plots of several stories expanded the Frankenstein theme into an all out war between men and machines. In "Paradise and Iron" for example, war broke out between the men who dwelt in the "City of Beauty" and the automatic machines that resided in the pointedly named "City of Smoke" under the rule of the Squid, a tangled oily piece of machinery with long metal tentacles and an electric brain. Ultimately, the Squid was defeated but at the cost of civilization. Like other stories featuring human-mechanical warfare, "Paradise and Iron" was rife with eschatological imagery. In "The Mentanicals," what was termed "machine life" threw off "the yoke of man and destroyed him."[69] In "Cities of Ardarthia" and "He Who Shrank" humans become extinct in a totally mechanical world.

The vision of "huge, grotesque metal structures and strange

·mechanical contrivances"[70] functioning without human presence evoked a major concern preoccupying the country during the Depression namely, human displacement by the machine, technological unemployment.[71] Directly voicing this concern was "The Mentanicals" in which the observer of a future society was not surprised that the human worker had been finally "ejected from the industrial process and cast out to . . . perish."[72]

Postscript

During his struggle with the Squid in Breuer's "Paradise and Iron," the hero, Davy Breckinridge, passed out. He awakened to find that the locus of the story, a mysterious island run by automatic machinery, had taken on familiar geographic dimensions:

> He recognized the Missouri and Mississippi Rivers and Great Lakes and Appalachian Mountains. In lovely valleys in Texas and Missouri and Indiana were beautiful cities like little glimpses of Paradise. . . . Then there were other cities, huge, smoky, congested clots, in mining districts and in oil areas whose streets were congested with clattering machines and totally devoid of human beings.[73]

The identification of the United States as the place where the future of technological society would be determined was not confined to *Amazing Stories*. In 1926 an article which equated American society and "machine civilization" appeared in the *New York Times*. Written by Capek, the European playwright, the article grew out of the author's displeasure with American failure to understand that his play about a robot world had been meant as a "protest against Americanization and its technological culture."[74] Condemning the values of that culture, Capek argued that they resulted in concern "with the increase of output and not with the increase of life"[75] and in interest focused more "in the size of things than in the soul of things."[76]

Responding to Capek's warning "against making mechanization the spiritual mistress of our existence," Glenn Frank, president of the University of Wisconsin, argued that it was better to view machine civilization as something to be domesticated rather than destroyed.[77] Objecting to Capek's desire to return to a "leisurely and gossipy handicraft world,"[78] Frank concluded that the machine was here to stay and that the sooner we quit sighing wistfully about the loss of world which preceded it and directed our efforts toward making the machine enhance our lives the better. He recognized that the transition from Arcadia to a "civilization based on machine production, minute division of labor, standardization of production and quantity of output"[79] had been, relatively speaking, a recent one: "It was not until the day before yesterday, historically speaking, that the apparatus of machine civilization had reached the size and the efficiency that really justified the hope that under statesmanlike guidance, it might become the savior instead of the slayer of mankind." In Frank's mind, the issue of the interwar years was whether mankind would master its machines or be mastered by them.[80]

The debate between Capek and Frank over the future course of machine civilization occurred in 1926, the year which witnessed the birth of *Amazing Stories*. Echoing the concerns of the surrounding society, *Amazing Stories* reflected both postwar misgivings about technology and the "hopes of progress by mechanization in a day when the airplane and the radio were at the threshold of conquest of the popular imagination."[81] Playing upon technology's captivation of the American mind in the interwar decades, the magazine speculated about the ways in which technology would alter American life. Offering contemporary insights into the "Machine Age" which rivaled those of more traditional sources, the publication revealed how Americans of the 1920s and 30s accepted the inevitability of technological culture, adjusted to the new standards which that culture introduced, and grappled with the dilemmas which the new era presented.

Notes

1. Melvin Kransberg, "Technology: The Half Full Cup," Abstract for *Technology and Pessimism: Affirmations, Refutations, and Reflections* edited by Howard P. Segal (1981) p. 8.

2. Edwin E. Slosson, "Twentieth Century Science and Invention," in *Science and Social Change*, compiled by Jesse Thornton (Washington: The Brookings Institution, 1939), p. 173.

3. Cf. Floyd W. Parsons, "Science and Our Everyday Life," *Saturday Evening Post* 195 (March 10, 1923): 10, 154, 157-58; "Is Scientific Advance Impeding Human Welfare?" *Literary Digest* 95 (October 1, 1927): 32-33; James J. Davis, "Science and the Worker," *Monthly Labor Review* 26 (February 1928): 29-36; Robert A. Millikan, "Science and Modern Life," *Atlantic Monthly* 141 (April 1928): 487-96; Fabian Franklin, "Einstein and America," *Scientific Monthly* 28 (March 1929): 279-82; "Revolt Against Science," *Christian Century* 51 (January 24, 1934): 110-12; J.W.N. Sullivan, "Science and the Layman," *Atlantic Monthly* 154 (September 1934): 330-37.

4. Books of the period which engaged in this debate include Stuart Chase's *Men and Machines* (1929), Ralph Flanders's *Taming Our Machines* (1931), Arthur Dahlberg's *Jobs, Machines and Capitalism* (1932), Harold Rugg's *The Great Technology* (1933), William F. Ogburn's *Living with Machines* (1933) and Lewis Mumford's *Technics and Civilization* (1934).

5. Thomas West, *Flesh of Steel* (Nashville, Tennessee: Vanderbilt University Press, 1967) p. x.

6. James O. Bailey, *Pilgrims Through Space and Time* (New York: Argus Books, 1947), p. 2.

7. Emanating from *Science and Invention*, a popular scientific magazine of the early twentieth century, *Amazing Stories* was established and edited by Hugo Gernsback, author of "Ralph 124C41▷"(1911), the first story to be officially named science fiction. Bearing an extraordinary name, sporting a lurid enameled cover, printed on rough wood paper, costing a quarter, boasting a circulation of 100,000, averaging one hundred pages of fiction and offering an array of features which included contests, readers' preference coupons and brazen advertisements, the magazine fell into the category of popular reading material known as pulp magazines. A bit more refined in physical appearance but less ambitious in its sense of purpose, *Amazing Stories* (in combination with *Fantastic*) is still being published today.

8. J. Roy Chapman, "The Amazing Value of 'Scientifiction,'" *Amazing Stories Quarterly* 2 (Spring 1929): 147.

A quarterly supplement to the monthly *Amazing Stories* was published from 1928 to 1933. From 1928 to 1931 the quarterly publisehd readereditorials such as the one by Chapman cited in this footnote.

9. Abner J. Gelula, "Automaton," *Amazing Stories* 6 (November 1931): 688.

10. This essay is based upon reading every issue of *Amazing Stories* cover to cover from April 1926 to April 1938. During that time period more than 2,000 letters to the editor appeared in the "Discussions" column. Written by real people, interpreted as representative of the reader body, largely unabridged, capturing attitudes which would otherwise be lost, providing a sense of immediacy, these letters to the editor offer the means to study the available contemporary views of early science fiction readers and to assess editorial response to those views. They also offer information about who read a magazine like *Amazing Stories*. The average reader who contributed a letter to *Amazing Stories* during the interwar decades was male, under thirty, well educated, engaged in a profession if not in school, from a large metropolitan center, and not necessarily from the United States.

11. Hugo Gernsback, "The 'New' Science and Invention," *Science and Invention* 11 (October 1923): 527.

12. Editorial Response to Milton Goldsmith, *Amazing Stories* 6 (May 1931): 187.

13. George Simpson, Letter to the Editor, *Amazing Stories* 5 (September 1930): 572.

14. Robert Withers, "'Scientifiction,' The Literature of Science and Life," *Amazing Stories Quarterly* 2 (Winter 1929): 141.

15. Miles Breuer, "The Future of 'Scientifiction,'" *Amazing Stories Quarterly* 2 (Summer 1929): 291.

16. Fred Barclay, "The Troglodites," *Amazing Stories* 5 (September 1930): 486.

17. Bertram Schumpf, Letter to the Editor, *Amazing Stories* 6 (April 1931): 91.

18. C. A. Livingston, "What Science Fiction Means to Me," *Science Wonder Stories* 1 (June 1929): 93.

Science Wonder Stories was a science fiction magazine established by Hugo Gernsback, first editor and owner of *Amazing Stories*, after he was squeezed out by a rival publisher in 1929. Because a number of the early readers of *Science Wonder Stories* were channeled to the publication via subscription lists from *Amazing Stories*, readership of the two publications overlapped rather frequently.

19. David Speaker, "'Scientifiction,' Interpreter of Science," *Amazing Stories Quarterly* 2 (Spring 1929): 285.

20. P. Schuyler Miller, Letter to the Editor, *Amazing Stories* 3 (March 1928): 1209.

21. Editorial Response to William Keller, *Amazing Stories* 4 (April 1929): 80.

22. J. Roy Chapman, "The Amazing Value of 'Scientifiction'" *Amazing Stories Quarterly* 2 (Spring 1929): 147.

23. Floyd Anderson, Letter to the Editor, *Amazing Stories* 8 (May 1933): 192.

24. Earle Brown, Letter to the Editor, *Amazing Stories* 1 (February 1927): 1078.

25. Douglass Benson, Letter to the Editor, *Amazing Stories* 3 (July 1928): 377.

26. Editorial Response to Thomas Clark, *Amazing Stories* 3 (April 1928): 87.

27. Catherine Moran, Letter to the Editor, *Amazing Stories* 2 (October 1927): 710.

28. Neil Tasker, "What Science Fiction Means to Me," *Science Wonder Stories* 1 (June 1929): 94.

29. Marguerite Robbins, Letter to the Editor, *Amazing Stories Quarterly* 2 (Summer 1929): 429.

30. Eric Sharf, Letter to the Editor, *Amazing Stories* 8 (July 1933): 376.

31. Richard Goodwin, Letter to the Editor, *Amazing Stories* 11 (October 1937): 141.

32. L. E. Connerley, Letter to the Editor, *Amazing Stories* 6 (June 1931): 286-7.

33. Robert Wait, Letter to the Editor, *Amazing Stories* 3 (June 1928): 281.

34. Madlyne Riegel, Letter to the Editor, *Amazing Stories* 3 (November 1928): 765.

35. Editorial Response to J.L. Cobra, *Amazing Stories* 2 (February 1928): 1112.

36. Bryon Dunlavey, "What Science Fiction Means to Me," *Science Wonder Stories* 1 (July 1929): 187.

37. Lamentation over the undemocratic implications of scientific development had appeared earlier in scientific journals. Edwin E. Slosson, for example, noted in 1921 that "the rapid advance and increasing complexity of modern science has made it difficult for the general reader to follow its course and he has often given up the attempt in despair" — Edwin E. Slosson, "A New Agency for the Popularization of Science," *Science* 53 (April 8, 1921): 321.

38. Writing in 1933 about the average man, William Wickenden asserted that "John Doe isn't quite so cocksure as he used to be that all this science is a good thing" — William Wickenden, "Science and Everyday Philosophy," *Science* 78 (November 24, 1933): 467.

39. David Daniels and Marshall Gilula, "Recommendations," in David Daniels, Marshall Gilula and Frank Ochberg eds., *Violence and the Struggle for Existence* (Boston: Little Brown and Company, 1970): 436.

40. In *Technics and Civilization,* Lewis Mumford observed that "In the development of the neutral valueless world of science, and in the advance of the adaptive, instrumental functions of the machine, we have left to the untutored egoisms of mankind the control of the gigantic powers and engines technics has conjured into existence."

41. Garet Garrett, "Machine People," *Saturday Evening Post* 28 (April 1928): 6.

42. "Faustian" is used here in allusion to the sixteenth century magician charlatan's intent of obtaining superhuman power/knowledge; "Marxian" is used in reference to Karl Marx's theories about victimization of the worker on the modern production line.

43. The term "mechanomorphic" is used by Frederick Crosson in his discussion of the way in which organic processes are described "in terms of cybernetic concepts" — Frederick Crosson, Introduction, *Human and Artificial Intelligence* (New York: Appleton-Century-Crofts, 1970), p. 22.

44. Edwin Megargee, "A Critical Review of Theories of Violence," in Donald J. Mulvihill and Melvin Tumin, Co-Directors, National Commission on the Causes and Prevention of Violence, *Crimes of Violence* (Washington, D.C.: U.S. Government Printing Office, 1969), p. 1084.

45. Daniels and Gilula, "Recommendations," p. 436.

46. Frederick D. Wilhelmsen and Jane Bret, *The War in Man: Media and Machines* (Athens, Ga.: University of Georgia Press, 1970), p. 17.

47. Lewis Mumford, *Technics and Civilization* (New York: Harcourt Brace and Company, 1934), p. 310.

48. Frederick Hoffman, *The Mortal No: Death and the Modern Imagination* (Princeton, N.J.: Princeton University Press, 1964), p. 155.

49. Miles Breuer, "Rays and Men," *Amazing Stories Quarterly* 2 (Summer 1929): 367.

50. Miles Breuer, "The Book of Worlds," *Amazing Stories* 4 (July 1929): 298.

51. Charles W. Diffin, "The Power and the Glory," *Astounding Stories* 3 (July 1930), 108.

52. Breuer, "The Book of Worlds," p. 298.

53. Miles Breuer, "Paradise and Iron," *Amazing Stories Quarterly* 3 (Summer 1930): 310, 315.

54. Gelula, "Automation," p. 684.

55. This independence was noted in the non-fiction of the period as well. The author of a 1922 article in the *Yale Review* described the machine as representing "a new race of beings with purposes independent of our own" — John M. Clark, "The Empire of Machines," *Yale Review* 12 (October 1922): 143.

56. Henry Hasse, "He Who Shrank," *Amazing Stories* 10 (August 1936): 40-1.

57. Waldo Frank, "The Machine and Metaphysics," *New Republic* 44 (18 November 1925): 330.

58. Breuer, "Paradise and Iron," p. 329.

59. John Scot Cambell, "The Infinite Brain," *Science Wonder Stories* 1 (May 1930): 1077.

60. Julian Kendig, Jr., "The Eternal Mask," *Amazing Stories* 7 (February 1933): 1023.

61. Francis Flagg, "The Mentanicals," *Amazing Stories* 8 (April 1934): 70.

62. Gelula, "Automaton," pp. 684, 694.

63. Edmond Hamilton, "The Comet Doom," *Amazing Stories* 2 (January 1928): 932.

64. Gelula, "Automaton," p. 693.

65. *Ibid.*, pp. 682-83.

66. G. K. Chesterton identified the curse of the modern world to be man's assumption that the "machine must go on working him. The motor drivers the motorist. The typewriter dictates to the typist" — G. K. Chesterton, "A Plea That Science Now Halt," *New York Times Magazines* (October 5, 1930), p. 1.

67. Despite Henry Ford's 1926 contention that "the fear that man may become the slave of his own mechanical creations is voiced by more or less secluded persons" — Henry Ford as quoted by William A. McGarry, "Man and His Machines," *Saturday Evening Post* (1 May 1926), p. 33 — and George Boas's feeling "that man is no more a slave of his machines now 1932 than he has ever been" — George Boas, "In Defense of Machines," *Harper's Monthly* 65 (June 1932): 93 — several authors of magazine articles of the period echoed the fears of contemporary science fiction writers. Austin Freeman found man's "independence and self-reliance . . . readily subjected to regimentation" his "sense of personal liberty . . . abated while his sensibilities are blurred and debased" — Austin Freeman as quoted by Stuart Chase, "Slaves of the Machine?" *Harper's Monthly* 158 (March 1929): 480. And the author of a 1930 article entitled "Men or Machines?" found that the "slavery of the specialized machine worker makes him a mechanized creature full of despair" — Gabriel Reuillard, "Men or Machines?" *Living Age* 338 (April 1930): 165.

68. Stanton Coblentz, "The Sunken World," *Amazing Stories Quarterly* 1 (Summer 1928): 319, 330.

69. Flagg, "The Mentanicals," p. 74.

70. Hasse, "He Who Shrank," p. 38.

71. Acknowledging that "the replacment of the workers by machines has been going on ever since the beginning of the factory system," the author of a 1930 article argued that "the amazing thing about the last ten years is that changes affecting thousands of workers have taken place almost overnight. In some industries, machines have been introduced so rapidly that in a few years' time changes have occurred comparable to a century of earlier progress" — William Green, "Labor Versus Machines: An Employment Puzzle," *New York Times* (June 1, 1930) III, p. 5.

72. Flagg, "The Mentanicals," p. 67.

73. Breuer, "Paradise and Iron," p. 360.

74. "Karel Capek Dies, 48," *New York Times* (26 December 1938), p. 23.

75. Karel Capek, "We Alarm and Amuse M. Capek," *New York Times Magazine* (16 May 1926), sec. 4, p. 1.

76. Glenn Frank, "In Defense of American Ideals," *New York Times Magazine* (6 June 1926), sec. 4, p. 1.

77. *Ibid.*

78. *Ibid.* p. 22.

79. *Ibid.*, p. 1.

80. *Ibid.*, p. 22.

81. "Karel Capek Dies, 48," p. 23.

4 Tabloids as an Urban Response

James E. Murphy

The tabloid newspaper that emerged during the 1920s in urban America, for all the scholarly scorn it would endure, performed a significant social function. The mass appeal paper helped the urban dwellers to order, to understand and to cope with their own experience in relationship to a new and increasingly complex society. The "tab" provided also a lively, dramatic picture of the city and the world that gave its readers a measure of escape from often narrow and stultifying lives.

Such a radical perspective on the widely vilified tabloids contradicts most of the conventional criticism of "respectable" journalists, historians, and media scholars. The literature of the period reveals an outpouring of disdain for the tabloid, a chorus of criticism that generally held the papers to have no redeeming social value.[1]

This chapter will offer an alternative perspective. To cast the tabloids in a new light, the effort will be to consider the kinds of social functions served by the papers. A series of overlapping, specific functions will be suggested and supported by reference to material in selected tabloid newspapers of the era. For the sake of manageability, the analysis is here restricted to selected New York City tabloids.

Although the tabloid represents but one media development among many during a particulary fertile period in American history, study of the tab offers some possibility of unique insight into the era. The tabloid bears study both to better comprehend it as the cultural artifact that it is and to better locate it in the cultural mosaic of the time.

The Social Context

By the first decades of the twentieth century, the United States had become a predominantly urban society. The inexorable rural-to-urban population shift, one that every industrializing nation experiences,

55

had been working its will on America through much of the preceding century. Industrialism and urbanization had proceeded apace, as the U.S. lived through its own "Long Revolution."[2] The economic and cultural promise of the cities had lured the masses from rural areas and small towns alike: census figures show that by 1920 more than half of all Americans lived in urban places and, for the first time, the actual number of people living on farms had declined. Concurrently, immigration from abroad was at its height, with many of the new Americans heading for the cities, especially the industrial cities of the Northeast.

Modern industrial processes, by now firmly in place, had fueled the influx — just as the factories, the foundries, and the assembly lines had themselves been fueled by the ever-increasing labor pool. The country's growing appetite for and economic ability to consume the new products also gave impetus to the urban phenomenon, as did increasingly efficient farming methods that required a small rural work force. Thus, the lure of the cities was primarily economic. Life in the city meant a job, money, the possibility of an easier life.

But the city was more than a job. It was excitement and cultural diversity. It was a wonder-full place, a place of action and noise and speed and bright lights, far different from rural and small town life. As the popular song of the era put it, "How ya gonna keep 'em down on the farm after they've seen Pa-ree?"

For many of the new city dwellers, however, that image of the exciting city doubtless ran headlong into a harsher reality of sweat shops, mind-deadening and backbreaking industrial routines, long hours, and short pay. Markham's "Man with the Hoe" had simply moved from field to foundry. Dreiser's *Sister Carrie,* which appeared in 1900, is a powerful statement of the contrasts of urban life as it traces the unhappy journey of young Caroline Meeber from innocence to woman of the world. The lure of the city, and then its vastness and impersonality, conspire to work their will on this simple, archetypal country girl.

The essence of the cities' problems and their promise was captured well by Michael Schudson: "with the movement from country to city, from self-sufficient family economies to market-based commercial and manufacturing economies, people came unstuck from the cake of custom, found chances to form individual personalities, and faced new possibilities of impersonality in the social realities of modern life."[3] In Tonnies' words, "society" came to replace "community."[4] Or, as Dewey wrote, a new public was being created, but it came to be dominated by impersonal and mechanistic organizations, creating a tension between democratic ideals and the increasing lack of personal control over life and events.[5]

Along with the city itself, the radical cultural uprooting experienced by the urban immigrants produced its own trauma. Family, ethnic, and class clusterings in part provided the security that the new urbanites needed, but that support was in turn offset by other major problems. Among the better documented of these were the racial and ethnic polarities of city life, the widening gaps between rich and poor, and the very speed at which urban society itself was moving, growing, changing. By the early twentieth century the rate of change in the modern American city, both social and technological, had become dramatic.[6] Along with the ascendancy of the city, another social phenomenon was drastically altering the world and its impact on Americans during the early twentieth century: nations themselves were fast becoming interrelated, their fates inextricably bound with one another. Despite moves the United States would make after World War I toward isolationism, a League of Nations had become part of life in the twentieth century.

The history of growing urban complexity and international interdependence is reflected fairly accurately in the development of the American newspaper industry. The very industrialization that had created (and reflected) the phenomena of modernity in the first place also gave rise to a fast-changing mass media institution.

The modern metropolitan newspaper had emerged in the first half of the nineteenth century. American cities, with their large, accessible masses of buyers and advertisers and their never-ending sources of story ideas, formed a natural newspaper market. The technologies for reproduction and distribution became more and more sophisticated. Simultaneously, consumer demand for the product grew. The newspaper—and eventually magazines, film and radio — rose to fill a socially created need. In his "Natural History of the Newspaper," Park discusses this close, almost symbiotic relationship between expressive forms and cultural needs. "The growth of great cities," he wrote, "has enormously increased the size of the reading public. Reading, which was a luxury in the country, has become a necessity in the city. In the urban environment literacy is almost as much a necessity as speech itself."[7] By the end of 1800s the daily newspaper was clearly an integral part of urban life. The industry was securely in place. Then, in the 1920s, newspapers soared to levels of daily and especially Sunday readership never before experienced. A major share, though certainly not all, of the circulation success could be attributed to the tabloid, an essentially urban journalistic phenomenon that heightened and capitalized on the mass appeal aspects of the newspaper that had preceded it for a century.

Description of the Tabloids

The name "tabloid" was simply a reference to the paper's size — a tablet half the size of the standard broadsheet newspaper. Its compact size lent itself to compact stories, full-page pictures, and large headlines.

Although the small paper became a significant feature of American journalism in the 1920s, its roots extended back to the late 1800s when tabloid-sized papers first appeared in Britain. Indeed, the British publisher Lord Northcliffe was often credited with introducing the first tabloid to America with his publication, on January 1, 1901, of the New York *World* as a tabloid.[8] After the one-day experiment, commerically successful though it was, *World* editors returned to the broadsheet format. The first regularly published tabloid in this country was the New York *Illustrated Daily News*, begun on June 23, 1919. Chicago newspaper barons Joseph Patterson and Robert McCormick created the paper, with Patterson the major driving force behind it.[9] Although the first issues of the *Daily News* suggested a modest, tentative effort, the paper quickly caught on and gradually became a circulation success. Advertisers were at first reluctant to climb aboard — indeed, issues of the paper in its first few years boasted sparse ad lineage. But the numbers turned that around. Within two years of its first appearance, the *Daily News* reached a circulation of 400,000. By March of 1926, it had reached one million. Through the same period, circulation of the so-called quality New York dailies — the *Times,* the *World,* the American — remained fairly constant. Indeed, by 1925 the *Daily News* had become the undisputed circulation leader among New York dailies, a position it would maintain for more than half a century. William Randolph Hearst's *Daily Mirror* and Bernarr Macfadden's *Evening Graphic* entered the New York tabloid race for readers in 1924. Within couple of years the *Mirror* would become the nearest circulation competitor to the *Daily News,* while the *Graphic* was to fail after a six-year race that would never see the paper grow into a serious contender.[10]

Obviously, the identity — and the appeal — of the tabloids lay in more than their size. The papers served up a lively, drama-filled daily diet of "news" unabashedly aimed at entertaining their adherents ("90 percent entertainment, 10 percent information — and the information without boring you," Hearst said about his *Mirror*).[11] The tabloids established sensationalism, poignancy, and pathos as their stock in trade. Typically, they covered sex, sports, and sentiment, with healthy doses of crime news thrown in. For the first time in daily journalism, they made extensive use of photographs, running whole pages of pictures throughout each issue. The tabloids appeared every day on the newsstand, bold, outlandish (if predictable) compendia of narrative and pictorial drama.

Except for the photography, the formula was far from new. Nearly 100 years earlier Benjamin Day's New York *Sun* had begun the era of the penny press, producing the first newspaper for the masses. The new emphasis had been on local stories and on news of violence and human interest. Then in the 1890s had come the so-called yellow journalism of Hearst and Joseph Pulitzer. This "new journalism" trafficked in sensationalism — and was immensely popular. It also drew the continuing scorn of scholars. In 1962 Edwin Emery would write of a yellow press that "instead of giving its readers effective leadership, . . . offered a palliative of sin, sex, and violence."[12] The tabloids of the twenties were to elicit the same kind of commentary.

The *Evening Graphic* was widely considered the most outlandish of the breed. In its maiden issue of September 15, 1924, the paper frankly announced its intention "to dramatize and sensationalize the news and some stories that are not news." In its early days, in fact, the paper tried to make all its featured stories first-person accounts. The gimmick quickly faded, but the paper retained its reputation as the most sensational of the tabs. Unlike Patterson and McCormick, Macfadden was not a newspaperman. A health and physical culture buff, he saw the *Graphic* as a vehicle for support of or opposition to a variety of causes. Among other gimmicks tried by the paper in its effort to get a toehold in New York journalism, perhaps its most notorious was the "composograph," a euphemism for the faked photo. Not content to fill the paper with pictures as the other tabs were doing, *Graphic* editors took to staging photos, using staff members to represent people in the news. Critical reaction to the composograph was loud and swift. But critics of the tabloid did not restrict their comment to that device, or to the *Graphic*.[13]

The Criticism

Journalists, media scholars, and critics of the time made much of the supposed contrast between the "quality" urban dailies and the tabloids — and the latter were widely vilified for their evil practices. The *Saturday Review of Literature* in a 1927 article entitled "Tabloid Poison," referred to them as "that new black plague."[14] The *New Republic* called the tabloids "jungle weeds in the journalistic garden."[15] *The Forum* sponsored a debate in 1927 posing the headline question, "Are Tabloid Newspapers a

Menace?" O. G. Villard, editor of *The Nation*, answering in the affirmative, called the papers a "gutter type of journalism," and the "degradation of journalism." They serve "no other purpose than to lure the pennies from the pockets of immaturity and pruriency," he claimed.[16]

A press critic, Silas Bent, writing in *The Nation*, dubbed the new form "journalistic jazz"[17] in a metaphoric putdown of the new form of popular music that was itself criticized as vulgar, undisciplined, and filled with sexual innuendo.[18]

Press critics during the 1920s worried in print about the harmful influence that the tabloids were wielding over the better newspapers. Wrote the *New Republic:* "We find today that even papers which seem safely beyond the reach of the tabloids are alarmed by their mushroom growth and tend to imitate many of their most undesirable characteristics."[19] A later critic would react in similar terms: "Sin, sex, and sensation appealed to broker and hodcarrier, society matron, and Woolworth counter girl, and it was not long before the conservative dailies were caught in the tabloid whirlpool."[20]

It should be pointed out, however, that such criticism assumed a dichotomy between "quality" journalism and "popular" journalism that did not exist, at least in this country. More accurate was the media criticism of Silas Bent, who in 1927 decried the "Ballyhoo" of American journalism generally. Wrote Bent: "The news which startles, thrills and entertains is still blown up as vigorously as the toy balloon of Queen Marie's visit. Thus does the American press exemplify day by day the grandiose, the Brobdignagian art of ballyhoo." Later, he added, "The picture pages [i.e., the tabloids] . . . have done nothing in the way of headlines or of news that their predecessors and contemporaries have not done and are not doing."[21]

A similarly balanced perspective was offered at about the same time by Douglass Miller, who restricted his analysis to the New York tabloids. They were, he wrote, not much better, or worse, than other U.S. newspapers: "The *News* is cheap and frothy but not, as a rule, antisocial. It is, from the social point of view, on a par with a considerable portion of the American press which, like this first of the tabloids, is given its character by triviality and slight constructive contest. The *Graphic* and the *Mirror* are far more objectionable. They too frequently emphasize the antisocial but are, after all, no worse than the more sensational representatives of the standard press."[22]

The humorist H. Allen Smith, writing about his experiences as a New York wire service writer and newspaperman a few years later, put the tabloid reputation into an appropriate light: "Though we were in the same building we saw very little of the newspapermen involved in the production of the tabloid *Daily News*. Even at this late stage of the game there was something not quite acceptable about the tabloids. I never liked the *Daily News* because it pandered, in a blatant and unashamed way, to the basic instincts and the vulgar tastes of the lower orders — the same as I do."[23]

Development of the Tabloids

However much the tabloid would be denigrated, it represented more or less a logical extension of U.S. journalism, at most a slightly more brazen assertion of journalistic practices and formulas for success in evidence since the 1830s. The true function of the newspaper, as Bennett put it back then, was not to instruct or inform, but to startle. Viewed in this light, the tabloid emerged as but a little more adept at startling the reader than was the rest of the nation's press.[24]

It should be stressed, however, that although differences among American newspapers ultimately were fairly slight, a far greater difference existed between the American and the European urban press. European newspapers, reflecting a greater class consciousness and struggle for political freedom of their readers, typically constituted instruments of ideology. The divergence in press systems rather accurately reflected the distinctions between American and European cities.[25] Indeed, the growth of U.S. democratization had as much to do with the development of a market economy as it did with politics in this country: the market was the greater social equalizer.[26]

Nonetheless, changes both technological and conceptual were at work in American journalism throughout this period. The speed of news gathering, preparation, production, and distributing all increased. Reporting and storytelling techniques became streamlined and standarized. By the 1890s, the chronological approach to telling the news had largely given way to the summary "lead," with its formulaic "Who, what, when, where, and why." "News" itself became further defined. By the end of World War I, the concept of "objectivity" was fully developed and had become something of an industrial ritual and safeguard, albeit an "unattainable goal."[27] Between 1900 and 1930, a new industrial-elite class of editors and reporters emerged and began to reproduce itself.[28] Its role in the consumer society was to offer a colorful, emotive brand of ephemeral literature to a vast and eager audience.

The rapid rise of the tabloid format provided a clearcut example of the symbiosis between expressive form and cultural need that Park referred to. The newspaper did not require a great deal of time, and time was increasingly in short supply in the cities. It did not demand a high degree of literacy. Its large pictures and loud headlines could appeal even to those segments of the urban mass who were poorly schooled or understood little English.

Social Functions

Beneath such factors as technology, brevity, and low literacy requirements however, lay a more central need served by the tabloid: it functioned (as did other dramatic forms such as film, books, and radio drama) as one repository of a relevant contemporary folklore for the urban masses. Helen McGill Hughes in 1940 would ground the development of the modern newspaper feature story in the traditional oral folk ballad. "In a period of rapid social change," she wrote, "the newspaper is perhaps the most robust medium the *demos*, or even sophisticated people, have found for expediting an understanding of themselves."[29]

The thesis put forth here, then, is that the tabloids helped to order the bloomin,' buzzin' confusion by reducing a complex and confusing stream of events to a series of recognizable themes. In other words, as a specific journalistic genre, the tabloids helped to create and sustain an urban reality for millions, through the use of simple and compelling images.[30]

Discussion of such a journalistic response to cultural needs should not imply any consciousness on the part of journalists or publics that the metaphoric process were at work. The cultural (i.e., artifactual) form of journalism was institutionalized and habitualized.[31]

The thesis advanced here likewise should not suggest that the appeal of the postwar tabloids was restricted only to the new urban masses, that vast tide of immigrants seeking to make sense out of a new and confusing environment. Given what has been argued here about the metaphoric mission of the tabloids and of journalism generally, it seems clear that the appeal of the tabs should have extended beyond class lines. Indeed, studies of circulation patterns at the time reveal just that — despite the elitist conception of mass popular literature as restricted in its appeal to the lower classes.[32]

The urban tabloid newspaper of the 1920s was one form of dramatic, mass-appeal story-telling that was aptly suited to the cultural needs of its time and place.

Some specific sense-making (or metaphoric) functions of the tabloids, with reference to some material from the papers themselves, are now offered in support of such a thesis. The following functions, although discussed separately, overlap. Some that can be identified are the following:

1. *Providing escape from the deadening "reality" of immediate personal lives:* The tab's formula included high drama, fantasy, hype and excitement. It represents an explicit attempt to add verve to individual lives — which doubtless were drudgery for many of the new (and "old") urbanites locked into endless, mindless work. In its inaugural issue, the *Daily News* promised that, "Because the doings of the very fortunate are always of interest," they would be covered extensively. The same introductory column explained that significant quantities of fiction would be carried, because of the presumed universal appeal of fiction. The first issue promised also the widespread use of pictures and short features: "Pictures and stories together will supply a complete understanding of the events of the day, and that is a liberal education."[33]

Five years later, in its own first issue, the *Evening Graphic* frankly acknowledged its intent: "We intend to interest you mightily. We intend to dramatize and sensationalize the news and some stories that are not news . . . We want this newspaper to be human, first, last and all the time. We want to throb with those life forces that fill life with joyous delight."[34]

Martin Weyrauch, assistant managing editor of the *Graphic* and one of the few critical defenders of the tabloids, argued strongly on their behalf in the *Forum* debate cited earlier. Referring to the comment of the New York retailer regarding tab readers and their needs, he said:

> These people (ninety-five percent of the population) are intensely human. To them the primary appeal of the metropolitan tabloids, the presentation in pictorial form of daily divergences from routine, is of compelling interest. They tread their daily grind in the home, the office, the workshop; but they are potential adventurers — we all are. And the tabloids dish up to them, everyday, food which keeps alive an unexpressed part of their nature, makes them feel they belong in the human chorus, though not in the spotlight.[35]

Another aspect of escape from boredom was the armchair adventure that tabloids afforded. "Real" adventure implied risk and usually required considerable capital. But to read about the real-life exploits of heroes like Lindbergh and Earhart, movie stars and dukes was much cheaper — and far less risky. In addition to their many stories of actual heroes, the tabs offered a fairly heavy dose of serialized fiction, together with "true story serials" of romance and intrigue. Park put this function into high relief with his comment about the tabloid's "persistent search in the drab episodes of city life for the romantic and the picturesque, its dramatic accounts of vice and crime, and its unflagging interest in the movements of personages of the more or less mythical high society."[36]

Thus, no matter how dull one's own life might be, the tabloid-a-day could reveal an exciting world beyond oneself, and show that world at its thrilling finest or worst. Pictures of "New York's most beautiful girls every morning in the *Illustrated Daily News,*" stories of heroes and villians, of a stunning movie star who "Quits Screen to Love Baby," of a "Love Nest Murder," of a "Family of Six Starving" — all were powerful antidotes to immediate dullness.

Nor was the adventure limited to the city. Stories from the rest of the country told of Prohibition and reactions to it, of coal strikes and race riots around the nation. Europe and America were being linked by dirigible and airplane flights as well as by the complex international treaties.

Thus, no matter what the humdrum activity of individual lives, the folklore was that of a brash and brazen, action-filled, troublesome but fascinating world. Expectations of good and evil were being fulfilled.

2. *Establishing and reinforcing the idea of the city and the world beyond as a wonderful, or wonderfully terrible, place:* This is a corollary to the first function, though distinct from it. As Walter Lippmann stated, "Certainly for the most part, the way we see things is just a combination of what is there and of what we expected to find."[37] The tabs satisfied the people's urge to know what was "going on" beyond their senses — not the conventionally "newsworthy" goings-on, however, but the hoped-for wild and erotic, the weird and exotic, those that are called (usually without much definition) the sensational — which Warren Franke would describe, in his "argument in defense of sensationalism," as the "journalistic tendency to shape dry facts into damp stories."[38]

The front page of a typical *Evening Graphic* (September 10, 1928), for example, is instructive in this regard. The 120-point headline read, "D'Olier Feared Murdered." Just under that, a 72-point head: "Cops Mobilize for Gang War." Then came side-by-side pictures of beauty ("Ziegfield girl Lillian Lorraine operated on 'under knife'") and the beast (an Irish baronet holding a tiger cub). Two bottom-of-the-page heads rounded out the page: "Drunk Nothing! He's Croaked, Gang Girl Confesses, p. 20," and "I Hope You Win — Millicent Prize Ring to Society, p. 18." Page two of the June 5, 1929, issue carried stories under these headlines, all of them glaring: "Glimpse of Slim Blond Girl in Bed Wins Decree for Furrier's Wife," "Left Waiting at Church, Minus Fiance and $250," "Love-Crazed Ex-Priest Shoots Girl, Kills Self," "Seeks Murder Clues in Death of Merchant," "Armed Bandits Get $1,425 in Newark Hold-Up." Or these juicy heads from page three of the June 2, 1932, issue (soon before the Graphic's own demise): "5 Beauties Take Man for a 'Ride,' Attack and Torture Him with Fire," "Year of Grief for Boy Who Died Led Family of Five to End Lives," "Pittman Made Love to His Maid When Wife Died, Court Hears."

3. *Inculcating and reinforcing urban norms and values:* Hughes in her 1941 book would speak of human interest news as challenging the ancient local ways and drawing people from their ancestral slumber.[39] And Bent referred to the *Daily News* as pushing piety, patriotism, and prurience — ostensibly promoting the old and the traditional, while subtly titillating readers with stories in which the old values were flouted. A classic example of propaganda for behavior change, in this case away from a restrictive sexual ethic, could be found in the *Graphic* column by Mrs. Bernarr Macfadden on September 22, 1924: "Life knowledge and sex knowledge are fast eliminating the old-maid type. In this age when advancement waits on mental and physical ability, there is no excuse for a girl growing up into a senseless, sexless thing who is an abomination in the sight of God and man."

Throughout much of the copy, however, ran an undercurrent of reportorial cynicism that perhaps only the most astute readers sensed. In the Ben Hecht-inspired 1931 film, *The Front Page,* the reporter, Hildy Johnson, saw a "hell of a story" in the heart-rending drama of a convict hiding in the press room of city hall. Throughout the film, reporters were portrayed as manipulating the emotions of the public for circulation's sake. Emile Gauvreau, a top editor at the *Graphic,* wrote a subsequent novel called *Hot News* about "a world of emotions and sensation called tabloidia. In this new world, you do not have to wait for exciting things to happen. You can make them happen."[40]

4. *Institutionalizing gossip:* In the non-mediated rural or village environment word-of-mouth gossip had been a fairly all-encompassing fact of life and an effective social control mechanism. The city newspaper, especially the kind of newspaper for which gossip-type stories were the more manifest fare, provided simultaneously a way to urbanize the gossip function and to simplify the overwhelming urban complexities. In place of village gossip that had drawn everyone into its net, urban gossip of necessity concentrated on the lives of a few — the important, the infamous, the attractive, the highly visible. In the tabloids, where gossip stories were a mainstay, the gossip columnist Walter Winchell perfected the form. He accurately perceived the tremendous popular appeal of writing the "inside story" of the glamorous film stars. Focusing on Broadway and Hollywood, Winchell turned gossip to a high art, first at the *Graphic,* and later at the *Mirror.* The column was crammed with tidbits, as in this example from the September 10, 1928 *Graphic:* "Katherine Zimmerman returns from Yurrop

next Monday . . . The Jesse Crawfords are out of tune. F.P.A., the
newspaper comedian, holds both ears with his hands at show when a pistol
is brought into play, the big pansy! . . . The best white wine in town can be
had at certain Ghetto Romanian restaurants for a $ a quart, and one quart
is enough."

Moving eventually to the *Mirror*, Winchell wrote a column that
for years afforded the paper's key attraction. The critic, Simon Bessie,
attributed 200,000 *Mirror* readers to Winchell's column alone.[41] While
Winchell held the pinnacle, scores of other columns ran in other tabloids.
In addition to literal (i.e., inside story) gossip columns, the bulk of the tab's
daily offering of features was cast in the same gossip-centered mold:
readers were to be let in on the "real" story, the "true" story behind
whatever.

5. *Emphasizing the social importance of private experience:* The
tabloid decision as to what "news" to feature typically highlighted the
importance of the personal. So-called important news (i.e., consequential
data or that which might have been deemed vital to self-preservation)
appeared infrequently in tabloid pages. Instead, the human interest elements were accentuated. Moreover, among the countless daily items the
tabloid could feature on its," "Broker Stole $1,000,000."[42] The tabs
eschewed importance for interest, thus providing conversational material
close to the proverbial pulse of human life. A *Newsweek* story of the era
said of the *Daily News:* "Peace conferences got a paragraph in the *News*.
Ripe, juicy divorces got a page."[43] Similarly, Weyrauch wrote: "If there is
one thing more than their size that distinguishes tabloids from their big
brothers I should say it is humanness. They talk in their columns about the
things that people talk about on the streets and in their homes. They are
not so far above the common herd as to have no concern in the interests of
everyday life."[44]

6. *Legitimizing the emotional response to human experience:*
Closely related to the elevation of the personal and private was the
acknowledgment that feelings are permissible. The tabs said, in effect, that
the expression of feelings was legitimate. Bent referred to the appeal of the
news "to unconscious passions and hungers."[45] The scholar of newspaper
ethics, Nelson Crawford, asserted that the press of the 20s expressed and
satisfied "herd" lusts for sex, gold, and blood — and permitted readers to
live vicariously through extremes of experience without performing the
acts themselves.[46] The appeal of virtually everything in the tabloids was to
the heart. Whether written by cynical reporters or not, the stories tugged at
the heart-strings.

7. *Legitimizing leisure:* In its daily dramatization of the world in

word and picture and in its comics, columns, and contests, the tabloid served up a fare of entertainment and relaxation that was cheap and portable. It was not time- or space-bound, as was watching a movie or listening to the parlor radio. Bessie referred to the tabloid as the urban equivalent of such old-fashioned country fun as hay rides, fireside yarns, and quilting bees. Life in the industrial city may have taken away these outlets, but the need to relax remained. In Bessie's words: "The daily grind of office, factory, and home produced a restless longing for diversion and adventure which was answered by the movies and the radio. In competition with these new media of entertainment, the newspaper was forced to increase its relaxation content."[47] An example was the *Graphic* interest in beauty, as in a story on "Venus of 1928 Crowned a Queen Before 15,000 at the 'Hearts' Ball." The lead read: "Troubles and cares were thrown to the winds by 15,000 members and friends of the Lonely Hearts Club, sponsored by the *Graphic*, when in gay mood and gala attire they wended their way to the annual ball and beauty pageant held at Madison Square Garden on Saturday night."[48]

8. *Offering the comfort of predictability:* For all their appeal to the new and senational, the tabloids conveyed a picture of the world that had a high degree of continuity and predictability. The names and the faces in the news may have changed each day, but the stories (i.e., the action) did not. Even in change, there was permanence. Like journalism of every age and persuasion, the tabloids told the story of an urban — and wider — world that remained fairly constant from day to day and year to year. In addition, the journalistic form itself was reassuring: whatever might happen, it said, this dramatic story-telling way of sorting it out still applied — and would appear every day, same time, same place.

Conclusion

Viewed in the light of the functions discussed here, the appeal of the tabloid newspaper of postwar America — along with that of film and radio — appeared to be a natural development. The new urbanites, and the "old" ones as well, dealt with new complexities, uncertainties, and tensions in age-old ways: by simplifying, ordering, and making sense out of them. Simply stated, coping with the very nature of the Twentieth Century urban, national, and international experience required such sorting out and mediating. In the tabloid newspaper, such sorting and mediation took the form of dramatic story telling. Ultimately, it always does.

Notes

1. For example, this statement from "Tabloid Poison," an editorial in *Saturday Review of Literature* (February 19, 1927), p. 590: "We no longer exploit the bodies of the masses — at least in America. They are too powerful. We exploit their minds." The anti-tabloid criticism of the period is reviewed more fully below.

2. See Raymond Williams, *The Long Revolution* (London: Chatto & Windus, 1961).

3. Michael Schudson, *Discovering the News: A Social History of American Newspapers* (New York: Basic Books, 1978), p. 59.

4. Alfred Tonnies, *Community and Society (Gemeinschaft und Gesellschaft)*, translated and edited by Charles P. Loomis (New York: Harper & Row, 1963), pp. 33 ff.

5. John Dewey, *The Public and Its Problems* (New York: Henry Holt, 1927), pp. 3 ff.

6. By the early 1900s, the American city was becoming recognized as a legitimate and important area of sociological study. See, for instance, Robert E. Park and Herbert A. Miller, *Old World Traits Transplanted* (Chicago: University of Chicago Press, 1925).

7. Robert E. Park, "The Natural History of the Newspaper," *American Journal of Sociology* (November 1923): 274.

8. Silas Bent, *Ballyhoo: The Voice of the Press* (New York: Boni & Liveright, 1927), p. 185. Bent actually found that the first U.S. tabloid appeared on February 1, 1891. The paper, the (New York) *Daily Continent*, was not a commercial success.

9. For studies of the *Daily News*, see John Tebbel, *An American Dynasty* (New York: Doubleday, 1947) and John Chapman, *Tell it to Sweeney* (New York: Doubleday, 1961).

10. *American Newspaper Annual and Directory* (Philadelphia: N. W. Ayer & Son, 1925-).

11. As quoted by Simon Michael Bessie, *Jazz Journalism: The Story of the Tabloid Newspapers* (New York: Russell & Russell, 1969), p. 139.

12. Edwin Emery, *The Press and America* (Englewood Cliffs, N.J.: Prentice-Hall, 1962), p. 416.

13. See Lester Cohen, *The New York Graphic: The World's Zaniest Newspaper* (Philadelphia: Chilton Books, 1964), pp. 95 ff.

14. "Tabloid Poison," *Saturday Review of Literature* 19 Feburary 1927, pp. 589-90.

15. "Who Reads the Tabloids?" *The New Republic*, 25 May 1927, p. 6.

16. O. G. Villard, "Tabloid Offenses," *The Forum* 77 (March 1927): 487, 491, 486.

17. Silas Bent, "Journalistic Jazz," *The Nation*, 31 March 1926, p. 341.

18. See Leroy Ostransky, *Understanding Jazz* (Englewood Cliffs, N.J.: Prentice-Hall, 1977), p. 40.

19. "Who Reads the Tabloids?" *The New Republic*, 25 May 1927, p. 7.

20. John L. Spivak, "The Rise and Fall of a Tabloid," *American Mercury* (July 1934): 311.

21. *Ibid.*, p. 192.

22. Douglass W. Miller, "The New York Tabloids," *Journalism Quarterly* 5 (1928): 39-40.

23. H. Allen Smith, *The Hell in a Handbasket* (New York: Doubleday, 1962), p. 276.

24. As quoted by Bessie, *Jazz Journalism*, p. 40.

25. Gunther Barth, *City People: The Rise of Modern City Culture in Nineteenth-Century America* (New York: Oxford University Press, 1980), p. 108. The British press is perhaps the point of convergence of both American and European press systems, containing in its vastly divergent media offerings close parallels to both.

26. Schudson, *Discovering the News*, p. 58.

27. See Schudson, *ibid.,* pp. 144 ff, and Gaye Tuchman, "Objectivity As a Strategic Ritual," *American Journal of Sociology* 77(1972): 660-79.

28. For a general discussion of the rise of the professional journalist, see Alvin Gouldner, *The Future of Intellectuals and the Rise of the New Class* (New York: Seabury Press, 1979), p. 15. See also Hans Magnus Enzensberger, *The Consciousness Industry* (New York: Seabury Press, 1974); Alvin Gouldner, *Dialectic of Ideology and Technology* (New York: Seabury Press, 1976); Arthur J. Kaul, "The Social Ecology of the Newspaper" (Ph.D. dissertation, Southern Illinois University, 1982).

29. Helen MacGill Hughes, *News and the Human Interest Story* (Chicago: University of Chicago Press, 1940), p. 291.

30. Such an argument is distilled from, and greatly informed by, the following: David L. Eason, "Telling Stories and Making Sense," *Journal of Popular Culture* (Fall 1981): 125-129; Gaye Tuchman, "Telling Stories," *Journal of Communication* (Autumn 1976): 93-97; James W. Carey, "A Cultural Approach to Communication," *Journal of Communication* (Winter 1975): 1-22; and Lee Thayer, "Communication and the Dilemma of Modern Man" (paper presented to the First International Colloquium on Communication, Mexico City, October 1980).

31. As Peter Berger and Thomas Luckmann would assert in 1966 in reference to cultural forms generally, the journalistic form appears neutral and transparent, a "natural" way to know about the world as it exists "out there." *The Social Construction of Reality* (New York: Doubleday, 1966), pp. 23 and *passim.*

32. Bessie, *Jazz Journalism,* pp. 220-28. The author cites detailed statistics to show that circulation of the tabloids transcended class lines. In one of his studies, the *Daily News* sold approximately 80 percent of its 1.3 million papers in middle class neighborhoods, 11 percent in upper class neighborhoods and 9 percent in lower class neighborhoods. Miller ("The New York Tabloids," p. 40) cites similar figures compiled by the New York University Bureau of Business Research.

33. *Daily News,* 24 June 1919, p. 5.

34. *Evening Graphic,* 16 September 1924, p. 20.

35. Martin Weyrauch, "The Why of the Tabloids," *The Forum* 77 (April 1927): 496. Weyrauch is here quoting W.D. Walker, who is identified only as "director of sales and publicity of one of New York's big department stores."

36. Park, "Natural History," p. 286.

37. Walter Lippmann, *Public Opinion* (New York: Harcourt, Brace, 1922), p. 115.

38. Warren Francke, "An Argument in Defense of Sensationalism: Probing the Popular and Historiographical Concept," *Journalism History* 5 (Autumn 1978): 73.

39. Hughes, *Human Interest Story,* p. 104.

40. Emile Gauvreau, *Hot News* (New York: Macaulay, 1931), p. vii.

41. Bessie, *Jazz Journalism,* p. 151.

42. The dates of the stories cited (all from page 1) are 18, 19, and 22. September 1928, respectively.

43. "Tabloids: Mr. Hearst Points His Biggest Gun at the *Daily News,"Newsweek,* 24 November 1934, p. 19.

44. Weyrauch, "The Why of the Tabloids," p. 500.

45. Bent, *Ballyhoo,* p. 45.

46. Nelson Crawford, "Mental Health and the Newspaper," *Mental Hygiene* 6 (April 1922): 304.

47. Bessie, *Jazz Journalism,* p. 239.

48. *Graphic,* 10 September 1928, p. 12.

5 Women, Cigarettes, and Advertising in the 1920s

A Study in the Sociology of Consumption

Michael Schudson

American society became a "consumer society" gradually,[1] but many observers would point to the 1920s as a critical decade.[2] One of the most visible changes in consumption in the 1920s, and one that would be frequently cited as evidence of the new powers of advertising and marketing, was the spread of cigarette smoking, particularly among women. Between 1918 and 1940 American consumption of cigarettes grew from 1.70 pounds of cigarette tobacco per adult to 5.16 pounds.[3] In the same years advertising budgets of the tobacco companies bulged, movies pictured elegant men and women smoking, and public relations stunts promoted cigarettes.

Some contemporary observers concluded that advertising *caused* the increase in cigarette smoking among woman. For instance, in 1930, Clarence True Wilson, board secretary of the Methodist Episcopal Church, declared: "If the advertising directed to women ceased, it is probable that within five years the smoking woman would be the rare exception."[4] Scholars in later years would accept a similar view. Erik Barnouw would hold that advertising was responsible for bringing women into the cigarette market, and David Halberstam would subscribe to the same view.[5]

But this conclusion requires a second look. The historical record makes this position difficult to sustain for a number of reasons, the most important of which is the fact that tens of thousands of women began smoking cigarettes in the 1920s *before* a single advertisement was directed toward them. It is more accurate to observe that cigarette smoking among women led tobacco companies to advertise toward the female market than to suggest that advertising created the market in the first place. In the pages that follow, I will suggest that the mass media played a role in spreading the cigarette habit among women, but that it was primarily the information conveyed in news stories, not the persuasion attempted in advertisements, that helped legitimate smoking among women in the 1920s.

My aim, then, is not to dismiss the power of the mass media in influencing taste and consumption patterns, but I do seek to put the mass media in context. It is clear that advertising did not *cause* the increase in smoking among women in the 1920s. News stories recorded the increase and so helped accelerate it. But what began the social trend in the first place? To answer that, I will consider the sociology of consumption more broadly, examining the variety of factors that underlie changes in consumption.[6]

For all practical purposes, the story of cigarettes begins in 1881, when James Bonsack patented a cigarette-making machine that manufactured up to forty times what the best skilled workers could produce. Within a decade the cost of producing a cigarette was redued to one-sixth of what it had been. When James Buchanan Duke turned exclusively to machine production in 1885, he quickly was able to saturate the American market. Production was no longer a problem; the only task was to sell.[7]

Cigarette smoking grew steadily from 1880 on. By 1890 the consumption of cigarette tobacco equalled the consumption of snuff. Cigarette consumption continued even into the 1890s but declined in 1900-1905, equalling snuff again only in 1911. It did not reach the level of consumption of any other tobacco form until 1919 when it passed pipe tobacco, in 1921 when it passed cigars, and in 1922 when it passed chewing tobacco. By 1935 cigarettes represented more than half of all tobacco consumption.[8]

The cigarette available to men and women in 1920 was not the same product that had been produced a decade before. It was a more mild tobacco. Just before World War I blended tobaccos came into use, replacing some of the stronger Turkish tobaccos. When the war interrupted trade and cheaper Turkish brands lost out completely, the newer, mild cigarettes came to dominate the market.[9] This change, it is reasonable to assume, reduced the cost of "trial" to new smokers. Because the cigarette was more mild, the threshold for trying it was reduced, and the chances of being initally disgusted by it were minimized.

If the war helped promote the acceptance of blended American tobaccos, it also provided many young men and women with their first smoking experience. Cigarettes were shipped to the young men at the front, but women, too, took up a smoking habit during the war: "Women war-workers took up the habit abroad, and women at home in their men's jobs and new-found independence did likewise. Within the next three or four years cigarette smoking became the universal fashion, at least in cities, and children born since the war take smoking mothers for granted."[10]

This contemporary observation is clearly an exaggeration, but there is no reason to doubt that some women who had never smoked learned that the physical threshold to smoking was lowered by the mild tobacco and that the social threshold was lowered when laboring in a war industry. Controversy arose, for instance, over women smoking in a dormitory set up for women war workers in Washington, D.C. One woman held, "If a woman wants to smoke, she'll smoke. You might as well try to stop a volcano from smoking."[11]

While the cigarette was mild, resistance to it was not, especially with regard to women smokers. Throughout the 1920s, controversy over women smoking was a news item of interest. This was notably so in a number of areas: colleges, public transportation, and other public places.

Take the case of women's colleges, which the *New York Times* covered closely. The *Times* reported as early as 1921 that the University of Chicago banned smoking among women students.[12] By 1925 such stories were front page news. The Vassar College students' council polled students on whether they smoked away from school, on whether their parents approved of their smoking, and as to what school regulations for smoking should be adopted. This was a response to agitation over a rule prohibiting smoking, agitation mounted by women allowed to smoke at home who felt their liberties infringed upon at school. A week later the results were in, and the *Times* provided front-page coverage. Of Vassar women polled, 433 liked cigarettes, 524 did not smoke. About 400 sets of parents disapproved of their daughters' smoking, and 302 approved, according to the daughters. Some 278 students voted to continue the smoking prohibition while 539 favored more lenient rules. A month later the students nonetheless banned smoking on the grounds that "smoking is not yet established as a social convention acceptable to all groups throughout the country." Letters from around the country showed, the student officers said, that "smoking is not yet sufficiently approved to be accepted by Vassar without seriously menacing the best interests of the college."[13]

The *Times* in 1925 also reported on smoking at Radcliffe and at Smith.[14] It was front page news that MIT permitted women to smoke at dances, while Goucher banned smoking both at the campus and in public places in Baltimore for its students.[15] The MIT decision was a student council ruling that followed months of debate at a time when smoking was banned at Wellesley, Radcliffe, and for women at Boston University. A study at Bryn Mawr showed that less than half of Bryn Mawr women smoked, but the Self-Government Association petitioned the college president to set aside a smoking room in each dormitory. President Marion Edwards Park consented, saying that a change in attitude toward smoking by women had come about and that it was natural for this change to be reflected among college students. She repealed the 1897 ban on smoking. The *Times* editorially endorsed the Bryn Mawr decision, though in condescending tones, hoping that by allowing cigarettes in certain places, "what once was a feat of defiance becomes rather a bore."[16]

All of this reinforces the subsequent conclusion of historian Paula Fass that "smoking was perhaps the one most potent symbol of young woman's testing of the elbow room provided by her new sense of freedom and equality."[17] Fass shows that, while the *Times* might have approved the Bryn Mawr decision, many other opinion leaders were shocked. The President of Kansas State Teachers College said that "nothing has occurred in higher education that has so shocked our sense of social decency as the action at Bryn Mawr," and many other college presidents and deans agreed. But however shocked the authorities were, the Bryn Mawr decision was a recognition of the social fact that by 1925 large numbers of college women smoked cigarettes. One-third of the women at Ohio State said that they smoked at least occasionally; a student leader at Rhode Island State in 1924 claimed that "practically all the girls smoke." The student newspaper at the University of Illinois covered the smoking issue often in 1924 and 1925 and made it clear that enlightened student opinion felt it perfectly acceptable for women to smoke.[18]

At the end of the twenties there was still opposition to women smoking on campus. At their 1929 conventions, sororities Pi Beta Phi and Alpha Gamma Delta voted to ban smoking in chapter houses.[19] But the tide was turning. Goucher, which just a few years before had banned smoking, reversed itself in 1929. Acting President Hans Froelicher said, "This practice has become so general that public opinion in the student body demanded the change in the rule to bring it within the law, for fear that disregard for this law would breed disrespect for all laws enacted under the student government."[20]

The campuses were not the only locus of social conflict and comment over women smoking. A second center for conflict developed over women smoking on public transportation. News coverage in the *Times* occured as early as 1921 when a news item noted that the Canadian Pacific Railroad had installed smoking compartments for women in its cars.[21] In 1925 the Chicago, Milwaukee, and St. Paul Railroad added a women's smoker to its Chicago-Seattle run.[22] The Detroit streetcar system ruled that women could smoke on the streetcars despite the opposition of the city council, a development the *Times* bemoaned in an editorial the next day.[23] In New York, fifteen people were fined for smoking on the ferry between Barren Island and the Rockaways, including one woman — the only person named in the story.[24] Women were allowed in the smoking room of the White Star Liner, "Homeric," despite men's complaints dating back several years that women occupied seats in the smoking rooms.[25] The Erie Railroad decided to allow smoking in the dining room because women requested it.[26] A reporter in 1923 took a seat in the smoker between New York and Philadelphia and observed that many of the forty men, but none of the ten women in the car were smoking. An hour out of the station one woman lit up. "There was a general straightening of backs and turning of heads. The fat man opposite the women dropped his paper and frankly stared." The reporter felt that the social inappropriateness of a woman smoking was palpable: "It is being done, because railroads are opening their smoking cars to women, but it is not being done comfortably."[27]

Part of the reason for agitation by women for smoking inside was that smoking outside, in public, was still unacceptable. The people of Dayton, Tennessee, were shocked to see women smoking openly in the street as visitors streamed in for the Scopes "monkey" trial in 1925.[28] As late as 1937 a market research firm found that 95 percent of male smokers smoked in the street, but that only 28 percent of them believed it right for women to do likewise.[29] The extent of the problem as to where a smoking woman might smoke was indicated by this 1928 report:

> A few years ago an enterprising taxi driver did a thriving business in the Wall Street district during the noon hour by driving around women who wanted to smoke a cigarette or two before returning to their offices. None of the women rode any considerable distance. But the taxi driver had a continued run of passengers.
>
> The taxi was about the only place these women could smoke with any sense of freedom. In the restaurants they would have felt conspicuous. In the offices it was quite out of the question. An unwritten law said that women must not smoke in business houses. Today there is hardly any place except the street where a woman cannot smoke with equanimity.[30]

Women who smoked were conspicuous because people were not used to seeing women smoke. But they were conspicuous also because, wary of smoking outdoors where they feared disapproval, they smoked inside in places where men had never smoked — railroad diners, retail stores, and art galleries. Frances Perkins took out after women smokers in a 1930 essay in *The New Republic*, "Can They Smoke Like Gentlemen?" She noted that President Nielson of Smith College had announced that smoking would be restricted to two fireproof rooms after several dormitory fires caused by cigarettes. He had said, "The trouble is, my dear young ladies, you do not smoke like gentlemen." Perkins wholeheartedly agreed, complaining of women who smoked in restaurants all through their dinners and in railway dining cars; men, she observed, always politely retired to the smoking car. In years of gallery going, she added, she had never seen a man smoke in an art exhibition. "It remained for a couple of plain middle-aged women to mess up the floor and haze up the air, successfully obscuring the exquisite colors of Georgia O'Keeffe at a recent showing." Her main concern was that women smoked in retail stores including the major department stores. In men's clothing shops, hardware stores, or florist shops, there was, by custom, no smoking. But in stores frequented by women, the prevalence of smoking was a serious fire hazard.[31]

 Concern over *how* women smoked — or how badly — surfaced in the press from time to time. The *Times* reported that a Pennsylvania underwriter held that women's smoking cost $17 million in fire damage annually. Women smoked, he said for "braggadocio" and not for taste. "Women are amateurs at the practice and have not learned the hazards connected with it."[32] The *Times* also described the first "Smokers' Congress" in France in 1928 in which a "woman" was accused of "scattering ashes this way and that, of laying down cigarettes carelessly, thereby burning restaurant tablecloths and of wasting tobacco by smoking only a few puffs from her cigarette." The two women delegates at the Congress were the only ones who did not light up at the meetings.[33]

 Smoking, at least indoors, was more and more a commonplace for women by the mid-1920s. Writer Harry Burke observed in 1922 that many women, particularly at fashionable restaurants, were smoking. At one dinner party he attended, 13 of the 14 women present smoked, women ranging in age from 18 to 70. Leading Fifth Avenue jewelers in New York sold expensive cigarette cases and cigarette holders, and a new tobacco shop opened that catered exclusively to women. The proprietress noted that "nowadays dinner favors are usually cigarette accessories," and she boasted a complete line.[34]

 Thus, in a variety of ways, smoking among women came to be socially legitimated. The actions of colleges to establish smoking rooms in dormitories or to allow women to smoke openly on campus and the actions of streetcars, railroads, and shipping lines to allow women to smoke or to provide special facilities so that they could smoke helped legitimate the cigarette for women. Further, these changes were covered prominently in the press, and such coverage gave further support to the spread of the cigarette habit among women. In times past smoking had been associated only with scandalous women, but now the cigarette was in especially prominent use among the young and the wealthy. Such status among women smokers was also a legitimating factor. In 1925 an inspection

report by the State Commission of Prisons on the Women's Workhouse in
New York showed that smoking was very common among the inmates.
The report refused, however, to recommend that smoking be prohibited on
the grounds that "if a recent canvass of Vassar College showed nearly 50
percent of the girls to the manor born smoking, this is not surprising in a
women's workhouse."[35] Opponents of cigarettes believed crime and smoking to be connected, but by 1929 the prison at Joliet, Illinois lifted its ban
on smoking among women prisoners. "To deprive them of smoking is as
much a hardship as it would be to deprive the men, who are permitted to
smoke," an official reported.[36] Meanwhile, cigarette manufacturers were
cautious in appealing directly to women. Curtis Wessel, editor of the
United States Tobacco Journal, wrote in 1924 that "all responsible
tobacco opinion" found the habit of women smoking so "novel" that "it
would not be in good taste for tobacco men as parties in interest to stir a
particular toward or against a condition with whose beginnings they had
nothing to do and whose end, if any, no one can foresee."[37]

    When advertisers did begin to address women directly, they did so
cautiously. The first notable cigarette ad directed toward women was a
Chesterfield's ad in 1926 showing a romantic couple at night, the man
smoking, the woman sitting next to him, with the caption. "Blow Some My
Way."[38] Most ads for cigarettes, even ads with an audience of women in
mind, showed only men smoking. The New Yorker in 1926 printed a full
page ad for Miltiades Egyptian cigarettes that featured a drawing cap-
tioned, "After Theatre," with a man and a woman in evening dress. The
man was smoking and saying to the woman, "Somehow or other Shakespeare's
heroines seem more feminine in modern garb and smoking cigarettes." He
advised her to exercise care in choosing a cigarette — but she, as usual, was
not shown smoking.[39] A Camels ad in Time in 1926 showed two men
lighting up, two women looking on.[40] An ad in Time for Fatima Turkish
Cigarettes claimed, "It's What the Younger Crowd Thinks About It!" and
showed a man and a woman waterskiing, but only the man smoking.[41] A
Camels ad in The Outlook in 1927 showed two men and a woman at a
nightclub, both men smoking and the woman not smoking.[42] A Lucky
Strike ad in Literary Digest in 1927 coyly proclaimed, "Men like the flavor,
women enjoy the fragrance."[43]

    In 1928 and 1929 Camels ran a series of back page full-color ads in
Time. Some of these continued to show men smoking, women looking on.
But some made it clear that women smoked Camels, too, although the ads
did not always go so far as to show women smoking. In one ad, "Don't Be
Selfish," an elegantly dressed man offered a cigarette to his fashionable
woman companion.[44] In another a woman was shown in a classy shop,

buying a box of Camels which the clerk was carefully wrapping. The caption said, "Camels, of course. The more you demand of a cigarette, the quicker you come to Camels."[45] Another ad, "Well Bred," dared to show two women smoking at the track. The copy emphasized "breeding" and "a capacity for selection."[46]

A content analysis of the *New York Times,* the *San Diego Union,* and *Time* magazine revealed no ads picturing women or obviously appealing to women before the late 1920s. (The analysis examined four weeks of each year for *Time* from 1923 through 1935 and two weeks for each newspaper for the years 1918, 1921, 1924, 1927, 1930, and 1933.) Then, however, the appeal to women became increasingly direct. American Tobacco's campaign for Lucky Strike was the most notable, emphasizing in testimonial ads that Luckies were not harsh to the throat. One ad in the *Times* in 1927 showed opera star Schumann-Heink recommending Lucky Strike as soothing to the throat, and another pictured actress Florence Reed also recommending the cigarette that offered "no throat irritation."[47] Beginning in 1928 American Tobacco advertised Lucky Strike as a good alternative to eating candy. Their famous slogan, aimed at the female consumer, was "Reach for a Lucky instead of a sweet." In the *Forum,* for instance, in 1929, actress Nazimova urged, "Light a Lucky instead of eating sweets."[48] Chocolate manufacturers feared that women were doing exactly what the tobacco makers urged, and the complaints of confectioners made news.[49]

Note, however, that by the time these first ads appeared, tens of thousands of women had already become regular smokers. The tobacco companies had stayed away from advertising to women for fear they would elicit a backlash of public protest. In fact, their advertising did have that effect. Outrage against cigarette advertising to women reached the floor of the U.S. Senate in 1929 when Senator Reed Smoot rose to say: "Not since the days when public opinion rose in its might and smote the dangerous drug traffic, not since the days when the vendor of harmful nostrums was swept from our streets, has this country witnessed such an orgy of buncombe, quackery, and downright falsehood and fraud as now marks the current campaign promoted by certain cigarette manufacturers to create a vast woman and child market for the use of their product."[50] Senator Smoot was not alone. The National Education Association passed a resolution at its annual meeting in 1930 condemning "the fraudulent advertising of certain manufacturers in their efforts to foster cigarette-smoking." It urged schools to select for school libraries periodicals which did not carry tobacco advertising.[51] Both the Cleveland Boy Scouts Council and the Sioux Falls, South Dakota, City Commission objected to

billboards that pictured women smoking.[52] Bills were introduced to restrict cigarette advertising in Illinois, Idaho, and Michigan. Utah banned
billboard and streetcar cigarette advertising and there were many efforts in
1929 to ban American Tobacco's billboard showing what Senator Smoot
called a "girl of tender years actually smoking cigarettes."[53] This is not to
suggest that advertising precipitated the criticism of tobacco companies,
but for a brief time it intensified public opposition.[54]

Why, finally, did women take to cigarettes in the 1920s? I have
approached that question indirectly. I have not presented the extensive
literature on why people take up smoking, what kind of satisfaction they
get from it, why they tend to begin as teenagers, and so on.[55] Those
questions examine the psychology of the individual smoker and ask why
someone would deviate from a healthful norm to take up smoking. My
interest in the 1920s, in contrast, is to understand how the norm itself
changed, how smoking for women became socially acceptable.

Clearly, smoking a cigarette was a social symbol of considerable
power in the 1920s. Women used cigarettes to mark themselves as separate
from the past, different from past women. In all human societies, there are
markings that distinguish people in their social identity—men are different
from women, children from juveniles from adults. These are physical
differences, of course, but they are always reinforced and restated culturally by clothing or other body markings and differentiated forms of
behavior. In modern societies, people mark themselves not only in social
space but in social time, as the literature on fashion suggests.[56] People
indicate their relationship to one another and also accent their relationship
to the spirit of the times. They display their modernity or their resistance to
modernity. They mark their allegiance to groups that embrace social
change or to groups that hold to tradition. In the 1920s, cigarettes came to
be a personal and social marker for "the new woman," a sign of divorce
from the past and inclusion in the group of the new, young, and liberated.[57]

This study is a reminder that symbols may not only work to
confirm members of an emergent social group in a new identity but, at the
same time, may act like a prism in concentrating light on a subject and
generating heat, even fire. The conflicts over women smoking and the
extensive news coverage of the conflicts focused (though, simultaneously,
displaced) anxiety and antagonism about the "new women" and changing
sex roles at a single point. In its own way, advertising cigarettes to women
had a similar effect, although by the time the ads first appeared the
legitimacy, or at least familiarity, of women smoking was rather well
established.

As for advertising, it would be a mistake to dismiss its role in

shaping American life in the 1920s. Advertising was an increasingly obtru-
sive part of the American cultural landscape in that decade. It was an
increasingly important factor in affecting the country's language and in
articulating and emphasizing those parts of the nation's dreams that were
well suited to material and commercial form. But it would be a mistake to
see advertising as having magical powers to shape consumption. Economists who have examined the matter find only the slightest evidence that
massive cigarette advertising has influenced total cigarette consumption.[58]
Determining the relationship between advertising and sales is not as simple
as it might at first appear. Businesses tend to advertise most heavily in
product lines where sales are growing. Advertising dollars follow sales
trends. Thus there is a high correlation between sales and advertising, but it
makes as much sense to argue that high sales produce higher advertising
expenditures as to suggest that higher ad budgets produce more sales.[59] In
this respect, advertising tends to be conservative. It ventures to challenge
established ways in the population only when evidence of new market
patterns is in plain view.

　　　One of the consequences of attributing magical force to advertising is that it keeps us from thinking more seriously about what really
shapes our material lives and about ways in which our material lives are
also, inevitably, our symbolic lives, elements in our construction of mean-
ingful existence. Despite the importance of the commercial interests
involved in spreading the use of cigarettes among women, the change that
occurred was a cultural one that was sponsored in its political and social
battles more by a new class of women than by a handful of tobacco
companies. In the 1920s, a cigarette in the hands of a woman meant a
change in the language of social interaction. Such changes may be vigorously contested — as they were then, as they would be subsequently when
"Ms." and "he or she" entered the spoken language and came, over time, to
be used, at least in some circles, naturally. That advertising played a role in
the late 1920s and after in promoting smoking among women should not
blind us to the fact that this change in consumption patterns, like many
others, had roots deep in the kind of cultural change and political conflict
that advertising responds to, but rarely creates.

Notes

　　　1. This chapter is adapted from a forthcoming book, *Advertising in American
Culture* (New York: Basic Books, 1984). My thanks to Abbe Fletman and Mary Skelly for
their assistance with library research for this work.

2. Daniel Bell, *The Cultural Contradictions of Capitalism* (New York: Basic Books, 1976) p. 66.

3. Benno Milmore and Arthur Conover, "Tobacco Consumption in the United States, 1880 to 1955," Public Health Monograph No. 45 (Washington, D.C.: USGPO, 1956) p. 107. This is the appendix to William Haenszel, Michael B. Shimkin, and Herman P. Miller, *Tobacco Smoking Patterns in the United States*.

4. *New York Times*, 3 February 1930, p. 9.

5. Erik Barnouw, *The Sponsor* (New York: Oxford University Press, 1978) p. 95, and David Halberstam, *The Powers That Be* (New York: Knopf, 1979), p. 28. These and other observers seem to have been influenced by Edward Bernays' recollections in *Biography of an Idea: Memoirs of Public Relations Counsel Edward L. Bernays* (New York: Simon and Schuster, 1965) pp. 383-95. Bernays took pride in having arranged for ten women to light up cigarettes, their "torches of freedom" in the 1929 Easter Parade in New York. He smugly recalled that this created a storm of interest and front-page stories and photos. And yet, women smoking cigarettes in public had been making the front page for years without the help of Edward Bernays.

6. Part of the broader context for understanding cigarette consumption among women in the 1920s can be discerned from an analysis of changing tobacco consumption patterns among men in the same period. In fact, the shift of men from other tobacco forms to cigarettes in the 1920s was quantitatively more important than the entrance of women into the cigarette market. See "Women and Cigarettes," *Printer's Ink* 18 February 1932, pp. 25-27 for the estimate that women represented just 12 to 14 percent of total cigarette consumption in 1930. See also Lester Telser, "Advertising and Cigarettes," *Journal of Political Economy* 70 (1962): 474, and "The *Fortune* Survey," *Fortune* 12 (July 1935): 111, for other data on the prevalence of cigarette smoking among men and women. Why men moved from pipes and cigars to cigarettes in the 1920s is a somewhat different question from why women took up smoking in the first place, and I treat it in a forthcoming work, *Advertising in American Culture*

7. Alfred Chandler, *The Visible Hand* (Cambridge, Mass.: Harvard University Press, 1977), pp. 289-92.

8. Milmore and Conover, "Tobacco Consumption in the United States," p. 107.

9. Richard Tennant, *The American Cigarette Industry* (New Haven: Yale University Press, 1950) pp. 76-79.

10. Eunice Fuller Barnard, "The Cigarette Has Made Its Way Up in Society," *New York Times Magazine*, 9 June 1929, p. 18.

11. *Literary Digest*, 28 June 1919, p. 76.

12. *New York Times*, 10 December 1921, p. 10.

13. *New York Times*, 22 January 1925, p. 1; 26 February 1925, p. 24; 27 February 1925, p. 16.

14. *New York Times*, 2 March 1925, on Radcliffe and 20 November 1925 on Smith.

15. *New York Times*, 12 October 1925, p. 1.

16. *New York Times*, 24 November 1925, p. 1, and 25 November 1925, p. 20.

17. Paula Fass, *The Damned and the Beautiful: American Youth in the 1920's* (New York: Oxford University Press, 1977), p. 293.

18. *Ibid.*, pp. 295-297. But see also A. T. Allen, superintendent of schools in North Carolina who saw Bryn Mawr as the wave of the future for women's colleges. *New York Times*, 29 November 1925, Section II, p. 3.

19. *New York Times*, 5 July 1929, p. 19, and 11 July 1929, p. 48.

20. *New York Times*, 7 December 1929, p. 44.

21. *New York Times*, 15 July 1921, p. 5.

22. *New York Times*, 9 April 1925, p. 18.

23. *New York Times*, 16 July 1925, p. 1 and 17 July 1925, p. 14.

24. *New York Times*, 4 August 1926, p. 21.

25. *New York Times*, 14 August 1926, p. 5.

26. *New York Times*, 18 June 1928, p. 13.

27. *New York Times*, "Mixed Smoking Done Here," 14 January 1923, Section IV, p. 2.

28. *Baltimore American*, 15 July 1925.

29. Jack Jacob Gottsegen, *Tobacco: A Study of Its Consumption in the United States* (New York: Pitman, 1940), p. 151.

30. "Woman No Longer Hides Her Cigarette," *New York Times Magazine*, 21 August 1928, p. 19.

31. Frances Perkins, "Can They Smoke Like Gentlemen?" *The New Republic*, 7 May 1930, pp. 319-20. Perkins, later to be Franklin Roosevelt's Secretary of Labor, was at the time Industrial Commissioner of New York State.

32. *New York Times*, 26 June 1928, p. 41.

33. *New York Times*, 19 November 1928, p. 2.

34. Harry Burke, "Women Cigarette Fiends," *Ladies Home Journal* 39 (June 1922): 19.

35. *New York Times*, 9 March 1925, p. 1.

36. *New York Times*, 12 September 1929, p. 32.

37. Curtis Wessel, "The First 60 Billions are the Hardest for the Cigarette Industry," *Printer's Ink*, 31 January 1924, p. 6.

38. Robert Sobel, *They Satisfy: The Cigarette in American Life* (New York: Doubleday Anchor, 1978), p. 99.

39. *New Yorker* 1, 9 January 1926, back cover.

40. *Time*, 5 December 1927, back cover.

41. *Time*, 11 July 1927, p. 29.

42. *The Outlook*, 23 March 1927, back cover.

43. *Literary Digest* 9 April 1927, inside back cover.

44. *Time*, 1 April 1929, back cover.

45. *Time*, 4 February 1929, back cover.

46. *Time*, 14 October 1929, back cover.

47. *New York Times*, 2 February 1927, p. 52 and 2 December 1927, p. 48.

48. Forum 81 (January 1929): li.

49. *New York Times*, 27 November 1927, p. 30, and 30 August 1928, p. 30.

50. *New York Times*, 11 June 1929, p. 51.

51. *New York Times*, 4 July 1930, p. 13.

52. *New York Times*, 13 July 1928, p. 19 and 22 May 1929, p. 21.

53. Senator Reed Smoot, *Congressional Record*, 10 June 1929, p. 2589.

54. Opposition to cigarettes had been powerful at the turn of the century when Lucy Page Gaston organized the National Anti-Cigarette League. Many states, especially in the midwest, banned cigarette sales, and Indiana banned cigarette possession. See Gordon Dillow, "Thank You for Not Smoking," *American Heritage* 32 (February/March 1981): 94-107. Women's groups kept up the fight during the 1920s. The National Council of Women in Philadelphia sought to prohibit cigarette sales to women. See the *New York Times*, 16 November 1921, p. 10. The Woman's Christian Temperance Union campaigned to prohibit smoking in places where food was exposed for sale and, by 1927, twenty-one states had laws to that effect. See *Report* of the 53rd Annual Convention of the Woman's Christian Temperance Union, Minneapolis, Minn., 1927, pp. 129-33.

55. See *Smoking and Health: A Report of the Surgeon General* (1979), especially chapter 16.

56. See Edward Sapir, "Fashion," *Encyclopedia of the Social Sciences* (1933); Georg Simmel, "Fashion," in Donald Levine, ed., *Georg Simmel: On Individuality and Social Forms* (Chicago: University of Chicago Press, 1971), pp. 294-323, and Anne Hollander, *Seeing Through Clothes* (New York: Vintage, 1979).

57. On the role of the cigarette as a symbol of new womanhood, see Peter Gabriel Filene, *Him/Her/Self: Sex Roles in Modern America* (New York: Harcourt, Brace, Jovanovich, 1975), pp. 148-49, and also his bibliography on pp. 312-13 for other newspaper and magazine coverage of the smoking controversy in the 1920s.

58. See Richard Tennant, *The American Cigarette Industry* (New Haven, Ct.: Yale University Press, 1950), pp. 137-42, and Neil H. Borden, *Advertising in Our Economy* (Chicago: Richard D. Irwin, 1945), pp. 52-71, for the view that advertising probably helped accelerate, but did not cause, increased cigarette consumption. See Gideon Doron, *The Smoking Paradox: Public Regulation in the Cigarette Industry* (Cambridge, Mass.: Abt Books, 1979), for a study of the effects of the TV cigarette advertising ban — which did not hurt and may have helped cigarette sales. The research on the overall effects of advertising on aggregate consumer demand for different products is clearly and simply reviewed in Mark Albion and Paul Farris, *The Advertising Controversy: Evidence on the Economic Effects of Advertising* (Boston: Auburn House Publishing, 1981), pp. 79-86.

59. A. J. San Augustine and W. F. Foley, "How Large Advertisers Set Budgets," *Journal of Advertising Research* 15 (October 1975): 11-16, and Colin Gilligan, "How British Advertisers Set Budgets," *Journal of Advertising Research* 17 (February 1977): 47-49. See also Borden, *Advertising*, p. 57. Richard Schmalensee, in his case study of American cigarette advertising, finds no support for an effect of advertising on industry or firm sales. See Schmalensee, *The Economics of Advertising* (Amsterdam: North-Holland Publishing, 1972), p. 213.

Section II
Betrayal

A scavenger digging for the disgusts and abnormalities of life, is the press. A yellow journal of lies, idiocies, filth . . . Yet each evening comes the two-penny minstrel — a blear-eyed croaking minstrel — and the good folk give him ear. No pretty words in rhythms from his tongue. No mystic cadences quiver in his voice. Yet he comes squealing out his song of an endless "Extra! All about the raptures, lusts and adventures . . . from dreamers and lawbreakers. Extra!" Thus the city sits, baffled by itself, looking out upon a tick-tock of windows and reading with a wonder in its thought. "Who are these people?"

Bem Hecht, *Erik Dorn* (1921)

The essays in this second section range widely in their topics, but a common disturbing motif appears in each—sense of expectations raised and then betrayed. Here, sharply delineated, appears the paradoxical relationship between culture and mass communications. The essayists portray media which seemed to soothe unease while provoking it, to cement relationships while frustrating them, to give people a way to see themselves and their environments while simultaneously trivializing or blocking the view. Media professionals as well as consumers felt more isolated, less able to shape their own patterns of communication and behavior.

Tracing the development of old and new forms of mass communication and of public policy toward them between the wars, Richard A. Schwarzlose sees the frustration of hopes for more effective person-to-person communication and a steady encroachment by institutional mass media at the expense of individual voices in public affairs discussion.

Both Marion Marzolf and Michael Kirkhorn discern a failure in journalism to convey to readers the realities of their time. Focusing on the debate over immigration restriction, Marzolf identifies a weakness in the developing ideal of objectivity which, she believes, allowed the press to sidestep divisive issues, to avoid moral commitment, and in effect to stifle robust debate. Kirkhorn perceives a pervading journalistic cynicism, expressing the fatigue of reporters and editors who, he argues, felt required to distract and insulate the public from great social and economic problems.

Sally F. Griffith traces the changing focus of William Allen White's *Emporia Gazette* in the 1920s from local events to far away people and places, from the lives of neighbors to the abnormality of strangers. Readers, she suggests, may have experienced a sense of a growing marginality of small town life, a waning legitimacy of their own lives.

Questions stemming from these essays include the following: How aware were people of communications in their lives? What did they think about communications? How were the mass media shaped by the large economic, social and political realities? Protect, shield, disconnect them from such realities and from each other? How did mass communications shape people's ideas about themselves or give them ideas about what their lives should be?

6 Technology and the Individual
The Impact of Innovation on Communication

Richard A. Schwarzlose

The waves of new technology which periodically swept nineteenth century America increasingly asserted the paradox of innovation: while today's invention is the hoped for solution to yesterday's social turmoil, it also sows the seeds for tomorrow's social dilemma. The broad message, nonetheless, of nineteenth century world's fairs, national celebrations, and literary utopias was "to discount the present for the future."[1] Hence the literary critic James Russell Lowell could believe that the nineteenth century newspaper and telegraphy would resurrect the town meeting. And as late as 1927, the historians Charles and Mary Beard could believe that the automobile, radio, and electrification would emancipate and make human beings more cosmopolitan and integrate urban and rural life.[2]

The same year the Beards surveyed the twentieth century's first wave of innovation with hope, John Dewey examined the social structure "created by steam and electricity," concluding that it "may be a society, but it is no community."[3] Dewey represented a growing number of skeptics who between the turn of the century and the Great Depression fretted over the nation's headlong rush into the technological future, believing nineteenth century inventions to be at least as pernicious as they were beneficial to the sociocultural fabric. Technology and the impersonal institutions it spawned were, to these social critics, the chief causes of the disintegration of communication, community, and individualism.

These observers abhorred the steady encroachment of mass produced and consumed messages emanating from distant and impersonal media voices. Such technocultural notions as propaganda and public opinion gained literary currency as sinister and potentially destructive social forces.[4] There was also reason to distrust the new disorienting experiences of communicating over long distances at the speed of light, of traveling on trains at speeds exceeding a mile a minute, of seeing halftone media reproductions of scenes occurring hundreds of miles away, and later of viewing sequences captured at other times in other places on motion picture film.[5]

Meanwhile in the broader sociocultural sphere Charles H. Cooley was detecting the significance of self, primary groups, communication, and disorganization and underscoring the delicate balance between individual and social setting.[6] Perhaps the most forceful assault upon the developing technoinstitutional system was Thorstein Veblen's discussion in *The Theory of the Leisure Class* of interaction between production and consumption, a discussion largely ignored when first published in 1899, but gaining respectability as each passing year of "conspicuous consumption" reproved his theory.

Following World War I, according to Robert M. Crunden, "intellectuals thought that the individual was alienated from society, and they valued individualism in all its manifestations."[7] Steam, telegraphy, and telephony, these writers believed, encouraged dislocation, uprootedness, disembodied communication, impersonal business and government, and blindly followed group values. Independence and self-confidence were yielding to alienation and self-consciousness, as these intellectuals saw it, as messages, policies, and forces reaching out from remote institutional sources controlled the thoughts and actions of a growing number of citizens. These writers, as perceptive individuals and as critical narrators of the human condition, sensed the beginnings of that gradual twentieth century American drift which Henry Steele Commager summarized after World War II as being "from certainty to uncertainty, from faith to doubt, from security to insecurity, from seeming order to ostentatious disorder."[8]

It is from the perspective of these World War I skeptics that this chapter examines the nation's most rapid and pervasive technological revolution to date. These writers' desire to see control of sociocultural forces returned to the individual and the community collided with a technological explosion in the years surrounding World War I which for its breadth and speed of impact eclipsed even the most spectacular nineteenth century innovation. The nation, which in the 1800s was not fully subdued by steam transportation and electronic communication until six decades had passed, was overwhelmed within only a few years after 1918 by feasible auto and air transportation and radio communication.

This chapter traces the interwar development of old and new systems of communication and conveyance and of public policies selectively encouraging their growth. Such an examination is set against a backdrop consisting of (1) the individual-institutional dichotomy suggested by the intellectual movement opposing the new technologically based society, and (2) the transportation-communication dichotomy implicit in both nineteenth and twentieth century technological evolution. Would the individual gain significant access to either the recently discovered radio spectrum or the existing telegraph and telephone systems as the twentieth century advanced? Or would the individual remain relegated to transportation systems for his communication needs, as had been largely the case in the nineteenth century? And would national policy supporting and shaping new technology favor the individual or institutions as the internal combustion engine and radio emerged?

Auto and eventually air adaptations of the internal combustion engine would, of course, greatly expand the individual's transportation options. The family automobile offered appealingly private and individually-controlled transportation, vis-a-vis the common carriers. Historically, intercity flow of information had been wholly dependent upon transportation systems until the introduction of telegraphy in 1844.[9] In any age, however, transportation is less equipped to move information than to move goods and people, its principal advantage being to allow face-to-face communication. While it is true that transportation systems multiplied and improved during the nineteenth century, they could not challenge the telegraph's speed and efficiency of moving information from place to place. Telegraph users chiefly sacrificed face-to-face communication.

Meanwhile radio technology promised the private citizen the possibility of inexpensive, individually controlled, person-to-person communication that did not depend on the institutional wired systems of telegraphy and telephony. Some hoped, moreover, that radio might be spared institutional exploitation as a mass medium, being instead turned to the task of resurrecting and encouraging the individual citizen's voice in the public arena.

The history of communications in this nation is the story of steady encroachment by institutional mass media voices at the expense of individuals' voices in public affairs discussion. This gradual realignment of voices may be glimpsed by comparing eighteenth and early twentieth century community communication. Colonial newspapers and magazines were highly personal affairs — merely technical extensions of publishers' own voices — and were often overshadowed by other, more effective and intimate communication systems, such as pamphlets, broadsides, gossip, tavern conversation, and church and town meetings.

By the early 1900s, however, daily and weekly newspapers were nearing the peak of their numerical growth, and magazines were having their first successful fling with the mass circulation formula. Media voices increasingly dominated political debate and public opinion while the media themselves grew into large departmentalized and impersonal corporate factories which packaged and sold sensational and inoffensively "objective" reportage. By the turn of the century the individual's voice was heard, if at all, increasingly in the collective company of proliferating unions, trade associations, fraternal or secret orders, or political movements on the fringes of political life. The lone turn-of-the-century voice was likely to emanate from an individual confined to the top of an overturned crate, placed in a specified public place at a specified time of the day or week.[10]

Nineteenth Century Norms

The steam engine and electronic communication spread surprisingly slowly across nineteenth century America. Thirty-one years elapsed between Robert Fulton's 1807 experimental passage of his steamer on the Hudson River between New York and Albany and the arrival in New York harbor in the spring of 1838 of the *Sirius* and *Great Western* — appearing within six hours of each other and heralding the beginning of transoceanic steam navigation. Samuel Cunard, armed with a contract with the British Admiralty to carry the royal mail, introduced regularly scheduled transatlantic steamer service two years later.[11]

On land the steam engine's first commercial application to rail transportation came in 1830, ending a twenty-year boom of turnpike construction and threatening canal and waterway projects, even though steam railroad development remained spotty and experimental until the 1850s. Transcontinental rail service began in 1869, after nearly four decades of rail development in this country.[12] Only after one-third of a century did steam finally reach the beginnings of its ocean-going influence, and only after another third of a century did it span the North American continent. Likewise, telegraphy after its 1844 birth took roughly two decades to emerge as a national monopoly, to link the United States and Europe via submarine cable, and to span the American continent.[13] Even telephony, introduced in 1876, developed slowly, spanning the continent in more than twice the time needed by the telegraph to accomplish the same feat half a century earlier.[14]

Nineteenth century steam and electronic networks grew in direct proportion to the nation's advancing frontier. Although the multifaceted national enterprise of building transportation lines, extending communication networks, taming the frontier, and moving millions of migrants would not be duplicated in the twentieth century age of internal combustion engines and radio, the slower pace of technological progress in the last century gave the nation ample opportunity to devise a well considered and appropriate national policy for encouraging and shaping such innovation. That slowly emerging national policy became the "norm" even for twentieth century policy-makers.

The booms of canal and turnpike building and the early development of railroads made repeated demands upon the nation's still limited pool of private investment capital, inevitably calling for government aid when private sources dried up, as they periodically did. State and municipal assistance readily appeared in the form of grants of funds and land, engineering consultation, and even formation of construction and operating companies. George Rogers Taylor reports that pre-Civil War Americans "believed that economic conditions should constantly improve and that the government had a simple and direct obligation to take any practicable measure to forward such progress. Why should they fear the power of the state? Was it not their own creation in which the people themselves were sovereign?"[15]

By contrast, the same pragmatically generous philosophy did not prevail in Congress, where regional jealousies and heated debates over federal versus state responsibility forestalled serious federal support until the 1850s. Although the U.S. Constitution empowered Congress to "establish Post Offices and Post Roads" and the federal treasury recorded surpluses during most of the years prior to 1850, the federal government gave relatively little assistance to transportation projects during the first half of the century[16] and only half-heartedly supplied Samuel F. B. Morse with a meager $30,000 appropriation to assist in erecting the first experimental telegraph line between Washington, D.C., and Baltimore in 1844.[17]

The logjam of federal support for railroad construction was finally broken in 1850 when a coalition of Western and Southern congressmen proposed a north-south rail route between Chicago and ports on the Gulf of Mexico. The resulting Illinois Central Railroad, while at the time considered a special case, set a precedent on which federal land and aid grants after the Civil War were based. Harold Underwood Faulkner notes that between 1865 and 1914, in addition to direct financial aid, charters with extraordinarily lenient provisions, and tax exemptions, the federal government handed the railroads 242,000 square miles of right-of-way.[18] Faulkner explains that "the attitude of the legislatures and the public was that transportation should be encouraged by every possible means. . . . The fundamental fact that transportation was essential to the building up of the nation was apparent, and nowhere was the willingness to speculate on the country's progress better seen. But before private capital went into railroads, the government was expected to do much to make the way easy."[19]

Meanwhile, except for the initial experimental grant, Congress would not be moved to assist telegraphy's development. Between 1838 and 1845 inventor Morse conducted a continuous campaign to convince the federal government to take control of the telegraph, at one point offering his device to the government for a mere $100,000.[20] The government's early inaction effectively threw the nation's prototypical communication system into the eager arms of private developers and eventually led to the formation in 1866 of the nation's first privately owned and national industrial monopoly, Western Union.

The appearance of this monopoly, in turn, spurred reformers and some congressmen to propose legislation periodically over the next three decades which would have brought telegraphy under federal control. Most proposals were modeled after the British system, which nationalized telegraphy under the post office in 1870. Nineteen times between 1845 and 1900 U.S. House or Senate committees studied, and reported reaction to, so-called postal telegraph proposals, all but twice supporting such proposals. Still no bill attracted a congressional majority, leaving telegraphy —and its telephonic cousin — in private hands.[21]

How did these developments and policies affect the individual? Newspaper correspondents and editors, government agents, military officers, and private letter-writers were all equally dependent upon inefficient transportation for their intercity communication needs prior to telegraph's appearance in 1844. Beyond the personal life-space encounters one experienced at meetings and in the streets, or with billboards, handbills, friends, associates, and the local newspapers, the individual in pretelegraph America could receive and send information only through the postal service, express companies after 1838, personal travel, and the portable printed media from distant localities. All such communication required transportation, which conveyed both the message and its storage medium[22] — the message in handwritten or printed form on paper or remembered by the human brain.

Transportation was a cumbersome, sluggish, and irregular communication system, and only late in the pretelegraph period did some of society's professional communicators seek ways of squeezing better intercity communication out of transportation. Between 1836 and 1838, for example, the postal service inaugurated a pony express among major Atlantic coast cities and inland to St. Louis and New Orleans, operating around the clock. This service was primarily for newspaper correspondence, news slips or proofs, and whole newspaper exchanges, having been designed by Postmaster Amos Kendall, himself a former newspaper editor.[23] A few aggressive and wealthy newspaper publishers intermittently between 1827 and the appearance of the telegraph operated their own transportation systems for gathering or moving news, but the prohibitive expense limited such activity to short spurts, usually induced by news-gathering competition.[24]

Even more than three-quarters of the way through the twentieth century, newspapers still receive some of their news via transportation-bound postal service and books and magazines receive most of their published content via this channel. At the distribution end of all print media until well into the 1970s, transportation systems were the only means of getting the published word to the public. Historically various accommodations between print media and postal or transportation authorities continued from an early date. The Post Office, even before the American Revolution, permitted free exchanges among newspapers and granted special low rates for transporting printed matter of all kinds to the public. By the Civil War press runs and train departures were being adjusted to mesh and thus widen the distribution of newspapers, and for a period late in the nineteenth century "newspaper trains," leased by big-city publishers to deliver papers to distant communities, represented perhaps the closest relationship between print media distribution and transportation.[25] Despite experiments with facsimile home delivery of newspapers before and after World War II,[26] all print media and the postal service through the 1970s remain transportation-bound.[27] Newspapers still depend on the carrier bicycling through the neighborhood or the truck rumbling down the street, magazines depend on mail carriers, and both media plus books depend on the consumer-readers traveling to a newsstand or book store.

At the news-gathering end of their operation, however, newspapers had immediately realized and availed themselves of telegraph's unique value as a mover of news dispatches. While it would not entirely replace newspaper exchanges and correspondents' letters, telegraphy quickly prompted the appearance of newsbrokerages, or wire services, which began supplying a daily newspaper report to subscribing newspapers.[28] Other institutions also rapidly adopted telegraphy's skill at separating message from medium and transmitting only the former at the speed of light over long distances. By 1860, it has been estimated, between 70 and 80 percent of all telegraphic traffic was generated by business customers.[29] A complicated and high tariff structure which favored institutional customers, the result of declining competition in telegraphy and a hands-off policy by government, had priced Morse's invention out of reach of most private citizens. Postmaster General A.W. Randall, writing Congress in 1869 in support of a postal telegraph proposal, observed

> There is a growing conviction in the public mind that a method of transmitting intelligence now so little used is capable of a greater extension; that an instrumentality which affects the interests of the whole community in so many ways should not be controlled by private individuals as private property.... The cheapness of the mails is compared with the high rates of the telegraph; the simplicity and uniformity of the one with the frequent changes and complex charges of the other. The public instinctively feel that it would be desirable to have the same simplicity and uniformity in the rates of the transmission of telegraph as by mail.[30]

Despite such pleas, even from high places, a national policy of not disturbing electronic communications persisted, leaving the private citizen sitting at his writing table, turning out letters which would be transported as message and medium across the physical expanse. Allan R. Pred's study of pretelegraphic urban growth and information dissemination comments that pretelegraphic news movement in the United States was a function of existing transportation technology, "synonymous with human spatial interaction." "Thus, the construction of turnpikes, the adoption of the steamboat for passenger and freight purposes, and the initial diffusion of the railroad in the 1830s contributed to the increased rapidity of information dissemination."[31]

Beyond the scope of Pred's study, however, would be the fact that from most individuals' viewpoint transportation technology continued to define information dissemination even after telegraphy arrived — and indeed even after telephony appeared three decades later. And outside of the use made by the postal service of coastal and inland steamers and a growing railway network, much of the transportation technology available to the communicating individual especially the majority living in rural areas, was an unimproved, dusty or muddy road system dating from colonial or frontier days. Taylor says "the failure of the plank-road movement left most short-haul land transportation literally stuck in the mud, there to remain until the later age of the rigid-surface road and the internal-combustion engine."[32]

After a brief turnpike boom, attention turned to canal building, steamers, and railroad development, which satisfied the merchant and industrialist, but which left the farmer and rural resident "almost the only element interested in better roads," says Wheaton J. Lane. "Practically no assistance was given to local governments for roads between 1845 and 1903" in Pennsylvania.[33]

Twentieth Century Tensions

Turn-of-the-century rekindling of interest in good roads was in large part agriculture's effort through new technology to rid itself of problems caused by an entrenched older technology, steam railroads. While the cyclist may rightly claim credit for a small part of the Good Roads movement around 1900, agrarian discontent with railroads' abuse of monopoly[34] and the beginnings of rural free mail delivery[35] were the movement's cornerstones. Although the postal service introduced home delivery of mail in selected cities in 1863, rural home mail delivery was not begun until 1896.[36] Therefore, when the prospect of circumventing the railroad with highway transportation of farm products was joined by the promise of having one's mail left at the end of the lane rather than several miles down the main road in town, road improvements became inevitable, first administered by the states, and eventually directed in large measure by federal agencies. As a matter of national policy, the Good Roads movement was not a response to a glut of automobiles on the highways. Motor vehicles did not begin to have a significant presence on the roads until 1920.[37]

At the start of the interwar period with the auto, aircraft, and radio beginning to move to the center of America's stage, the average private citizen was still relying on the postal system for any of his communication that could not be conducted by face-to-face travel. Local travel for a privileged few involved an automobile, even though rural touring was a perilous undertaking on roads only beginning to receive state and federal attention. For the vast majority, horses and feet remained the prevailing local technology, except in metropolitan areas where mass transit had made steady strides since the mid-nineteenth century.[38] Intercity travel by private vehicle was adventuresome, arduous, and beyond the reach of most people, the nation's railroads at the zenith of their development providing a safer and more luxurious alternative. Meanwhile no evidence suggests that individual use of telegraph and telephone systems had improved over pre-Civil War levels of telegraph use.

When the average citizen, faced with the need to communicate, surveyed his options in 1921, he found transportation systems far more accessible than communication systems. Total surfaced highway of 387,000 miles was rapidly approaching the miles of railroad track in operation and would in 1922 surpass the rail mileage. While there was one mile of surfaced highway for every 280.5 persons and one registered auto for every 11.8 persons, each person averaged 9.8 trips per year on railroads.[39] Telegraphy's 1,787,000 miles of wire in 1921 had been surpassed by telephony's network in 1900, the later standing at 32,331,000 miles in 1921. Moreover, there was one telephone in 1921 for every 7.9 persons, one local call per day for every 2.1 persons and one toll call per day for 66.3 persons. On the other hand, each person averaged 1.3 telegraph messages per year. Despite telephone's apparent availability and usefulness to the private citizen, compared to the older telegraphy, only 35.3 percent of the households had phones in 1921, a surprisingly low percentage, which suggests that, like telegraphy before it, telephony was primarily the tool of institutions. (Census data reveal that the highest percentage of households with phones during the interwar period was 41.6 in 1929, dropping off the 31.1 in 1933 and rebounding only to 39.3 percent in 1941.[40])

The data suggest that the average private citizen infrequently, at best, used the nation's communication media of telegraphy and telephony, relying instead on transportation-bound postal service and personal travel. The interwar innovations of surface and air travel would obviously provide new options for the individual's communication needs. Whether, on the other hand, the citizen could acquire access to radio for his personal communication needs would be, as will be seen, another matter entirely.

Most of the expansion or decline in communication and conveyance systems in the interwar period can be traced to the absence or nature of governmental policy. Direct government support has historically been directed at the fields of public health, radio and telecommunications, agriculture, and defense, including surface craft, aircraft, and jet propulsion.[41] Indirect government support or control arises from efforts to facilitiate and upgrade mail delivery and from regulation of telecommunications. Post-World War I federal involvement in the expanding highway network arose from postal and defense considerations.

Clearly the automobile was the interwar period's chief growth industry. David A. Shannon, noting that 1920s prosperity arose from "a few relatively new industries," dubbed motor vehicles "the most spectacular new industry of the period, causing the very appearance of the country to change and affecting some of society's most personal habits.[42] The the first federal road aid was a grant of $500,000 for highway improvements in a 1912 Post Office appropriations bill.[43] Four years later $75 million in highway aid to the states was tied to the post road provision of the U.S. Constitution.[44] The 1921 Federal Highway Act, acknowledging postal and defense needs, established a system of 200,000 miles of designated federal highways and federal-state matching-fund financing. Congress may have been moved by reports that a convoy of army vehicles took sixty-two days to go from coast to coast that year.[45]

To the private citizen the automobile afforded an opportunity for local communication which, unlike early telephone service, was private and face-to-face and which, unlike public transportation systems, was controlled by the individual. There was one mile of surfaced highway in 1921 for 280.5 persons, but in 1941, resulting from massive local, state, and federal funding, there was one mile of surfaced road for 82.8 persons. Meanwhile, vehicular saturation of the population more than doubled during the interwar period. In 1921 there was one vehicle for 10.3 persons, one auto for 11.8 persons, and one truck for 84.7 persons. Twenty years later there was one vehicle for 3.8 persons, one auto for 4.5 persons, and one truck for 25.8 persons. Or to put it another way, 55 billion miles of vehicular travel in 1921 amounted to 507 miles of driving for each person in the nation. In 1941, 333.9 billion miles of travel represented 2,506.5 miles of driving for each person.[46]

During the same two decades the operating intercity rail system shrank by nearly four thousand miles, leaving one mile of track for 330 persons in 1941 as compared with one mile of track for 266 persons in 1921. Rail passengers declined from 1,061.1 million in 1921 to 488.7 million in 1941. Each person was taking 9.8 rail trips, on the average, in 1921, and only 3.7 trips in 1941.[47] Meanwhile rapid transit railway track mileage dropped from 28,500 in 1934 to 18,342 in 1941, a trend contrasting sharply with steep increases in trolley coach and motor bus route mileage during the same time.[48] Although the railroads claimed deficits for their passenger service each year after 1928,[49] Congress, viewing railroads as monopolies, passed the Transportation Act of 1920 which imposed tight regulation on railroad rates, schedules and operations. Relief from heavy-handed regulation, coming too little and too late, appeared with the Emergency Railroad Transportation Act of 1933.[50] While railroads fought the governmental regulatory apparatus with requests to implement efficiency measures, to shut down unpopular runs and unneeded stations, they watched other arms of government assist highway building and airline development projects. One especially bitter pill for the railroads was the Post Office's inauguration of airmail service between New York City and Washington, D.C., in May 1918, followed soon by transcontinental airmail service.[51]

Although competition for passenger service from airlines was largely a post-World War II phenomenon, air postal service and some freight service both in the air and on the highways began impinging on railroad revenue at the start of the interwar period. Between 1918 and passage in 1938 of the Civil Aeronautics Act, air service was under repeated investigation by various legislative bodies with "significant" legislation passed five times between 1925 and 1935. The principal governmental preoccupation with air service during most of this interwar period, however, had to do with moving the mail.[52]

The net effect of these national policies was a tremendous growth of the highway network on which vehicular traffic depended. Thus government contributed substantially to the emerging new private industry of manufacturing, servicing, financing, and fueling the internal combustion vehicle — an industry employing an estimated 3.7 million workers, or one-tenth of the nonagricultural labor force by 1929.[53] And for the fledgling aeronautics industry governmental support extended to handling airmail, developing military aircraft, and building airport facilities. Stiffer regulation of air service arrived at the end of the interwar period, after the railroads had had twenty years of regulation and of being forced to watch helplessly as these competitors reaped governmental benefits.

With one in every 34.5 persons an air passenger in 1941, air transportation found itself roughly where automobile transportation had been at the start of World War I. But during the interwar period the growth of auto travel had freed the worker to commute to work in the privacy and flexibility of a personally operated vehicle. It had freed the shopper from mass transit systems gravitating to the central business and shopping district; the disintegration of the central city and of mass transit was about to begin. The car became the family's chief means of reaching and communicating with a wider circle of local businesses and professional services. For intercity transportation and communication, efficiency measures sustained the railroads up through 1941, despite passenger service deficits, but intercity buses and the family car assisted by government highway programs, were cutting into railroads' business.

While the private citizen benefited from the increased transportation options, both for personal face-to-face communication and for indirect communication via the postal service, his access to the nation's new communication system of radio was painfully reminiscent of his grandfather's first encounter with the telegraph or telephone. The first blow to the "scattered brotherhood" of amateur radio operators was the 1912 Radio Act which confined "hams" to the broadcasting bands of 200 meters and above.[54] It was to be the law of the land for fifteen years, a congressional slap on the wrist for those who filled the airways in the precommercial broadcast days with chatter which sometimes interfered with institutional or governmental radio. Depicted as a flock of either irresponsible or fun-loving youths, these early experimenters were neither organized nor numerous enough to convince the federal government after World War I that radio's prime or exclusive purpose ought to be the transmitting of individuals' messages.[55] At a time when telephone service in many communities was anything but private, the possibility of widespread person-to-person communication via radio was not outlandish.

In the years following World War I, the U.S. Navy, the Post

Office, and the Department of Commerce each voiced claims of control over radio when it, like other communication systems, awaited postwar denationalization. Had Congress honored some of these claims, radio might have become a governmental monopoly, greatly affecting the balance of commercial and private radio uses which eventually emerged. In the vacuum of congressional indecisiveness, however, radio's future was largely preordained by creation of the Radio Corporation of America in 1919 as a vehicle for pooling patents and thus paving the way for private sector manufacturers of radio equipment to begin shaping radio's commercial future. Broadcasting, which received its chief impetus from manufacturers' two-pronged program of establishing broadcasting stations and selling receivers by which the public could hear those stations, marked a radical departure from long-standing uses of electronic communcation systems. Radio's "free" service to the listening public broke sharply with telegraph's and telephony's tradition of delivering private messages. And it was left to Secretary of Commerce Herbert Hoover after 1920 to strike a balance between radio's new broadcast service and vestiges of its older private function.[56]

In the world of what might have been, one must guard against erecting straw men to topple and hypthesizing "widgets" which would have altered the course of history if permitted to develop. It seems clear, however, that some persons knowledgable about radio hoped for radio's conversion to private use following World War I. W. Rupert Maclaurin gives an idyllic shading to the amateur movement as a vehicle which might have shown the way to widespread private use of radio if given an opportunity.

> By the 1920s wireless had become the hobby of thousands of young Americans. No other modern industry had been supported by so many ardent participants. It is hard [in the late 1940s] to recapture the spirit of this period: amateur clubs were started in every state, comprising all types of classes — schoolboys, professors, electricians and ex-servicemen who had operated radios during the war. Radio was a new toy, not only technically interesting, but the means by which people could reach out into unknown regions and communicate with new-found friends.[57]

But because this "new toy" appeared to be only a "hobby" for most amateurs, the large-scale private use of radio could be seen as justifiably pushed into the background. President Woodrow Wilson's call for a postwar communication policy in the "public interest" on the eve of communication's denationalization could have been understood to mean that radio would be developed either *on behalf of* the public or *by* the public.[58] Hoover, urged on by a young but powerful radio manufacturing industry, chose the former interpretation.

Secretary Hoover, addressing the first conference on radio convening on February 27, 1922, in one stroke acknowledged the possibility of private use of radio and dismissed such use as ludicrous, opting for station broadcasting.

> I think that it will be agreed at the outset that the use of the radio telephone for communication between single individuals, as in the case of the ordinary telephone, is a perfectly hopeless notion. Obviously, if ten million telephone subscribers are crying through the air for their mates they will never make a junction; the ether will be filled with frantic chaos, with no communication of any kind possible. In other words, the wireless telephone has one definite feature, and that is for the spread of certain predetermined matter of public interest from central stations.[59]

Private use of radio meant "amateur" radio, and for Hoover the amateur was condescendingly perceived as "the American boy," one of a group of harmless, if sometimes noisy, kids.[60] Hoover's remarks at the third radio conference in 1924 reflect his view of the low standing of person-to-person communication as represented by the amateur.

> Nor have we overlooked in . . . previous conferences the voice or interest of the amateur, embracing as he does that most beloved party in the United States — the American boy. He is represented at this conference, and we must have a peculiar affection for his rights and interests. I know nothing that has contributed more to sane joy and definite instruction than has radio. Through it the American boy today knows more about electricity and its usefulness than all of the grown-ups of the last generation.[61]

Thus, with phenomenal speed after 1920 commercial broadcasting developed, jumping from one station in 1921 to 556 stations two years later, and reaching 955 by 1941, of which fifty-six were newfangled FM stations and two were television stations. Meanwhile, the total of 5,717 licensed amateurs in 1920 grew to 60,000 by 1941, but their ranks during the interwar period never exceeded 0.05 percent of total resident population. (The addition of citizens band service in 1950 brought total private involvement in radio to the point that in 1970 the total of 1,170,412 authorized CB and amateur stations was only 0.6 percent of total population.[62])

Electrification, in turn, brought the growing number of radio stations after World War I into more homes. National electrification stood at 34.7 percent of all dwelling units in 1920 with only 1.6 percent of rural dwelling having been reached by electricity. In 1941, 80 percent of all dwellings in the nation and 35 percent of all rural dwellings had electricity.[63] Concurrently households with radio sets rose from 0.2 to 55.2 percent in the decade after 1922, and continued to grow to 81.5 percent on the eve of World War II.[64] Broadcasting with the blessing of government and through industry's eager effort had introduced another mass medium to compete with newspapers and magazines.

Conclusion

As World War II approached, the American citizen found himself more mobile, yet no more plugged into the nation's communication systems than he had been at the end of World War I. His communication was still largely via transportation, either through personal travel or the postal service. A national policy of encouraging and shaping transportation technology, a policy borrowed from the nineteenth century, had given the individual a growing opportunity during the interwar period to conduct his communications on a face-to-face basis. That was a melody which Dewey and his friends might happily have hummed. But the contrapuntal themes of governmental policies — involved too intimately in transportation's development and too little interested in urging upon communication institutions a responsibility to individual voices — would be dissonant to that skeptical World War I crowd.

The individual, left sitting at his writing table at the end of the nineteenth century, was for the most part still there on the eve of World War II, if he was not sitting behind the wheel of the family car. Except for the less than one percent of the population licensed as "hams," people experienced radio, and eventually television, only as recipients. The interwar period, beyond dusting off and extending nineteenth century policies regarding new technology, had been marked by success principally in developing more ways for individuals to communicate inefficiently among themselves and for institutions to communicate with speed and precision to the populace at large.

Each innovative revolution breeds its curative and unexpected sequel, and the interwar explosion of internal combustion power and broadcasting was no exception. The "horseless carriage" and "wireless telephone," as these early terms imply, were perceived as harmless extensions of existing technology, exciting new innovations based on nineteenth century American life. Consequently, the tensions created by the automobile, the airplane, and radio and by national policies which applied outdated perspectives to these innovations were not perceived until the country had become dependent upon foreign petroleum, had allowed American cities to spread in all direction like spilled milk, and had permitted the rust to begin to form on the national rail network.

As this chapter is written we talk blithely of the coming revolution in "cable television," "word processing," and "video display terminals." Yet these innocent sounding words, borrowed from existing technology, camouflage a powerful new interactive communication medium based on a cable-computer-satellite system which will doubtless displace the bulk of our present electronic communications and mass media and could eliminate most face-to-face communication. We await the verdict on the individual's status at the conclusion of our present technological trial.

Notes

1. James W. Carey and John J. Quirk, "The History of the Future," *Communications Technology and Social Policy, Understanding the New "Cultural Revolution,"* ed. George Gerbner, Larry P. Gross, and William H. Melody (New York: John Wiley and Sons, 1973), p. 488.

2. *Ibid.* pp. 499, 489, citing *The Writing of James Russell Lowell,* vols. (Cambridge, Mass.: Riverside Press, 1890-92), 5:239, and the Beards' *The Rise of American Civilization* (1927; New York: Macmillan, 1940), p. 746.

3. John Dewey, *The Public and Its Problems* (New York: Henry Holt, 1927), p. 98.

4. Public opinion acquires its modern dimensions of news and audience psychology in the writings of Walter Lippmann, notably *Liberty and the News* (New York: Harcourt, Brace and Howe, 1920) and *Public Opinion* (New York: Harcourt, Brace, 1922).

5. An interesting exploration of half tone photographic reproduction as "an iconographic revolution of the first order" that caused a generation of Americans between 1885 and 1910 to experience a "visual reorientation that had few earlier precedents" is Neil Harris' "Iconography and Intellectual History: The Half-Tone Effect," pp. 196-211, in *New Directions in American Intellectual History,* ed. John Higham and Paul K. Conkin (Baltimore: The Johns Hopkins University Press, 1979). The above quotes are from p. 199.

6. Of Charles H. Cooley's three major volumes, the one most relevant to this discussion is *Social Organization, A Study of the Larger Mind* (New York: Charles Scribner's Sons, 1909).

7. Robert M. Crunden, *From Self to Society, 1919-1941* (Englewood Cliffs, N.J.: Prentice-Hall, 1972), p. x.

8. Henry Steele Commager, *The American Mind, An Interpretation of American Thought and Character Since the 1880's* (New Haven, Ct.: Yale University Press, 1950), p. 407.

9. Allan R. Pred, *Urban Growth and the Circulation of Information: United States System of Cities, 1790-1840* (Cambridge, Mass.: Harvard University Press, 1973).

10. The author elaborates on the changing historical mix of individual and institutional voices in the marketplace of ideas in the historic outline of a bibliographic essay on "Newspapers," pp. 232-40 in *Handbook of American Popular Culture,* vol. 3, ed. M. Thomas Inge (Westport, Ct.: Greenwood Press, 1981). A further and more specific elaboration is the

author's "The Marketplace of Ideas: A Measure of Free Expression," an essay prepared for *Free Expression in a Democratic Society*, being edited by James W. Carey and Clifford Christians for the University of Illinois Press.

11. Steam navigation's history is depicted in Carl D. Lane, *American Paddle Steamboats* (New York: Coward-McCann, 1943); John H. Morrison, *History of American Steam Navigation* (New York: W. F. Sametz, 1903); and David Budlong Tyler, *Steam Conquers the Atlantic* (New York: Appleton-Century, 1939). The Cunard Line history is told in F. Lawrence Babcock, *Spanning the Atlantic* (New York: Alfred A. Knopf, 1931).

12. For historical accounts of national transportation generally and of railroad development in particular, see George Rogers Taylor, *The Transportation Revolution, 1815-1860*, vol. 4 of The Economic History of the United States (New York: Rinehart & Co., 1951); Balthasar Henry Meyer, ed., *History of Transportation in the United States before 1860* (Washington, D.C.: Carnegie Institution of Washington, 1917); Jean Labatut and Wheaton J. Lane, eds., *Highways In Our National Life, A Symposium* (Princeton, N.J.: Princeton University Press, 1950); Alvin F. Harlow, *Old Towpaths, The Story of the American Canal Era* (New York: Appleton-Century, 1926); and John F. Stover, *American Railroads* (Chicago: University of Chicago Press, 1961).

13. Telegraphy's history is told in: Robert Luther Thompson, *Wiring a Continent, The History of the Telegraph Industry in the United States, 1832-1866* (Princeton, N.J.: Princeton University Press, 1947), and in Alvin F. Harlow, *Old Wires and New Waves, The History of the Telegraph, Telephone, and Wireless* (New York: Appleton-Century, 1936).

14. The transcontinental telegraph was completed in 1861, seventeen years after the first Morse line went up. Transcontinental telephone service was first available in 1915, thirty-nine years after Bell's first successful phone calls. Telephony's history is available in: Frederick Leland Rhodes, *Beginnings of Telephony* (New York: Harper & Brothers, 1929); N. R. Danielian, *A.T.&T., The Story of Industrial Conquest* (New York: Vanguard, 1939); and Horace Conn, *American Tel & Tel, The Story of a Great Monopoly* (New York: Longmans, Green, 1939).

15. Taylor, *The Transportation Revolution*, pp. 352-53. See also pp. 24-26, 48-52, 92-94.

16. *Ibid.*, pp. 19-22.

17. Thompson, *Wiring a Continent*, pp. 16-19.

18. Harold Underwood Faulkner, *American Economic History*, 8th ed. (New York: Harper & Brothers, 1960), p. 481.

19. *Ibid.*

20. Alfred Vail, *The American Electro Telegraph: With the Reports of Congress and a Description of All Telegraphs Known, Employing Electricty or Galvanism* (Philadelphia: Lea & Blanchard, 1845), p. 81; Edward Lind Morse, comp. and ed., *Samuel F. B. Morse, His Letters and Journals*, 2 vols. (Boston: Houghton Mifflin, 1914), 2: 84-86; and Thompson, *Wiring a Continent*, pp. 27-31.

21. Harlow, *Old Wires and New Waves*, pp. 322-39.

22. James W. Carey and Norman Sims, "The Telegraph and the News Report" (paper delivered at the meeting of the Association for Education in Journalism, College Park, Maryland, July 1976), p. 1.

23. Carl H. Scheele, *A Short History of the Mail Service* (Washington, D.C.: Smithsonian Institution Press, 1970), pp. 68-69.

24. The most complete attempt in print to survey these pretelegraphic activities by newspaper publishers is Alfred McClung Lee, *The Daily Newspaper in America, The Evolution of a Social Instrument* (New York: Macmillan, 1937), pp. 477-92. Such activities

included running horse expresses from Washington, D.C., to New York City, operating news boats in and beyond Eastern harbors, and employing express agents to carry news dispatches on chartered locomotives and steamers.

25. George Everett, "Newspaper Trains — America's First Fling at High-Speed Transmission of the Printed Word" (paper delivered at the meeting of the Association for Education in Journalism, Boston, August 11, 1980).

26. See Charles R. Jones, *Facsimile* (New York: Murray Hill Books, 1949), pp. 58-74, and Lee Hills and Timothy J. Sullivan, *Facsimile* (New York: McGraw-Hill, 1949).

27. At this writing numerous authors are speculating on the possible integration of the printed word into developing cable-computer-satellite information systems. See notably Anthony Smith, *Goodbye Gutenberg, The Newspaper Revolution of the 1980's* (New York: Oxford University Press, 1980), esp. pp. 241-99, and Alan L. Sorkin, *The Economics of the Postal System, Alternatives and Reform* (Lexington, Mass.: Lexington Books, 1980), pp. 107-31.

28. The general dimensions of early newsbroking history may be found in Victor Rosewater, *History of Cooperative News-Gathering in the United States* (New York: Appleton, 1930). For indications of how rapidly telegraphy brought newsbroking onto the scene, see the author's "Early Telegraphic News Dispatches: Forerunner of the AP," *Journalism Quarterly* 51 (Winter 1974): 595-601, and "The Nation's First Wire Service: Evidence Supporting a Footnote," *Journalism Quarterly* 57 (Winter 1980): 555-62.

29. Richard B. Du Boff, "Business Demand and the Development of the Telegraph in the United States, 1844-1860," *Business History Review* 54 (Winter 1980): 465, 479.

30. A. W. Randall, *Postal Telegraph. Letter from the Postmaster General Transmitting a Report of G.G. Hubbard, esq., of Boston, Relative to the Establishment of a Cheap System of Postal Telegraph*, H.Rep., 40th Cong., 3d sess., Ex. Doc. 35, January 9, 1869, p. 1.

31. Pred, *Urban Growth and the Circulation of Information*, p. 13.

32. Taylor, *The Transportation Revolution*, p. 31. An excellent and graphic summary of antebellum road conditions is in Meyer, *History of Transportation in the United States*, pp. 54ff.

33. Wheaton J. Lane, "The Early Highway in America, to the Coming of the Railroad," ed. Labatut and Lane, *Highways in Our National Life*, p. 75.

34. James J. Flick, *The Car Culture* (Cambridge, Mass.: MIT, 1975), p. 8.

35. Wayne E. Fuller, *RFD, The Changing Face of Rural America* (Bloomington: University of Indiana Press, 1964), pp. 177-98.

36. *Ibid.*, pp. 13, 37.

37. Census data on total registered vehicles, total resident population, and total mileage of surfaced road in the nation reveal that vehicular traffic is not a signficant phenomenon until after World War I. U.S. Bureau of the Census, *Historical Statistics of the United States, Colonial Times to 1970*, 2 pts. (Washington, D.C.: USGPO, 1975), 1:8, 2:710, 716.

38. In Chicago, for example, horse-drawn streetcars appeared in 1859, followed by cable-operated streetcars in 1882, electric streetcars in 1890, steam-powered elevated rapid transit trains in 1893 which were converted to electric power two years later, and motor buses in 1927. Public Information Department, Chicago Transit Authority, *Chicago Transit Authority, History and Accomplishments* (January 1967), pp. 4-7.

39. Total resident population in 1921 was 108,538,000; total operating railroad track was 407,531 miles; total registered autos was 9,212,100; and 1,061,131,000 rail passengers were recorded in 1921. *Historical Statistics*, 1:8, 2:710, 716, 728-29.

40. *Ibid.*, 1:8, 2:783, 785-87, 789.

41. Jesse W. Markham, "Inventive Activity: Government Controls and the Legal Environment," Universities-National Bureau Committee for Economic Research, *The Rate and Direction of Inventive Activity: Economic and Social Factors* (Princeton, N.J.: Princeton University Press, 1962), p. 587.

42. David A. Shannon, *Between the Wars: America, 1919-1941*, 2nd ed. (Boston: Houghton Mifflin, 1979), pp. 98, 108.

43. Dudley F. Pegrum, *Transportation, Economics and Public Policy*, 3rd ed. (Homewood, Ill.: Richard D. Irwin, Inc., 1973), p. 459.

44. H. Jerome Cranmer, *New Jersey in the Automobile Age: A History of Transportation*, vol. 23 of the New Jersey Historical Series (Princeton, N.J.: Van Nostrand, 1964), p. 57.

45. *Ibid.* and Pegrum, *Transportation*, p. 460.

46. *Historical Statistics*, 1:8, 2:710, 716, 718.

47. *Ibid.*, 1:8, 2:728-29.

48. Between 1934 and 1941 route mileage for trolley coach routes rose from 423 to 2,041 and for motor bus routes from 54,700 to 82,100. *Ibid.*, 2:721.

49. Stover, *American Railroads*, p. 211. Since 1929 the railroads could claim profits for passenger service only during the four war years of 1942-45.

50. *Ibid.*, pp. 219, 269.

51. *Ibid.*, pp. 214-15.

52. Richard E. Caves, *Air Transport and Its Regulators, An Industry Study* (Cambridge, Mass.: Harvard University Press, 1962), pp. 123-25.

53. Shannon, *Between the Wars*, p. 98.

54. Erik Barnouw, *A Tower in Babel*, Vol. 1 of A History of Broadcasting in the United States (New York: Oxford University Press, 1966), pp. 31-32, 296.

55. See Harlow, *Old Wires and New Waves*, pp. 468-70, for a derisive account of amateur activity, concluding with "as in the case of movie censorship and Prohibition, unbridled liberty had become license and slain itself." For a more balanced treatment of amateur radio see Gleason L. Archer, *History of Radio to 1926* (New York: The American Historical Society, 1938), pp. 98-210 passim, and Barnouw, *A Tower in Babel*, pp. 28-38.

56. The story of interdepartmental conflict over the postwar governmental policies regarding communications systems has ben told in several places. For a recent, well researched, version see Philip T. Rosen, *The Modern Stentors, Radio Broadcasters and the Federal Government, 1920-1934* (Westport, Ct.: Greenwood Press, 1980), pp. 15-36.

57. W. Rupert Maclaurin, with the technical assistance of R. Joyce Harman, *Invention & Innovation in the Radio Industry* (New York: Macmillan, 1949), p. 112.

58. Woodrow Wilson's message to Congress, May 20, 1919, reprinted in Wilson, *War and Peace, Presidential Messages, Addresses, and Public Papers (1917-1924)*, ed. Ray Stannard Baker and William E. Dodd, 2 vols. (New York: Harper & Brothers, 1927), 1:485ff. "Public interest" as a theory buttressing government regulation of private broadcasting became national policy at the third annual radio conference in 1924 in statements made by Secretary of Commerce Hoover. James C. Malin, *The United States After the World War* (Boston: Ginn, 1930), p. 172.

59. Portions of this quote appear in Herbert Hoover, *The Memoirs of Herbert Hoover, The Cabinet and the Presidency, 1920-1933* (New York: Macmillan, 1952), p. 140, and in "Asks Radio Experts to Chart the Ether," *New York Times*, February 28, 1922.

60. Hoover, *Memoirs*, pp. 139-48.

61. U.S. Department of Commerce, *Recommendations for Regulation of Radio Adopted by the Third National Radio Conference Called by Herbert Hoover Secretary of*

Commerce (Washington, D.C.: USGPO, 1924), p. 8.
    62. *Historical Statistics,* 1:8, 2:796, 799.
    63. *Ibid.,* 2:827.
    64. *Ibid.,* 1:43, 2:796.

7 Americanizing the Melting Pot
The Media as Megaphone for the Restrictionists

Marion Marzolf

The image of the immigrant as a menace in America became increasingly visible in the mass media of the early 1920s. The loyalty of the millions of hyphenated Americans already in the country had been questioned and tested during the first World War. Now came predictions of hordes more, crowding the embarcation ports of Southern and Eastern Europe, clamoring for passage to America.

And with them came the fears. A flood of cheap labor appeared to threaten American workers' hard-won standard of living. The new immigrants lacking experience in self-government would provide ripe ground, it was feared, for the growth of radical labor movements and Bolshevism. The war had increased American awareness of the "dangerous" radical elements and "unassimilated" aliens in the nation. Widely publicized Americanization campaigns to turn aliens into good citizens seemed ineffective. The melting pot had overheated. Adding more foreigners would strain an already depressed economy and create a potentially explosive social tension between native and foreign, rich and poor.

Thus the eugenics movement stepped up its campaign to bar the "inferior stock" immigrants from Slavic and Latin Europe. According to the eugenicists' pseudo-scientific evidence, the new immigrants' "gene plasma" inclined them toward anti-social behavior, crime, and mental deficiency.

American popular magazines and the daily press amplified these frightening messages in headlines, news articles, pictures, feature stories, and editorials as the issue of immigration restriction boiled up in the early 1920s. The media, in paying little attention to opposition views and opinions on immigration policy and to the quality of the new immigration, effectively served as a national megaphone for the well-organized publicity efforts of the restrictionists. This essay will argue that a weakness in the professional ideal of "objectivity" allowed the press to be manipulated by the publicists.

At the core of the restrictionist movement was the Immigration Restriction League founded in 1894 by New England intellectuals. Its educational and publicity campaigns eventually drew in others — politicians, labor unions, the American Legion and other patriotic groups as public opinion crystallized on the issue. [1]

The first World War made Americanization a "great popular crusade," the historian John Higham would explain. "At the deepest level, what impelled the restriction movement in the early decades of the twentieth century was the discovery that immigration was undermining the unity of American culture and threatening the accustomed dominance of the white Protestant people of northern European descent." [2]

Americans realized that the country was much more ethnically divided than had been presumed. Immigrants, it was felt, should be an integral part of society, but many Americans had lost faith in the ability of the melting pot to assimilate the foreigners. Furthermore, it was not at all certain that all foreigners wanted to be merged; many seemed to want to stay huddled in their ghettos, and others came only to work and take their profits home to Europe. Immigrant loyalty, despite a record 450,000 foreign-born volunteers in the armed forces and impressive Liberty Bond campaign efforts among the hyphenates, was still not completely trusted.

Lapse of the wartime passport act presented the restrictionists of the early 1920s with the opportunity to renew efforts to stop or at least limit immigration. Instead of simply passing a law to continue orderly processing of passport applications, they redoubled efforts to whip up sentiment against the aliens. Rising unemployment and fears that the flood of immigrants would create economic chaos and threaten social stability became popular arguments for restriction.

Opponents of restriction — a smaller group of intellectuals and politicians, some ethnic groups (especially Jews, who were hit hard by the new laws and by political conditions in Europe), businessmen and industrialists — were not well organized. Some were vulnerable to the restrictionists' charges of self-serving interest in the matter — the industrialists after cheap labor and the ethnics concerned about kin. The philosophical issue, America's long-cherished role as home of the oppressed and land of opportunity and equality, as well as the validity of the eugenicists' race theories were rarely debated, however, as the country moved to passage of a permanent quota act in 1924.

In only four years, from 1920 to 1924, the restrictionists over-

turned America's traditional open door immigration policy. With passage
of the Immigration Restriction Act of 1924 the melting pot image of
America as a land of continually fusing new people was abandoned. The
new law made national loyalty and political and social conformity to the
Anglo-Saxon Protestant tradition the new standards. The American character and nation had been forged. From now on there would be just
enough of the foreign element to add some spice, but not enough to spoil
things.[3]

Coverage of the issue was typified by the urban newspapers which
by the 1920s had become big businesses; many were parts of chains and
interested primarily in profits. Competition had declined, except in the
largest cities. National and international news was increasingly provided
by the newsgathering agencies, the wire services. Their "objective," factual
accounts of the day's events served papers and readers of all shades of
political opinion. What was called "objectivity" had become the standard
for urban news reporting. News was to be shorn of obvious partisan bias;
opinion, reserved for the editorial pages. The reader must decide.

This prized objectivity was thought to enhance the democratic
process, to encourage robust and open debate. Yet in this instance,
journalistic objectivity actually aided the manipulation of the issue by the
best-organized forces, the restrictionists. The objective journalist did not
seek out the opposing views: he waited for them to emerge. If they failed to
appear, they went unnoticed. Reporting was reactive, event-oriented, fact-
based. The ideology and values that lay behind the events and political
maneuvering were not evaluated in the news columns, even though they
might be embedded in the quoted statements of the interested parties.

It is relevant to note that, although press histories ignore it, a new
profession was developing in the post World War years that would have
increasing influence on the content and style of American mass media. It
was public relations.[4] The profession of publicity grew out of experiments
in wartime propaganda, opinion manipulation and behavioral psychology. The careers of early practitioners would be detailed in biographies,
but their influence on the print media would be largely ignored.[5]

This relationship of journalism's news orientation and standard of
objectivity to the democratic marketplace and the rise of public relations
and the big corporation is probed by Michael Schudson in *Discovering the
News*. He asserts that journalists lost confidence in the ideal of the democratic market place as corporate power came to replace it by the 1920s.
Objectivity was a means of escaping from journalists' own doubts; the
objective journalist was an impartial observer who stayed above the
action. At times, objectivity also camouflaged the real power of the press,

says Schudson.[6] The new power of the press was that of setting the terms of the debate, determining the public agenda and speaking to great masses at once.

The press coverage of the restrictionist debate illustrates this new power and the ways in which a press cherishing notions of "objectivity" as a professional norm could be manipulated by publicists. The essential weakness in this ideology of "objectivity" was revealed as journalists pursued the main immigration story and covered testimony in Congress, major speeches and statements but failed to point out that several of the Congressmen and Senators sponsoring the legislation and managing the investigating committees were active restrictionists and eugenicists.[7] The official sources and leaders of organized groups drew the largest press coverage, while immigrant editors and ethnic groups, opposing intellectuals and scientists gained little attention. The reporting was straightforward, but it was one sided.[8]

Media Coverage of the Immigrants

Although the objective urban daily press and the more openly subjective national magazines had different editorial objectives and policies, their coverage of the immigration issue was remarkably similar. A diversity of views could be found in 1921, but by 1923 most coverage favored some kind of restriction. After that the only real questions were "Who?" and "How much?" Such narrow conceptualization gave the restrictionists a decided advantage. They had been rehearsing their arguments for two decades and were ready with hundreds of letters, pamphlets, articles and books. They set forth the argument that as native-stock birth rates dropped, America would be overcome by inferior, non-Nordic stock whose birth rates would remain high.

On the other hand, the actual subjects of the debate — the foreign born as a group — had been rarely pictured or discussed in newspapers and magazines, even though by 1920 a third of the nation's population was foreign-born or children of foreign-born, and was concentrated most heavily in the cities and industrial areas. Some nationalities had been stereotyped as dangerous, comic, or quaint, and occasionally had been thus depicted in the media. Mostly, however, they had been given little serious attention. Indeed, conditions of life among the poor and ordinary of any kind had usually escaped mass attention.[9]

In the 1920s, however, urban immigrants became both danger and event. Immigrant hordes crowding at Ellis Island, outbreaks of typhus, labor unrest and crimes involving immigrants were perceived as "news."

The media also picked up and used the colorful "old" and "new" immigrant labels first promoted by the Immigration Restriction League to separate the acceptable old pioneers, the English, German, Scandinavians, Dutch, and French, from the strange new folks, the Poles, Bohemians, Russians, Greeks, and Italians so visible in the modern cities. Negative stereotypes about the Irish and German, for example, were modified and toned down in order to fit the problem as the restrictionists saw it.[10] Splitting the immigrant image this way was a successful example of image making. It allowed America to cherish the positive image of pioneering immigrants while decrying the dangerous elements. This split image would remain in the popular media and textbooks, shaping immigration policy for decades, long after the charges and statistics had been proven faulty.

Role of Media: The Newspapers

The immigration restriction debate was not a major story for the newspapers. It was covered mainly on inside pages with occasional editorials and letters. Page one treatment was reserved for Congressional action or a statement by a powerful figure or group. A few democratic-liberal daily newspapers took strong editorial stands against restriction, but most of the press accepted the "need" to control immigration.

Editorially, the *New York Times* stood unwaveringly for restriction. Even though the *Times* thought existing laws already ample to exclude undesirable immigrants, it was convinced that the current widespread unemployment, drastic wage cuts, lack of efficient Americanization, and inability to enforce laws argued for a prompt and strong new law that would "strictly limit" immigration and "would never again allow it to exceed our capacity for useful and wholesome assimilation."[11]

The newspapers in 1921 were reporting the steadily rising number of immigrant arrivals, anticipating two million in a year when four million were already unemployed. They reported on crowded and filthy conditions at Ellis Island and the louse-infested immigrants bringing in typhus. This set off cries for better health inspection and treatment. It also strengthened the image of the new immigrants as inferior, unclean, and harmful.[12]

An immigration bill before Congress in that year had been introduced by Senator William Dillingham. He proposed a limit of 356,461 immigrants per year, with each national group to be allowed entry up to 3 percent of the total of that nationality in the country as recorded in the 1910 Census.[13] This amounted to 202,213 from Northern Europe and 153,240 from South and Eastern Europe.

The Inter-Racial Council called for a presidential veto on the basis

of the bill's "inhumanitarian policy which is contrary to America's traditional attitude of asylum and opportunity."[14] The Hebrew Aid Society
attacked on the same grounds, calling the bill "unscientific and contrary to
the highest dictates of humanity,"[15] and asked at least for amendments to
permit reunification of families separated by the war and a more just
attitude toward those minority groups in the new and enlarged countries.

This bill was killed by pocket veto, but passed in the 1921 summer
session and was signed May 20 by President Harding. During the debate
Secretary of State Hughes referred to "undersirables" from Balkan cities
Armenia, Russia, and Georgia. He cited examples of large numbers of
Jews excused from Romanian military service if they were emigrating to
America, of 35,000 in Poland waiting for third-class passage, and of Letts
and Lithuanians fleeing the slums of the Baltic states, most of them "Jews
of an undesirable type."[16] This story rated page one in the *New York Times*

The *Times* also expressed its pleasure over what it called the
intelligent and clear policy of the new temporary quota act and its plan for
"scientific selection and efficient distribution." The paper was relieved that
the menace to unity and solidarity would be averted. The *Times* linked the
revolutionary industrial unions of recent years to men of the "new immigration" and endorsed the idea of a permanent bill soon, one to provide
overseas inspection and selection.[17]

"Typhus is not the worst thing the undesirables can bring in,"
editorialized the *Chicago Tribune*. That is "merely indicative of the stra-
tum of human life which the U.S. is tapping for its future citizenship."[18]
The *Detroit News*, while favoring the legislation, praised local efforts to
Americanize the foreign American homes through the mothers. It described immigrant women who wept on the shoulders of social workers in
homesicknesses, and who were transformed into good citizens and reu-
nited with their estranged children through classes and work of the social
centers.[19]

The *Washington Post*, the *Detroit Free Press*, and the *Chicago
Tribune* gave strong endorsements, expecting the bill to provide protection
from a "flood of undesirables, innoculated with the virus of Bolshevism
and Communism."[20] Some newspapers took a middle view. The *Washington Star*, The *Baltimore Sun* and The *Baltimore News* only approved the
bill because it was temporary.

The *New York World*, however, found the bill grossly unfair and
impolitic. It was "closing the haven of refuge to the oppressed." The
Brooklyn Citizen pointed out that the bill's support came from organized
labor, old Know-Nothing remnants, and anti-Semitic elements. It thought
the bill "disgraceful and unworthy of America . . . a reproach to the

administration."[21] Said New York Commissioner of Immigration F. A. Wallis, "We don't need to restrict immigration. Talk of reaching the saturation point is nonsense." He proposed more thoughtful distribution of immigrants throughout the country to meet labor needs.[22]

The *Boston Globe* gave one of the rare favorable portraits of immigrant ships in 1921: "The immigrants coming into Boston this week have caused some comment among officials because of the large number of women and children among them . . . eager mothers with their offspring, who spent long, happy hours by the rail, straining their eyes for the first glimpse of their new homeland . . . hundreds of these women are wives, or mothers, or sisters of foreign-born American citizens . . . practically all of them are being brought to the United States by their husbands, brothers, or fiances to begin life anew . . . there is a light in their eyes that is good to see and a smile that stirs the slumbering pulse of human brotherhood."[23]

Congress deferred hearings on proposals for a permanent quota law until late 1923, having renewed the temporary legislation for two years. During these hearings many of the familiar supporters of restriction and eugenics policies testified before the Congressional committees, as did some immigrant groups and editors.

There was testimony also from foreign editors and from two scientists in the early days of January 1924, but these were not reported in the daily press. The problems of immigrant-laden ships arriving after national quotas for the month had been filled and being sent back to Europe had occupied the press for some time. Now the largest coverage centered on a proposed Japanese exclusion, which would break an old "gentlemen's agreement" allowing some Japanese to enter, despite the Oriental Exclusion Act.

Majority newspaper opinion had backed restriction since the spring of 1923. "The mind of the country is clear on the matter . . . there will be no liberalizing of the immigration laws," said The *New York Times*.[24] The *Times* did not modify its editorial stand, continuing to approve each new and tighter version of the quota proposals while increasing its coverage from 60 articles and three editorials in the first six months of 1921 to 168 articles and 32 editorials in the first half of 1924.

With the passage of the permanent Immigration Restriction Act in the spring of 1924, most newspapers were convinced that it would bring a better standard of living and preserve America for the Americans. Only few newspapers, including The *Baltimore Sun*, The *Boston Transcript* and The *Brooklyn Eagle* condemned the Quota Act and lamented the end of America as a "refuge for the oppressed" and the beginning of new rule of "bigots and demagogues."[25]

Role of the Media: Magazine Selectivity

Diversity of opinion on social, cultural, and political matters was available to American readers through the national general-interest magazines. Though "selectivity" in content to meet perceived interests of special groups characterized magazine practice more than did adherence to the "objectivity" standard of the newspaper press, it is important to note magazine content for its role in informing and influencing large groups of readers.

About a dozen monthlies and weeklies commented regularly on newsworthy issues. They ranged in circulation from the five-cent weeklies (The *Saturday Evening Post* and *Colliers*) with 1-2 million circulations to the quality monthly magazines (*Atlantic, Harper's,* and *Scribner's*) with circulations in the few thousands. The *Literary Digest,* with a circulation of 1.4 million, was unique. It alone summarized and digested the nation's news and opinion and took no overt editorial stands of its own. The other general-interest magazines, large and small, had strong-minded editors with editorial slants ranging from conservative to liberal and aimed at like-minded readers.

Most of these magazines took up the immigration question only once or twice a year from 1919 to 1925; a few provided more coverage. The *New Republic,* a liberal weekly and opponent of racially based quotas, ran about four articles a year, with six and seven in 1920 and 1922. The *Outlook,* a weekly Protestant review, gave about the same amount of annual coverage with seven and eight articles in 1920 and 1923. Their 1920 articles, however, dealt entirely with Americanization, which they supported. The *Literary Digest* averaged an article per month throughout the period, while The *Saturday Evening Post,* a staunch proponent of the quota plan and Nordic theory, averaged one article or editorial every other month, with the pace stepped up to one per month during 1923. *Colliers* ran about three to four per year. The magazine coverage thus provided preponderance of discussion from the restrictionists' viewpoint. Even The *Literary Digest,* though it tried to report both sides, gave more coverage to the restrictionists and their fears and solutions.[26]

The *Literary Digest*'s coverage of the issue included stories on illegal immigration smuggled in through Canada, on machines, replacement of workers and on the "prized" Anglo Saxon heritage. Major stories in 1923 and 1924 included a thorough discussion of the effects of using the 1890 census as the basis for quotas, the Army intelligence findings and studies of criminal and antisocial behavior of the "new immigrants." When the bill passed, the *Digest* reported the "death of the Melting Pot theory," and observed that the majority approved the new principle of national origins.[29] The two years following contained fewer immigration stories, and those tended to concern smuggling of illegal immigrants, renewal of effort to liberalize the law and the improved quality of the latest immigrants.

Once the temporary quota act of 1921 passed, the *Digest* presented opinions of the press, including the foreign-language press. The *Digest* that observed public opinion seemed to favor race purity and admission only of aliens that could be assimilated, refusing Japanese and other unmeltables to avoid a mongrel race.[28] By October 1921, the new law had created its own crisis. Shiploads of immigrants were being raced to New York harbor to beat quota deadlines; on occasion entire shiploads of passengers were refused entry because their homeland's quota had been filled. This situation generated several articles deploring the inhumanity of the new system and prompted suggestions to move the immigrant inspection and passport approval to foreign consulates.

The *Literary Digest*'s coverage of the issue included stories on illegal immigration smuggled in through Canada, on machines, replacement of workers and on the "prized" Anglo Saxon heritage. Major stories in 1923 and 1924 included a thorough discussion of the effects of using the 1890 census as the basis for quotas, the Army intelligence findings and studies of criminal and antisocial behavior of the "new immigrants." When the bill passed, the *Digest* reported the "death of the Melting Pot theory," and observed that the majority approved the new principle of national origins.[29] The two years following contained fewer immigration stories, and those tended to concern smuggling of illegal immigrants, renewal of effort to liberalize the law and the improved quality of the latest immigrants.

The monthly *Forum* provides a typical example of the changes in magazine coverage between 1919 and 1925 on the immigrant matter. During the 1919-21 period, *Forum* articles called the immigrant threat "one of pure conjecture," and said there was nothing to fear.[30] *Forum* was still convinced that Americanization would work and urged readers to help foreigners become better citizens. The magazine attacked the hysteria in Congress in 1921, assuring readers that there was room for more immigrants in this country.[31] But in the 1923 debate, *Forum* agreed that there was a need for limits and some control of the mix. The magazine would not use race or nationality as a scale, but did approve of the plan for physical and mental inspection abroad.[32] The subject reappeared in 1925 when the leading Nordic superiority theorist, Madison Grant, and anthropologist Franz Boas wrote major articles on opposing sides. Grant explained the reasons for keeping "America for the Americans" while Boas denounced "This Nordic Nonsense," pointing out that there were persons of Nordic type throughout Europe. The only properly scientific basis for selection of immigrants was by reference to the individual and his genealogy, he declared. "Nationality is absolutely irrelevant."[33]

A liberal weekly journal of opinion, the *New Republic*, argued consistently against racist thinking and the quotas. Its editors advocated some limit on immigration, but suggested other ways to differentiate between the intelligent and ignorant.[34] The magazine promoted better understanding of the immigrant experience and the Americanization process and warned against stirring up animosities against foreigners as a result of the Palmer Red raids. One writer, E. H. Bierstadt, suggested in 1921 that groups trying to Americanize the immigrant were really "pushing false and misleading ideas" and using "Americanization as a mask to conceal selfishness, prejudice, and the desire for power."[35] Walter Lippmann, a regular contributor and founder of the magazine, wrote in 1922 a six-part series analyzing the intelligence tests used to screen immigrants and taking issue with the psychologists' claims that these tests could measure intelligence levels fixed by heredity. The tests, he asserted, measured a mixture of intelligence and learning and had their useful place. But the Army tests were being used to restrict immigration, and the interpretations being made in these instances were "nonsense."[36]

The *New Republic* attacked the quota law proposals as discriminatory against Jews, Slavs, and Armenians and deplored the tragedy of separation of families kept apart by arbitrary quota laws.[37] An editorial exploring the growing power of immigrants in the older American cities in 1922 speculated that these "upstart half-breeds will come to rule our cities," and pointed out how quickly the immigrants dropped their European culture as their Americanization was sped up through the movies, newspaper headlines and fashions.[38] The *New Republic* advocated a "humane" policy for selection of immigrants and hoped the new bill would fail.[39]

But what the masses of middle-class readers were hearing was just the opposite. The emotion-laden descriptions by popular journalists such as Kenneth L. Roberts, whose personal inspection tour of Europe resulted in a series of nine long, illustrated articles in The *Saturday Evening Post* between 1920 and 1924, went to some two million homes. The magazine's editor, Horace Lorimer, believed that he had his finger on the pulse of middle America. And he fought to keep "America for the Americans," as President Coolidge put it in 1924. Lorimer sent Roberts on the tour with careful instructions on what to research.[40] Roberts' vivid pictures of millions of louse-ridden, pathetic human beings crowding the harbors of Europe underscored the image of the alien horde about to descend on America. They would be the "lumps in the melting pot," he declared. Or they would be "birds of passage" who came only to earn money and run back to Europe. "Stop being sentimental," he warned in February 1921. It was a "matter of life and death," because in a few years the U.S. would be populated by a new "composite race" of people wholly different from the Americans of the present day, or by a number of racial groups that "would fight and bicker and haggle among themselves over their alien differences."[41] Later he attacked the Jews for falsifying papers to get in, and he described the Poles as the "lower type" who were forced to take their first baths at the European ports' delousing centers.[42]

Roberts and the *Post* kept up the pressure with stinging attacks on the sentimentalists who "believed the whimsical fairy tale of the melting pot." The immigrants were the ones who brought the filth and mess to Ellis Island, he explained. The Island was cleaned and sterilized daily. "Mongrelization," he warned, "will be the result . . . unless the Nordic balance is restored."[43] Roberts used studies by Dr. Harry H. Laughlin and Army IQ tests to document figures on the inferior migration. Nordics contribute most to the nation, he maintained, and have the highest rate of naturalization.[44]

Other *Post* authors included eugenicists Lothrop Stoddard, who wrote a twelve-part series on the persistence of racial types, and the new Commissioner of Immigration, Henry H. Curran, who characterized immigrants as of low quality.[45] All found ways to promote Nordic theory or attack its opponents. The *Post* labeled newspaper sob stories about immigration problems as "shams." In the fall of 1924, The *Post* was delighted to find the new law "doing the country a world of good, bringing in better quality people who were healthier and cleaner and who were being processed in a more humane way."[46]

Role of the Media: Immigrant Press

Had the mass media editors wanted other opinions, they might have turned to immigrant editors whose 1,300 newspapers served the thirteen million foreign-born population in forty languages. Some had testified before Congressional committees, but their voices were generally ignored except for two roundups in The *Literary Digest* in 1921 and 1924 as the laws were being passed. Immigrant editors were critical of restriction, and they raised humanitarian and philosophical issues that the rest of the nation seemed to want to ignore. Some favored restriction of some form, but most in 1921, at least, felt the laws already in place could be used effectively to keep out the mentally and physically impaired.

They raised the issue of racism directly. German, Italian, and

Jewish editors called this a revival of the old "Know-Nothing mentality" and found it hard to understand Americans who would first encourage immigration, benefit from immigrant labor and volunteer military service, and then turn around and call immigrants unfit, hateful, and objectionable. A Danish editor declared that "calling foreigners the firebrands of revolution is seeing spooks in daylight. The revolutionary ideas of Lenin and Trotsky would find poor soil among the foreign-born populations which gave indisputable proof of their loyalty during the war." A German editor maintained that the "immigrants are a national asset . . . but the masses have never understood this." Another said, "Not England, but all Europe is mother of our country." If conditions "compelled prohibition of immigration," declared one Italian editor, "the Government must show why that is so and apply emergency laws without showing any race discrimination. To stop immigration otherwise would be to violate the spirit of the American Constitution and offend sacred principles of humanity."[47]

Immigrant editors believed that more labor still was needed in some industries and on the farms and that the number of immigrants wanting to come had been vastly exaggerated. Much of the opposition was "partisan prejudice or selfishly motivated by the AFL and other special interests," speculated a Swiss editor. These editors, too, encouraged Americans to aid in the process of Americanization by getting to know immigrants and helping them learn how to function in society. "No country has a moral right to close its doors to newcomers who have peaceful intentions to better their lives or escape persecution," declared a Jewish editor, noting that this was a serious concern for Jews who more than any other nationality were fleeing from persecution."[48]

Similar views were expressed by immigrant editors testifying before the House Committee on Immigration and Naturalization in the winter of 1923-1924. Editors of Polish, Slovak, Italian, and Jewish newspapers opposed the new 2 percent quota bill. They discussed the racial inequities and asserted that the three percent bill had already been too stringent. They reminded the Congressmen that all nationalities and races provided outstanding as well as ordinary and inferior examples, and they confirmed the loyalty of America's immigrant groups during the past war as well as the importance of the immigrant press in America. Only three members of the committee agreed with these sentiments and filed a minority report.[49]

Responding to an article in *World's Work* of the previous December, Read Lewis, head of the Foreign Language Information Service which had been organized to work with immigrant editors during the war, wrote the *Times* in January 1924 to correct the impression that all immigrant papers were opposed to the quota law. Most are opposed, but some favored it. He cited examples of Italian, Polish, Slovak, Lithuanian, Swedish and German papers in New York City, Chicago, Pittsburgh, Milwaukee, and Omaha that supported selective immigration.[50]

A liberal Danish language newspaper, *Den Danske Pioneer*, of Omaha told its readers that the new law would not change the number of Danes coming very much, but criticized the law's "philosophy of to be enough to ourselves." The weak point, it said, is that without immigrants America would not be self-supporting. Immigrants have done the coarse, hard work and allowed others to move up. "We think it is a mistake and that our country will see that later, and the law will share the same fate of similar laws."[51]

When the 1924 act passed, The *Digest* surveyed twenty-one language group editors. Most called the bill unfair. America had now "picked up the curse of European civilization and was no longer the country for the oppressed," they felt. Immigrant editors were especially resentful because their people had helped to build so much of the nation since 1890 through their work in the mines, mills, factories, subways and railroads in jobs Americans refused to do. "Samuel Gompers, an immigrant, should be ashamed at his efforts to shut out others," said one. Another German editor approved of Nordic favoritism, but believed this bill discriminated excessively against other races. One feature of the new legislation did please the immigrant editors — the overseas inspection; still, overall the new act betrayed America's most noble ideals. Said a Greek editor, "The idea of discriminating between foreigners was certainly an imported product, for neither the American Constitution nor the ideals of this country ever allowed such a political conduct." A Jewish editor explained, "The ideal that distinguished America from the old world was the ideal of universal democracy, not democracy for a few racial types."[52] But the immigrant voices were not heard in the mainstream American press. No attempt was made to seek them out and amplify their voices for the rest of the nation to hear.

The bill cut the quota in half, to 161,990 the first year, but the "Italians, Poles, and Russians (chiefly Jews) will be the most severely cut," explained The *New York Tribune*. Italians would be reduced from 42,057 to 3,989, Poles from 30,979 to 8,972, and Russians from 24,405 to 1,892, while Great Britain would only drop from 77,342 to 62,558, Germany from 67,607 to 50,229, and Sweden from 20,042 to 9,661. Some of the "Nordic" countries probably would not even fill their quotas, while others would have many times the allotment wanting to immigrate.[53]

Scientists Let Eugenicists Dominate

Although the popular literature made it seem that scientists approved of the Nordic theory, some of the leading geneticists expressed deep concern in their private correspondence about the situation and in 1923 and 1924 discussed the pending legislation that was "based on prejudice rather than science.[54] Few spoke openly to counter the respected tesimony of Laughlin and the other eugenicists. It was too early for some of the careful scientific scholars to make generalizations about the implications of research in genetics. Some who had earlier supported the genetics movement quietly dropped out by mid-decade and began to voice their opposition. (By the end of the 1920s psychologists would be conceding the importance of environment and culture on intelligence. Anthropologists studying under Boas would add further evidence about the importance of culture. By mid-century Boas and others would be denouncing the Nordic myth and racism of Grant, Stoddard, and Osburn, but the immigration restriction would have long been in place.[55])

During the debate, four scholars publicly questioned the validity of Laughlin's studies of immigrant IQ tests. Herbert S. Jennings testified before the House Immigration Committee in January 1924, and he used Laughlin's own data to refute assumptions made about the inferiority of the "new stock." Jennings showed that some of the old stock had higher rates of some socially undesirable traits. He was given only a brief time to speak to the committee, and his written remarks were placed in the record. They went unreported by the press.[56] Another criticism attacking Laughlin's statistical errors was also inserted in the written record but not discussed. These were the remarks of Joseph M. Gillman of the School of Business Administration of the University of Pittsburgh. They appeared later in The *American Journal of Sociology*[57] Geneticist Vernon Kellogg in 1923 cautioned *New Republic* readers against thinking that racial mixing led to inferior stock. He asked for much more scientific study before any policies were to be made on these assumptions.[58] Edwin Grant Conklin, writing in *Scribner's* in 1919 and 1921, raised similar objections, further noting that America was an amalgamation of all its peoples and the ideas they brought with them. This "could produce" a great variety of human types, benefiting democracy. But even Conklin wanted some system that excluded the inferior and defective types in order to perpetuate the best.[59]

Scientists were represented in two of the largest journals, *Science*, and *Scientific Monthly*, mainly by the views of the eugenicists. Only three of fifteen articles on immigration or eugenics in The *Scientific Monthly* between 1919 and 1925 and none of the five in *Science* in the same period appeared to challenge the eugenicists. These three articles attacked as false the theory that cross-breeding of racial types always led to "deterioration."[60] Other specialized scientific publications might contain some discussion of these issues, but clearly the growing objections of scientists did not gain wide circulation even in journals of the scientific world before the passage of the 1924 Quota Act.

Conclusions

The restrictionists, having no well-organized or authoritative opposition, successfully steered the 1924 law through Congress; the arguments for the "national origins" approach that would preserve the distinct American type dominated the last stages of the discussion. Other types of immigration restriction plans were scarcely considered. *Outlook* had twice proposed the Canadian system of a flexible quota based on industrial labor and agricultural needs, but more often the magazines related stories about immigration limits imposed by other nations to validate the very idea of imposing limits.[61] The full implications of race purity theory would only become clear in the 1930s in Nazi Germany, giving rise to eventual opposition.[62]

Pluralistic notions about America would not find wide reception, however, until just before World War II when America would begin to reaffirm its old tradition of welcoming homeless and persecuted Europeans.[63] Despite a slowly increased popular appreciation for the contributions of the immigrants it would remain for the John F. Kennedy administration to press for a change in the "national origins" principle of immigration.[64]

The loss of confidence in the melting pot of the early 1920s reflected a disillusion by Americans in democracy's ability to work freely without manipulation, as well as a growing desire for national unity and cohesion following a disruptive and turbulent time. The mass media, which in the 1920s were already serving as an informal information network linking the nation, amplified the voices of the nation's leaders in politics, business, and labor. Newspapers had lost the aggressive muckraking energies of the prewar era, and many had become pillars of society, big institutions intent on profit and respectability. Their mission was not to stir up trouble and agitate for change; rather, they presented news from authoritative sources and let the readers decide what to think.

This represented the modern journalist's theory of objectivity, and it was thought to be a fair and reasonable way to safeguard the middle role of journalism between clashing views. In fact, it allowed the press to sidestep many emotionally divisive and ethical issues and to avoid making moral commitments. The press had become the lofty, detached observer. It had also become passive, complacent and successful. It no longer was zealous to investigate, expose, or exhort.

A new, as yet undiscussed or unrecognized, power had been attained by the "objective" press. Its news judgment and the prominence, space, photographic, and typographic attention given major issues told the public what to think about and often framed the arguments for them. At times this power could be even more effective than ringing editorials, because news treatment was thought to portray objective facts rather than *selective* facts and interpretations, often from those informed sources most interested and connected with the problem.

The sobering note sounded by this essay is the exposure of the hollowness of the ideal of journalistic objectivity when put to the test on a crucial social and philosophical issue. In the restrictionist debate, the mass media for the most part reflected the protectionist majority view. Unchecked by an organized minority viewpoint, the media became the megaphone for propagandists clever enough to play on the fears and self-interests of the middle-class majority, many of whom had benefited from the earlier open door policies toward immigrants. Except for the foreign-language press and a few small magazines, the media seldom raised the philosophical issue. The press allowed Americans to forget the lofty sentiments which they had enshrined on the Statue of Liberty, in the Constitution and on the nation's currency. The objectivity philosophy allowed a profession built by the idealism and activism of generations opposed to suppression of free speech to remove itself from the battle and to suppress speech in another less obvious manner — avoidance. The press hid behind its middle position of watchdog for the public interest and became primarily a passive, neutral and amoral observer and recorder. This stance by the press allowed the best organized, loudest, and most sensational voices to monopolize public attention, effectively stifling robust debate. It was a criticism that would be made of the modern press many times thereafter.

Notes

1. Kenneth M. Ludmerer, *Genetics and American Society: A Historical Appraisal* (Baltimore: The Johns Hopkins University Press, 1972), p. 32. His social history of genetics provides a thorough examination of the role of the eugenicists. See chapters 4-6. Also useful for the discussion of the forces supporting the IRL is: Barbara Solomon, *Ancestors and Immigrants: A Changing New England Tradition* (Cambridge: Harvard University Press,

1956), and Thomas J. Curran, *Xenophobia and Immigration, 1820-1930* (Boston: Twayne Publishers, 1975).

2. John Higham, *Strangers in the Land: Patterns of Nativism 1860-1925* (New York: Atheneum, 1965), p. 47. Other useful discussion of the treatment of immigration by American historians are: John Higham, *Send These to Me: Jews and Other Immigrants in Urban American* (New York: Atheneum, 1975), and Rudolph J. Vecoli, "European Americans: From Immigrants to Ethnics," *International Migration Review* 6 (Winter 1972): 403-434.

3. Higham, *Strangers in the Land,* pp. 330. Sources emphasizing the uniqueness of American allegiance to the ideology of democracy are: Arthur Mann, *The One and the Many: Reflections on American Identity* (Chicago: University of Chicago Press, 1979), and Jethro K. Liberman, *Are Americans Extinct?* (New York: Walker, 1969). For a thorough discussion of the term "melting pot," see Philip Gleason, "The Melting Pot: Symbol of Fusion or Confusion?" *American Quarterly* 16 (Spring 1964): 20-40.

4. For example, the comprehensive press history by Edwin Emery and Michael Emery, *The Press and America: An Interpretive History of the Mass Media,* 4th ed. (Englewood Cliffs, N.J.: Prentice-Hall, 1978), has no index entries under either "publicity" or "public relations."

5. For a discussion of propaganda and public relations in the World War I years see Edward L. Bernays, *Crystallizing Public Opinion* (New York: Horace Liveright, 1929).

6. Michael Schudson, *Discovering the News: A Social History of American Newspapers* (New York: Basic Books, 1978), p. 159.

7. Ludmerer, *Genetics,* p. 108.

8. The author looked at all articles on immigration in The *Saturday Evening Post, Colliers,* and The *Literary Digest* from 1920 through 1939 and in selected monthlies and weeklies from 1919 to 1939, including *Forum,* The *New Republic, Century, Outlook, Scribner's, Atlantic, Harper's, Science* and The *Scientific Monthly.* Also examined were issues of The *New York Times,* The *Chicago Tribune,* The *Boston Globe,* The *Detroit News* and The *Detroit Free Press* for dates around the passage of the quota legislation in 1921, 1923 and 1924.

9. Studies documenting the small amount of space given to social issues by newspapers include Michael Ryan and Dorothea Owen, "A Content Analysis of Metropolitan Newspaper Coverage of Social Issues," *Journalism Quarterly* 54 (Spring 1977): 634-640, and Paul J. Deutschmann, *News-page Content of Twelve Metropolitan Dailies* (Cincinnati, Ohio: Scripps Howard Research, 1959).

10. Solomon, *Ancestors,* pp. 152-175.

11. *New York Times,* 5 January 1921, p. 12.

12. *New York Times,* 14 February 1921, p. 1.

13. *New York Times,* 20 February 1921, p. 1. See also U.S. Immigration Commission 1907-1910, *Abstracts of Reports of the Immigration Commission, with Conclusions and Recommendations and a View of the Minority,* (Washington: U.S. Government Printing Office, 1911). See "Recommendations," pp. 45-48, and "Emigration Conditions in Europe," pp. 165-204.

14. *New York Times,* 2 March 1921, p. 9.

15. *New York Times,* 14 February 1921, p. 9.

16. *New York Times,* 20 April 1921, p. 1.

17. *New York Times,* 29 May 1921, II, p. 2.

18. *Chicago Tribune,* 16 February 1921, p. 8.

19. *Detroit News,* 17 April 1921, p. 8.

20. *Literary Digest* 68, 30 April 1921, p. 36.

21. *Ibid.*

22. *Literary Digest* 68, 7 May 1921, p. 13.

23. *Boston Sunday Globe,* 20 February 1921, p. 3.

24. *Literary Digest* 77, 5 May 1923, pp. 9-11.

25. *Literary Digest* 81, 10 May 1924, p. 12.

26. *Literary Digest* specialized in compilation and summarization of opinions and reports from the nation's newspapers and magazines. In the 1920's it was a serious contender with The *Saturday Evening Post* for the nation's middle-class readers. It had 1.4 million weekly circulation to the *Post's* 2 million. The *Post* did not try to be impartial, while the *Digest* did present clearly identified and varying views and editorial opinions.

27. *Literary Digest* 63, 30 November 1920, pp. 48-54.

28. *Literary Digest* 77, 5 May 1923, pp. 9-11.

29. *Literary Digest* 81, 7 June 1924, pp. 14-15.

30. *Forum* 61, March 1919, pp. 343-48.

31. *Forum* 65, June 1921, pp. 68-76.

32. *Forum* 70, September 1923, pp. 1866-70.

33. Madison Grant, "America for the Americans," *Forum* 74, September 1925, pp. 346-55 and Franz Boas, "This Nordic Nonsense," *Forum* 74, October 1925, pp. 502-511.

34. The *New Republic* 32, 22 December 1920, pp. 95-96.

35. The *New Republic* 26, 25 May 1921, pp. 371-373 and the *New Republic* 27, 1 June 1921, pp. 19-23.

36. The *New Republic* 32, 29 November 1922, pp. 9-11 and 8 November 1922, pp. 275-277.

37. The *New Republic* 29, 22 March 1922, pp. 93-94, and 8 March 1922, pp. 52-53.

38. The *New Republic* 31, 10 May 1922, pp. 301-302.

39. The *New Republic* 37, 27 February 1924, pp. 6-7.

40. Lorimer's views on restriction are discussed in John Tebbel, *George Horace Lorimer and the Saturday Evening Post* (New York: Doubleday, 1948) pp. 90-94 and p. 180.

41. K. L. Roberts, "Plain Remarks on Immigration for Plain Americans," The *Saturday Evening Post* 193, 12 February 1921, pp. 21-22.

42. K. L. Roberts, "Existence of an Emergency," The *Saturday Evening Post* 193, 30 April 1921, pp. 3-4.

43. K. L. Roberts, "Shutting the Sea Gates," The *Saturday Evening Post* 195, 28 January 1922, p. 11.

44. K. L. Roberts, "And West is West," The *Saturday Evening Post* 196, 15 March, 1924, pp. 12-13. Laughlin, affiliated with the Eugenics Record Office of the Carnegie Institution, was a favorite authority for restrictionists. His studies of I.Q. tests of immigrants, made in certain jails and hospitals, had detailed the inferior propensities of the "new immigrants," and were widely quoted in newspapers and magazines.

45. H. H. Curran, "Fewer and Better, or None," The *Saturday Evening Post* 196, 26 April 1924, pp. 8-9.

46. H. H. Curran, "Fewer and Better," The *Saturday Evening Post* 196, 15 November 1924, p. 6.

47. "Our Foreign-Language Press on Immigration," The *Literary Digest* 69, 28 May 1921, pp. 19-20.

48. *Ibid.*

49. "Restriction of Immigration," *Hearing before the House Committee on Immigration and Naturalization, 68th Congress, First Session* (Washington, D.C.: USGPO, 1924), pp. 225-426. The author's dissertation on the Danish-American press discusses the role of the

foreign-language press in more detail. See Marion T. Marzolf, *The Danish Language Press in America* (New York: Arno Press, 1979) pp. 151-179.

50. *New York Times,* 13 January 1924, section 8, p. 7.

51. *Den Danske Pioneer* (The Danish Pioneer), 29 May 1924.

52. "Our Foreign-Language Press on Immigration," The *Literary Digest* 81, 17 May 1924, pp. 17-20.

53. *Ibid.*

54. Ludmerer, *Genetics,* p. 123.

55. *Ibid.,* p. 126.

56. "Restriction of Immigration," *Hearings before the House Committee on Immigration and Naturalization, 68th Congress, First Session* (Washington, D.C.: USGPO, 124), pp. 510-512.

57. Liberman and Mann detail these criticisms. Joseph M. Gillman of the School of Business Administration, University of Pittsburgh, published in "Statistics and the Immigration Problem," *American Journal of Sociology* 30, July 1924, pp. 29-48, a criticism of Laughlin's survey which he called incomplete and biased.

58. The *New Republic* 36, 8 August 1923, pp. 278-80.

59. E. G. Conkin, "Biology and Democracy," *Scribner's* 65, April 1919, pp. 408-412 and "Some Biological Aspects of Immigration," *Scribner's* 69, March 1921, pp. 352-359.

60. For the eugenicists' views see: Robert De C. Ward, The *Scientific Monthly* 15, October 1922, pp. 313-319; 15 December 1922, pp. 561-569; 17 December 1923, pp. 527-534; 21 July 1925, pp. 45-53. For an alternative point see: "The Mechanics of Evolution," The *Scientific Monthly* 10, May 1920, pp. 496-515; C. C. Little, "The Relation Between Research in Human Heredity and Experimental Genetics," The *Scientific Monthly* 14, May 1922, pp. 401-414, and Ezra Bowen, "Mixing the Issue in Immigration," The *Scientific Monthly* 22, June 1926, pp. 30-32.

61. Higham, *Strangers,* p. 321; *Outlook* 135, 12 December 1923, pp. 619-620.

62. Ludmerer, *Genetics,* pp. 113 and 131. Also of interest is Richard Weiss, "Ethnicity and Reform: Minorities and the Ambience of the Depression Years," *Journal of American History* 66, December 1979, pp. 566-585. He points out that only 4.7 percent of the 1930 population were aliens.

63. Heywood Broun, "A Cheer for the Melting Pot," The *New Republic* 94, 6 April 1938, pp. 272-273.

64. Two decades would pass before wider circulation and acceptance would be accorded the cultural pluralism ideal expressed by Horace Kallen in "Democracy vs. the Melting Pot," in the *Nation,* 18 February 1915, pp. 190-194; 25 February 1915, pp. 217-220. See also: David A. Hollinger, "Ethnic Diversity, Cosmopolitanism and the Emergence of the American Liberal Intelligensia," *American Quarterly* 27, 1975, pp. 133-151.

8 This Curious Existence

Journalistic Identity in the Interwar Period

Michael Kirkhorn

In one of Miguel Covarrubias' caricatures from the 1920s Walter Winchell and Walter Lippmann are shown sauntering along Broadway.[1] They are unlikely companions. Winchell, the gossip, is natty, shrewd, sharp-eyed, smirking. He clasps Lippmann's arm, but the public philosopher scarcely notices. The author of *Public Opinion* and *The Phantom Public* is no casual saunterer. His bearing is impeccable. He seems entranced. Oratorically, he fingers his lapel, while in his other hand he holds a newspaper rolled as tightly as a scroll — probably the newspaper whose editorial page he governs, Pulitzer's *New York World*. Littering the background are a trash can, marquees, two-bit dance palaces. A tousled newsboy's tabloid blares the familiar bulletin — *Love Nest Raid*. Lippmann transcends the sordidness. He is (to use one of his favorite words) the embodiment of *disinterest,* and since the teeming street permits no neutrality, he seems otherworldly. Winchell is guiding him toward rough enlightenment, or taking him in for repairs.[2]

With this glimpse Covarrubias revealed an aspect of the confusion which beset American journalism between the world wars. The wise owl and the night owl; the personifications of highmindedness and lowmindedness — what were they doing side by side? What might they have sufficiently in common for one to be on the same street at the same time as the other? An answer may be found in the strained identities of journalists who interpreted the events of these decades for a presumably bewildered, nevertheless avid public. Reality was disjointed; it always is, but in this period journalists were expected to accentuate the glimmerings of social fantasy. Diversion was their duty. They inflated celebrities, flapped flappers, howled over calamities, ridiculed one another. Journalists themselves became celebrities, of a kind, and when they tired of their apprentice dreamerships they often found lucrative employment as full-time fantasizers in public relations or advertising firms. From these positions they looked back disdainfully and with some regret at the time they had spent as journalists. Their stranded colleagues, still working for newspapers, looked out disdainfully at the public they were expected to serve and at the pumped-up celebrities who provided the entertainment. In many ways the atmosphere was one of universal disdain. Serious readers of the news "continually dwindle," Ivor Brown wrote in 1933, not because "they are themselves hysterical cretins, but because they are intensely bored with solemn discussions about the doings of half-wits. It is not so much the reader who has mentally collapsed. It is the economist, the politicans, the rulers of the world who have tumbled into the tabloid arena." It is no wonder, Brown said, that "educated readers" preferred "the derisive cartoon whose swift, cynical values are in tune with their own despair. . . . The readers of the most modest sagacity know the rumpus is better summed up in a jest or a caricature."[3]

The slangy, sarcastic, knowing Winchell may have been a truer creature of this "Jazz Age," but Lippmann, concocter of a pessimistic doctrine deriding the public's seriousness and its ability to understand much of anything, held newspaper readers in no higher regard than the editor of any tabloid. It may be argued that Winchell's cynicism and Lippmann's solemnity both expressed a disaffection and that their disdain for the public was an indication of bewilderment in the journalistic mind and temperament. This essay argues that journalistic cynicism expressed the fatigue and resentment of reporters and editors who felt required to distract and insulate the public from great social and economic problems. In the process, the public itself was caricatured as a mob clamouring after sensation and celebrity.

Whatever else it may have been, the interwar period certainly was a time for brilliant caricature. The targets were irresistible and the caricaturists' insights inflicted wounds. When he ventured out from Baltimore to describe the Scopes Trial, H. L. Mencken discovered primitive religious devotion with a gleeful astonishment which suggested that his worst suspicions and happiest hopes had been confirmed. Don Marquis stung the arrogant and celebrated durability. His feline fatale, mehitabel, prone to any hint of "abduction," yowled over blasted hope and cruel deception, but she hung on: "arch your back and caper/ and kick at the gold moon; mebby some yeggs who sell butter and eggs/ will fling us a party soon." Rube Goldberg assembled machines of elaborate futility. In 1924 the *New York World* introduced to its readers H. T. Webster's Caspar Milquetoast, a figure so resolutely helpless that its meekness came to resemble a heroic defense against the pummelings of the time.[4]

But good nature was under strain. Gerald Johnson noticed contempt in the work of editorial cartoonists, and Heywood Broun offered this observation: "Post-war humor in this country tends to be slightly mad. It is fantastic and extravagant in the extreme. Even our funny men have caught the tempo of the jazz age. And since I know them as sensitive men I gravely suspect that their efforts to jingle bells are somewhat inspired by a fear that the world of actuality will catch up with them. They create their own sounds of merriment in order to shut out the din of despair."[5]

When it was over, even the hilarities of the Algonquin Round Table sounded unfunny: "It was the terrible day of the wisecrack," said Dorothy Parker, "so there didn't have to be any truth." The documentary film-maker Robert Flaherty (*Nanook of the North*) observed the American conversation flashed wittily and was essentially unkind.[6]

Sometimes good-naturedly, sometimes not, the public was lampooned, but there is no evidence to suggest that the citizens of the republic were more ridiculous during the worrisome period between World Wars I and II than they had been in the past; in fact, the debasing of the public's identity was nothing more than a contorted reflection of journalism itself. At the center of the issue was the journalist, and anyone who studies some of the statements in which journalists of the 1920s and 1930s scrutinized their trade is likely to come away with an impression of splintered indentity.

This vulnerability did not go unnoticed. In an ingratiating interview New York City's beguiling Mayor James Walker told *The American Press:* "Newspaper men are actors, putting on different masks for every story they cover. They are living paradoxes — by the very necessities of their lives at once hard and sentimental, possessing a keen, cold capacity for abstract questions and digestion of statistics along with imaginations of the utmost elasticity. The same reporter who can sit out a dry hearing and disgorge the mass of facts and figures in a readable story can cover some stark tragedy and interpret its underlying human values in words that drip blood and tears."[7]

The implication of theatricality — reporters doffing identities not only elastically but indifferently, playing successive roles at the editor's command or to meet the public's supposed expectations — contains a sharp perception about the nature of journalistic enterprise. It was substantiated by the reporters themselves. The journalistic humorist Irvin S. Cobb said of the newspaper reporter: "Essentially, he is an actor. He can mingle with millionaires and talk about billion-dollar deals when he doesn't have the rent money in his pocket. He can sleep in a stuffy hall bedroom and write knowingly about the revels of the rich. He's living the life of the people he writes about, and his own life is altogether out of the picture. That seems to me to be the lure of the game. And — I'm sorry I'm out of it."[8]

Frank Ward O'Malley, a retired New York *Sun* reporter who "made a speciality of 'nut' and 'weep' stories," complained that he had lost his public identity: "Since I quit newspaper work, I feel out of touch with life. When I go to a political meeting now, I don't sit next to the candidate. I'm just one of the crowd. At the theatre or circus the press agent doesn't come out and greet me as a long-lost friend."[9]

Even a journalist of Lippmann's eminence lapsed into sycophancy, first with President Woodrow Wilson, whom he served as journalistic advocate before joining the postwar planning group called The Inquiry, again with Franklin D. Roosevelt, later with John F. Kennedy. What seems remarkable about journalists of the interwar period is that so many of them would admit that they preferred to live vicariously as sidekicks or followers. This characteristic might be seen as evidence of a habitual evasiveness. In his writing about the careers of well-known correspondents, Leo Rosten observed a "flight from understanding in the narcotic pursuit of things outside the self."[10]

The misdirected desire to impersonate the powerful was not the only problem journalists encountered in this period. Worried complaints flew from all sides. Speaking at the 1934 convention of the American Society of Newspaper Editors, J. Charles Poe of the Chattanooga News applied the fashionable notion of cultural lag to journalistic habituation. If newspapers remained preoccupied with "petty policy court gossip, crimes of little or no moment, divorce cases, the doings of a movie star, town or county council meetings, ambulance runs, . . . resolutions by women's clubs denouncing war in time of peace and urging patriotism in time of war" or "the misadventures of a senator, or the daily doings of an air hero," it was because reporters and editors "generally follow the easiest path. They trail in packs, and follow formulae long since sterile and cold."[11]

Others asked whether newspapers that published syndicated columns would thereby sacrifice their individuality and strut an "editorial goosestep."[12]

"Would the tabloids ever go away?," the critics asked. Would journalists who wrote for confession magazines lose their integrity? Would reporters and editors ever stop their sentimental glamorizing of criminals? Of what disturbing advances in communications did movies, radio, newsreels and experimental television serve as forerunners? What consolation could be found by a young reporter, awakening "in the hall bedroom of a New York boarding house" to the realization that he had made an uncapturable error in yesterday's story? But it was with a special ambivalence that journalists worried about advertising and publicity — burgeoning enterprises which made daily journalism seem more difficult and even less attractive.[13]

Frank Cobb, Lippmann's predecessor as editorial page editor of the *World,* called publicity "private propaganda" and speculated that it had replaced government propaganda as a shackle for public opinion which had been "demobilized" after the Armistice but could not rid itself of its wartime habit of submission. "At this point," he wrote, "private propaganda stepped in to take up the work that government had abandoned, and when we deal with public opinion today we are dealing largely with private propaganda." Cobb was only one of many critics of the growing apparatus of publicity, which suavely restricted the flow of information from corporations and labor unions as well as from government. "No ruler in history ever had such a magnificent propaganda machine as Mr. Coolidge's," said *The New Republic,* "and certainly it would be impossible for anyone to use it more assiduously." Four years later the *North American Review* told its readers: "Of the four men in President Hoover's secretariat, three have had newspaper experience." One, George Akerson, "though he never writes a line can determine by a few verbal hints the tone and slant of much of the comment on national affairs that speeds over the wires from Washington every day. If it is power that the young journalist wants, let him by all means consider the field of publicity."[14]

Many journalists considered, and chose, publicity and advertising. More than a few reported that their satisfaction in their new work was compounded by relief from the vicarious dissatisfaction of daily journalism. Norman Klein, star reporter for the New York *Evening Post,* joined Benton and Bowles, the advertising firm, because, he said, "I have, I think, suddenly matured."

It is a rubber stamp to say that newspapering is a young man's game. But I think we have usually meant a reporter's birthdays — not his mental and emotional age. And a newspaper man is young only as long as he can successfully kid himself.

I kidded myself because I kept on thinking smugly that I was somebody — just because I interviewed or wrote about the stuffed shirts of our front pages — Lindberghs, the J. P. Morgans, the Babe Ruths, the Peaches Brownings, the Tex Guinans, the Florenz Ziegfelds, the Hoovers and Al Smiths. During the furor of a Page 1 story I have been asked to many a studio cocktail party, and doggone if I didn't kid myself into believing those fashionables were crazy about old Norm Klein — when the truth was, they only wanted some first-hand 'inside stuff' on the day's news.

> . . . It was a grand fifteen years of it, and I relished every minute.
> But lately I've had my doubts. . . . I began to feel that I had been taking
> millions of steps on a treadmill; and lately they were tiresome steps.
> . . . Well, I'm thirty-three. I've grown up at last. Retarded
> development, I suppose. And, boy, I'm out for the jack from now on . . .
> and when I get a nice big pile I'm going to buy me a newspaper somewhere
> and have some fun.[15]

Journalists tend to be sentimentalists, but, even so, it is hard to find in the accounts from this period of job migration even one which expresses regret about leaving newspaper work behind. Frank Ward O'Malley complained that retirement had deprived him of his public identity, but this was the insider's identity that the more dissatisfied Klein found so specious and humiliating. Journalists did not seem to suspect that the actorly adroitness which Cobb accepted so uncritically as an ingredient of the reporter's identity might in subtle ways falsify the news. Apparently it was assumed that an imposter or sycophant could report news as well as anyone else. In his writing about the responsibilities of the press, Lippmann, as we shall see, insisted that journalists exclude personal values from their reporting. But Lippmann also insisted on belittling the intelligence of ordinary people — the great body of newspaper readers — and this was a fissure in his thinking. Since his journalists were only to circulate information between the sanctums of disinterested speculation and decision, it mattered very little what they thought or felt about the situations they observed. The thinking and feeling were reserved for the experts. What could the members of these elites care about the assumptions of their journalistic servants? It may be that if Lippmann had seen (as the documentary film-maker and theorist John Grierson did) an imaginative way that journalists might have served the larger public more directly, as educators, he would not so readily have reduced reporter and editor to conduits. Certainly the inability of journalists employed by newspapers to depart from this mechanical function caused many of them to suffer feelings of deficiency.

In the July 1927 issue of *The Forum*, André Maurois offered readers a pessimistic and all-too-prophetic prediction of worldwide disaster followed by the resurrecting of civilization under the domination of five "dictators of public opinion." By 1962, Maurois wrote, New York, London, Berlin, and Peking would be rebuilt from the ruins of the World War of 1947, which would kill 30 million humans. Domination of the world's press, therefore of the world's politics, would by then have fallen to the five dictators, who, grasping the fact that monopoly of information meant monopoly of power, would establish a "tyranny in disguise." The master of the American press, Joseph C. Smack, "celebrated for the blunt brutality of his radiograms," would rule absolutely and command respect throughout the world.[16]

Nobody remotely resembling Joseph C. Smack ever appeared in the United States. None of the legendary journalistic innovators of preceding or subsequent generations (neither Dana, Hearst, Pulitzer, nor Luce) approached the power of Maurois' figment, and neither the insidious influence of propaganda — public or private — nor the concentration of power in public communications corporations has produced so commanding a figure.

In the interwar period another sort of man, endowed with subtler powers, appeared, and while it would be unfair and untrue to call him a "dictator of public opinion," his persistence over six decades as moralist and politician as well as journalist allowed him the opportunity to dictate much of the thinking of his time.

From the beginning of his career, and he was precocious, Walter Lippmann was marked by a clear intelligence, an eloquence and a dispassionate fairness and steadiness in his understanding of public affairs which impressed everyone he met. If he had written nothing about the press, he would still have had his reputation as a columnist, editor and popular philosopher (*A Preface to Politics, A Preface to Morals*), but between 1914 and 1927 he published four other books in which he set out his own rules for proper journalistic procedure and outlook: *Drift and Mastery, Liberty and the News, Public Opinion* and its sequel, *The Phantom Public*. In these books, product of more than a decade of thought about the obligations of a democratic press, Lippmann declared with increasing conviction that he believed in neither the good sense nor the inherent wisdom of the American people. His prescription for the press contained his belief that ordinary citizens were either unable or unwilling to gather enough information to understand the great issues of the world in which they lived.

Published in 1914, when Lippmann was only twenty-five years old, *Drift and Mastery* was a young man's book, vigorously clearing the way. From the uncertainty of the prewar period Lippmann wove a tapestry of general bewilderment which he called "the chaos of a new freedom." The powerful could not be blamed for this chaos. The confusion issued not from "the uncanny, malicious contrivance of the plutocracy, but the faltering method, the distracted soul, and the murky vision of what we call grandiloquently the will of the people." Journalists were part of the problem. The book's first chapter, called "Themes of Muckraking," criticized Lincoln Steffens and his colleagues for producing an aggressive and moralizing reporting which drew together the "clouds of accusation which hang over American life." But the true culprit was the excitable and gullible public, whose zealous desire to shame men for conventional misdoings was dismaying even for reporters. The "mere fact that muckraking was what people wanted to hear is in many ways the most important revelation of the whole campaign," Lippmann wrote. "For muckraking flared up at about the same time when land was no longer freely available, and large scale industry had begun to throw vast questions across the horizon. It came when success had ceased to be easily possible for everyone. The muckrakers spoke to a public willing to recognize as corrupt an incredibly varied assortment of conventional acts."[17]

An erring, moralizing press was keelhauled again in *Liberty and the News,* published in 1919, but now the press's problems were compounded by the onset of a complexity in the composition of public affairs which was so urgent in its implications that it seemed that every public question had been subdivided ten times over and recombined unrecognizably. Lippmann had completed his tasks for The Inquiry, President Wilson's postwar planning group, and it may be assumed that the responsibility he had been given — to provide Wilson with a map of Europe redrawn to avert future conflict — would have acquainted him with the complexity of the modern world, as well as the absurd devices sometimes devoted to its simplifying. Certainly there is evidence to suggest that Lippmann had an opportunity to study the complexity of affairs; whether he devoted as much time to the study of the companion assumption, that the public was incapable of understanding this complexity, is not clear. But the two assumptions would cleave together as he continued to interpret the workings of the press.

Church and school have left men unprepared to understand the intricacies of the world, Lippmann wrote. The press does not fill the gap in understanding because it does not even provide the pertinent facts. The moralizing editor believes that "edification is more important than veracity"; citizens wonder "whether government by consent can survive in a time when the manufacture of consent is an unregulated private enterprise. For in an exact sense the present crisis of Western democracy is a crisis in journalism.... The philosophy of the work needs to be discussed: the news about the news needs to be told."[18]

These themes would thread through other writings, and by the time he wrote *Public Opinion* (1922) and *The Phantom Public* (1927) Lippmann would have woven them into dogma. The world remained complex; the public remained bewildered; the press itself had to be reliable, factually, but its attention was too fragmentary to provide an accurate or complete reflection of society. It could be nothing more than a search light, he said, which illumined for a moment some event emerging from the field of social action. Certainly the press could provide no guidance for political decision. Those who made decisions would have to supplement their understanding with private sources of information. It is questionable whether Lippmann's fatherly chidings could have penetrated the thinking of a press as witless as the one he described, but members of the public must have been stung by the scorn he expressed in *The Phantom Public:* "We must assume that a public is inexpert in its curiosity, intermittent, that it discerns only gross distinctions, is slow to be aroused and quickly diverted; that since it acts by aligning itself, it personalizes whatever it considers, and is interested only when events have been melodramatized as conflict."[19]

As editor of the *World*'s editorial page from 1922 to 1931, as a syndicated columnist and author, Lippmann was powerful and influential. But behind his prolific outpouring, through the adulation which accompanied each new volume, his critics discerned the apologist's facility. "His learning is not too heavy, it is well distributed and limber," Benjamin Stolberg observed in 1927. "He is not so much a professional journalist as he is a man of considerable importance. There is something in his temper which tends to make him, as the years go by, more prominent than significant."[20]

Six years later, confessing a "feeling of awe" in the presence of this forty-four-year-old prodigy, by then author of eleven books and a syndicated column, Amos Pinchot nevertheless accused Lippmann of being a "salesman of plutocracy," eloquently restating what "his flock . . . has already heard on the piazza of the country club." Informed people could afford to disregard Lippmann, but Pinchot worried that those "unthinking people," for whose intellectual ability Lippmann felt such contempt, might be taken in by "the illusion of intellectuality" which his writings produced — "largely by references to irrelevant authorities but partly by a good journalistic technique." And, Pinchot said, Lippmann was callous: "He writes as though there were not hungry people in the world. He writes as though the privileged class in this country were ready to take its responsibilities seriously, and seriously become friends and shepherds of the people; and as if this were a desirable consummation."[21]

Lippmann's defenders sometimes paid him the sort of odd tribute which suggests how useful his elaborate formulations could be when they were stripped down and enlisted in the service of a conservative outlook. A *Time* Magazine cover story of March 30, 1931, said Lippmann "began with a stout faith in the workings of popular democracy. But his newspaper experience gradually bred in him a distrust . . . of so-called public opinion, the judgments of the Mass. As editor of the *World*, public ignorance was his field."[22]

Actually, Lippmann's lifelong distrust for popular thought originated in early manhood, when he renounced the socialist beliefs which he had embraced, somewhat defensively, after suffering discrimination as a Jew at Harvard College — the only time in his life that he was treated as an outsider. But it is not a mistake to see his belittling of the public's intelligence or interest as the central fact in his prescriptions for the press. For all of his career, down to the publication of his *Essays in the Public Philosophy* in 1955, he feared the anarchic excesses of uncontrolled public expression. In the *Essays* he would argue that the functioning of governments had been warped by the domination of those functions by public opinion. His journalism of restrained purpose would seem almost to have been designed to refuse nourishment to this encroaching public will.

This journalism without resonance, confined to bare factuality, was Lippmann's preference. It was not inevitable, however, that the journalist's job be seen as one in which he would gather, distill and distribute pertinent facts to a disinterested elite and an uninterested public. The limitations implied in this definition of reporting indeed partly explain why, in the 1920s and 1930s, so much memorable journalistic work was done by people who were not certified journalists. There were those, like Dorothy Parker, Edmund Wilson, or James Agee, who were journalists intermittently; others — artists such as Dorothea Lange or Paul Strand — took advantage of the political atmosphere and the support offered by Roy Stryker and other enlightened government officials to do outstanding photojournalism; the filmmakers described in William Alexander's *Film on the Left* and Erik Barnouw's *Documentary* saw in the restless dissatisfaction of this period opportunity to explore the lives of working men and women as they had not been explored before. One of these, John Grierson, whose ideas influenced the growth of a worldwide documentary film movement, used Lippmann's bewildered citizen as a starting point. Lippmann, Grierson said, "drew the sad portrait of John Citizen, tired after the day's work, being asked to express his free and rational judgment on matters he could not possibly be equipped to judge." Grierson, impressed not by John Citizen's helplessness but by the necessity that he participate in public affairs, dispensed with "the servile accumulation of fact" as a way of knowing how things worked. He thought a documentary film which "held the facts in living organic relationship" might provide a "shorthand method for world observation." His optimism was borne out in countless documentaries, among them *The Plough That Broke the Plains* and other films by the American director Pare Lorentz.[23]

Evident in much of the work of these documentarians, writers and photographers would be a concentration on the object, an attention, an emotional and intellectual involvement which simply would have been unavailable to journalists who followed Lippmann's rules of detachment. Presumably, these qualities were unnecessary; the dispassionate relaying of information did not require them. In any case, news executives were not overly concerned. In a patronizing way, sometimes with a tinge of bitterness, they blamed their readers for preferring diversion to information. "Some call it the Jazz age, but we all know what it is," Paul Bellamy of the Cleveland *Plain Dealer* had told a convention of the American Society of Newspaper Editors in 1927. "We all know, and I think most of us would admit, that the reading publics to which we generally appeal care less at the moment for the so-called serious and important concerns of society than at any time during the lives of all the men in this room. They do not care to analyze and improve their government or any other of their public institutions, including the press. They want to be entertained."[24]

An even more revealing example of the complacency which afflicted American journalism in this period is the comfortable assumption at the center of this statement by Kent Cooper, general manager of the Associated Press: "People like to read about themselves, about the things that might conceivably have happened to themselves, the dramas and the tragedies in which they might have been the heroes or the victims. A famine in China may wipe out a hundred thousand lives, or even a million, but it does not make a big story to the average American. China is far off, and famine is quite removed from the realms of your possible experience or mine." What is a genuine interest to the American newspaper reader? Floyd Collins, Cooper said,

> entombed in a Kentucky cave and fighting against time for his life. . . .
> Why? Because you and I and everybody have been in caves, or deserted
> houses, or dark passages. . . . We have known the sudden spasm of fear
> that comes with the thought "Suppose I should get shut in here alone, and
> nobody came along to release me. . . ." A hurricane may wipe out the
> entire population of an island in the South Seas without causing us to
> spend an extra minute over our morning papers. But when the "Shenan-
> doah" falls with its score of men the story grips us all. . . . We could
> imagine ourselves in its rocking cabin. The grinding crash when it broke
> in pieces, the horror of the breathless fall through the inky blackness, the
> shattering jolt.[25]

While famine and social disorder in China were of little interest to American readers in 1926, they certainly were more interesting in 1937 and in 1947. The reason Floyd Collins was more important than China was simply that the Associated Press and other news-gathering agencies took the time to make him interesting, and they generally disregarded China. It was ridiculous for Kent Cooper to compare Floyd Collins with China, but by the standards which guided American newspaper journalism it also was perfectly reasonable. American journalism always has had unspoken as well as proclaimed purposes, and one of those is to maintain a cozy social environment of diversion, reassurance, and acceptable anxiety. The entombing of Floyd Collins and the crash of the "Shenandoah" were accidents. They made sensational journalistic diversions because readers could be reasonably sure that such accidents would *not* happen to them. Famine was an immeasurable calamity. It broke down the boundaries of reassurance which the newspapers each day rebuild for their readers. The elevation of Floyd Collins was based on a convenient assumption. A more idealistic editor — say, Oswald Garrison Villard of the New York *Evening Post* and the *Nation* — would have found Cooper's excited discovery of the popular mind repulsive; a more worldly Associated Press general manager, such as Melville Stone, who hired Cooper, might have found his provincialism dismaying. But none of those who heard Cooper speak that day would have been surprised, for in periods of great social tension American journalism has tended to be more mindful of its mediating and insulating function. In the interwar period this renewed sense of duty was expressed in celebrity mongering, gossip and sensation, but the whole panoply rested on the very serious assumption, best expressed by Lippmann, that the public could not stand, or could not understand, the discoverable truths of its situation.

The consequences of the strategy of belittlement may be seen in the careers of journalists, and perhaps particularly in the careers of those who left newspaper work because it seemed indistinguishable from other kinds of daydreaming. The daydreams were indispensable; so were the celebrities who peopled them. The daydream shapers were called journalists, and those who accepted the responsibility wholeheartedly moved quite naturally into their lucrative positions in publicity and advertising, where they became full-time dreamers and prodders of the halfhearted who remained in the newsrooms. Once they got there, like Norm Klein, "suddenly matured," they wondered why they had spent so many years doing the same job at half the pay.

Notes

1. Advertisement, *Publishers Weekly* 115 (9 February 1929): 740.

2. *The Jazz Age, as Seen Through the Eyes of Ralph Barton, Miguel Covarrubias and John Held, Jr.* (Providence: Museum of Art, Rhode Island School of Design, 1968), p. 33.

3. Ivor Brown, "Can Journalism Be Restored?" *American Spectator* 1 (March 1933): 1.

4. Don Marquis, *the lives and times of archy & mehitabel* (1935, Garden City: Doubleday, 1950), p. 451.

5. Heywood Broun, "Those Earnest Jesters," *Reader's Digest* 18 (January 1931): 793.

6. John Keats, *You May As Well Live: The Life and Time of Dorothy Parker* (New York: Simon and Schuster, 1970), p. 299.

7. "Mayor Walker Calls Reporters His Best Friends and Critics," *The American Press* 46 (September 1928): 1.

8. "Irvin S. Cobb — Still the Reporter," *The American Press* 47 (June 1929): 25.

9. "O'Malley Misses Reporting Days," *The American Press* 46 (September 1928): 6.

10. Leo C. Rosten, *The Washington Correspondents* (New York: Harcourt, Brace and Company, 1937), p. 242. "Journalists are caught in the remorseless vitality of the moment. They are hyperactive persons. In the exhilarating chase after the Now there is refuge from the restraining past and the disturbing future."

11. *Problems of Journalism, Proceedings of the American Society of Newspaper Editors* (Washington, D.C.: American Society of Newspaper Editors, 1934), pp. 43-44.

12. *Problems of Journalism, Proceedings of the American Society of Newspaper Editors* (Washington, D.C.: American Society of Newspaper Editors, 1926), p. 33. "Personally, I am sorry to see this syndicated editorial comment. Facts in the news are facts wherever they are, and a press association report should be a fact report. But syndicated comment, interpretative or otherwise, starts an editorial goosestep up and down this broad land; readers will either fall in line by reading it or they will fall out of line by avoiding all editorials. And you really want them to do neither."

13. Alexander Woollcott, "Too Late to Mend," *Collier's,* 25 September 1926, p. 26.

14. John L. Heaton, ed., *Cobb of 'The World'* (New York: E. P. Dutton, 1924), p. 331. "Government by Publicity," *The New Republic,* 22 September 1926, p. 111. Oliver McKee, Jr., "Publicity Chiefs," *The North American Review* 230 (July 1930): 417-18. Harold Brayman, "Hooverizing the Press," *Outlook and Independent,* 24 September 1930, p. 123.

15. Norman Klein, "Why A Reporter Left His Paper For An Advertising Agency Job," *The American Press* 47 (October 1929): 2.

16. Andre Maurois, "The War Against the Moon," *The Forum* 78 (July 1927): 20.

17. Walter Lippmann, *Drift and Mastery* (New York: Mitchell Kennerley, 1914), pp. 4-5.

18. Walter Lippmann, *Liberty and the News* (New York: Harcourt, Brace and Howe, 1920), pp. 4-5, 8, 15-16.

19. Walter Lippmann, *The Phantom Public* (New York: Macmillan, 1927), pp. 64-65.

20. Benjamin Stolberg, "Walter Lippmann, Connoisseur of Public Life," *The Nation,* 7 December 1927, p. 639.

21. Amos Pinchot, "Walter Lippmann, 'The Great Elucidator,'" *The Nation,* 5 July 1933, p. 7; "Walter Lippmann, 'The New Tammany,'" *The Nation,* 12 July 1933, p. 36; "Walter Lippmann, 'Obfuscator de Luxe,'" *The Nation,* 19 July 1933, p. 67; "Walter Lippmann on Democracy," *The Nation,* 2 August 1933, p. 126.

22. "Piano v. Bugle," *Time* Magazine, 30 March 1931, p. 24.

23. Forsyth Hardy, ed., *Grierson on Documentary* (London: Faber and Faber, 1946), pp. 140, 288, 289.

24. *Problems of Journalism, Proceedings of the American Society of Newspaper Editors* (Washington, D.C.: American Society of Newspaper Editors, 1927), p. 153.

25. Bruce Barton, "How Did *That* Get in the Paper?" *The American* Magazine 102 (August 1926): 72.

9 Mass Media Come to the Small Town

The *Emporia Gazette* in the 1920s

Sally F. Griffith

In 1916 William Allen White celebrated the small-town newspaper in *Harper's Monthly Magazine:* "The country newspaper is the incarnation of the town spirit."[1] While acknowledging that city folks might find such papers provincial, White insisted that "the beauty and the joy of our papers and their little worlds is that we who live in the country towns know our own heroes."[2] In the cities, he argued, few were actually acquainted with the socialites, businessmen or criminals depicted in the daily papers, while his fellow Emporians knew all about the people in his *Gazette*'s stories.

> Our papers, our little country papers, seem drab and miserably provincial to strangers; yet we who read them read in their lines the sweet, intimate story of life. . . . When the girl at the glove-counter marries the boy in the wholesale house, the news of their wedding is good for a forty-line wedding-notice, and the forty lines in the country paper give them self-respect. When in due course we know that their baby is a twelve-pounder, named Grover or Theodore or Woodrow, we have that neighborly feeling that breeds the real democracy.[3]

In the years after World War I these and similar comments, together with his shrewd, colorful political commentary, created for White the reputation as not only "Sage of Emporia," spokesman for Middle America, but the quintessential small-town newspaperman. It is therefore significant that during the 1920s White's own newspaper underwent a drastic shift in emphasis, away from the normal life of small-town Emporia and the "sweet, intimate stories" of its marriages and births and toward the dramatic and sophisticated urban world of the mass media. This shift was caused by a combination of factors that included increased advertising and improved technology of printing and communications, as well as the much-discussed "ballyhoo" of the urban media. But for Emporians it meant the increasing marginality of their quiet small-town life.

In 1916 the *Emporia Gazette* was the only daily newspaper in Emporia, Kansas, a prosperous, stable community of around 10,000.[4]

While hardly meriting White's characterization as provincial, it was clearly an unsophisticated paper by urban standards. Typically, a little over half of the *Gazette*'s front page was devoted to national and international news, but its seven ruled columns were visually gray and the full-cap decker headlines rarely exceeded one column in width.[5] There were virtually no news illustrations on the front page or elsewhere in the *Gazette* — with the significant exception of occasional halftone photographs related to the war in Europe, probably supplied by Allied publicists. Like most small-town newspapers in this period, the *Gazette* lacked facilities to make halftone engravings from local photographs, and sending them away to be engraved was a time-consuming and expensive process. Therefore, photographs rarely appeared in the newspaper unless provided by outside agencies in the form of cuts or papier-maché matrices.[6]

The lack of banner headlines contributed to a general impression in the *Gazette* that local and outside news were of equal significance and that normal community happenings were as important as dramatic events. The shocking murder of Lyon County Sheriff Walter Davis received extensive coverage, but it did not call up more than a single column headline, nor was it given substantially more space than a report on an Adventist camp meeting.[7] On October 12, 1916 the *Gazette* carried a two column play-by-play report of the final game of the World Series, culminating the first direct wire Associated Press coverage of the event.[8] Yet the same issue contained a lengthy front-page account of the wedding of Ruth Jones and Wayne Traylor, with abundant descriptions of the ceremony, church and reception decorations, music, bridal gown and bouquet, and attendants.

Wedding stories more often appeared on inside pages, but as White indicated, they represented a major form of news. His "forty-line wedding notice" could have been referring to the Ingram-Donnellan affair:

> Miss Grace Ingram, daughter of Mrs. Alice Ingram, 820 Cottonwood Street, and Joseph J. Donnellan were married at 2:30 o'clock this afternoon, in the priest's parlor of the Church of the Sacred Heart by Rev. Doctor Berthold.
>
> The bride wore a blue silk suit with a rose hat and gray shoes. The couple was attended during the ceremony by Mr. and Mrs. Harry Norton. Mr. and Mrs. Donnellan left this afternoon on a wedding trip and several days' visit in Kansas City.

Mrs. Donnellan was for several years employed in the G.W. Newman store, and resigned her position about a month ago. Mr. Donnellan came to the Newman store as a decorator about three years ago from New York City. Mr. and Mrs. Donnellan will be at home at 1001 Walnut Street, after March 15.[9]

In addition to such notices, "locals" — columns of short news items from neighborhoods or rural townships — filled the bulk of the inside pages. These traced the day-to-day routines of residents' lives: visits, shopping trips to town, family reunions, holiday get-togethers, illnesses and recoveries. Other columns focused on happenings in local schools and churches and among Santa Fe railroad workers. Although urban dailies had developed special sections and departments such as sports, entertainment, and society, the *Gazette* demonstrated no such clear differentiation. A sports column, covering a mixture of local college teams and national college and professional events, appeared with the classified and legal advertising. Occasionally some — but not all — of the entertainment notices appeared there as well.[10] The *Gazette* was generous with free notices of all "cultural" events, particularly if there were also paid advertisements.

White's description of the country newspaper focused upon news, but of course a sizable portion of his *Gazette* consisted of advertising (see Table 1).[11] There again, the *Gazette* was far from being isolated from the

Table 1

Advertising in the *Emporia Gazette*

	1916	1917	1918	1919	1925	1926	1927
Advertising per issue (col. in.)	444	469	491	518	723	1014	870
Ave. no. of pages	6.8	6.8	6.8	7.7	9.6	12.7	10.4
Percent adv./issue	43	45	47	43	43	45	48

Averages were obtained from randomly selected issues. Figures for 1916-19 represent seven columns per page; for 1925-27, eight columns per page. Numbers in the sample: 1916, 9; 1917, 5; 1918, 10; 1919, 6; 1925, 10; 1926, 9; 1927, 10.

outside world; so-called foreign advertising comprised the most visually striking aspect of the newspaper. Ads for Ivory Soap, the National Biscuit Company's Uneeda Biscuit, Calumet Baking Powder, Sunkist Oranges, and Armour's Glendale Oleomargarine invariably stand out on the newspaper page by virtue of their superior design and use of clear, lively illustrations. But there was nothing about their appeals that conflicted with the rest of the *Gazette*'s contents. These manufacturers were pioneers in the development of brand name recognition, and they endeavored to endow their products with comforting and familiar associations of wholesomeness and trustworthiness.[12] For example, Calumet ads coupled images of the baking powder package with that of a puckish, roly-poly baby.[13]

Purely "foreign" ads comprised only a small percentage of advertising space in 1916, about 12 percent, while ads originating locally accounted for 88 percent (see Table 2). Whether they mentioned brand names or not, local ads were as unsophisticated in design as the rest of the paper. Appealing through words much more than illustrations, they were often composed wholly of type. Ads for movies in Emporia's theaters were exceptionally modest, being simply typographical announcements of the theater, the star's name, the producer, and the film title. A line in small, light type might describe the movie, as for "The Case of Becky" with Blanche Sweet, "A thrilling and dramatic story of a young woman possessed of two personalities."[14] Some local advertisers used simple decorative borders or electrotype cuts; the Citizens National Bank had a standing patriotic motif with an American eagle, and several lumber companies used cartoons to attract attention. But few attempts were made to relate image to verbal message, aside from a general appeal to the idea of thrift or service. A few local firms used pre-packaged ads for brand name lines of products, provided in the form of mats by the manufacturers. Ads for "Royal Tailored Clothing" and "High Art Clothes," lines of ready-to-wear men's clothing in Emporia dry goods stores, were some of the most striking in the paper. But, like the foreign ads, they appeared more concerned with giving their mass-produced products reputations for quality by emphasizing their appearance of fine tailoring than with setting new styles.

Though the *Gazette* in 1916 was perhaps not as provincial as White claimed, it was clear that Emporia, as a community and as a marketing center, was the center of the newspaper's universe. "Foreign" news and advertising were presented in terms which reflected local tastes and interests. For example, Progressivism was not merely a thing of cities, or of a remote Washington government, but pervaded local life, through campaigns for municipal ownership of utilities and drives to improve the

Table 2

Origins of Advertising in the *Gazette* (Percentages)

	1916	1917	1918	1919	1925	1926	1927
Local	53	42	53	54	53	52	35
Brand	31	40	36	31	30	32	47
Agents	4	4	5	3	7	6	6
Foreign	12	14	6	12	10	10	12

Source: See Table 1.

Local: mentioned only local firm name
Brand: mentioned brand name in ad for local firm
Agents: chains or dealerships

care of Emporia's children and to "swat the canker worm" from the town's trees.[15] News of outside events were balanced in the *Gazette* by the sheer numbers of references to Emporians and their life-cycle celebrations as well as their daily lives. The overall impression is of the continuity and centrality of family and community life.

The *Gazette* of the mid-twenties conveys a far different message. The emphasis is upon the new and the abnormal, and most importantly the center of action has shifted from Emporia to the Big City. At first glance, the paper is not dissimilar: the front page is nearly as gray as before, and the proportion of national and international, state and local news is approximately the same.[16] When one begins to read the news, however, and then turns to the inside pages, it is evident that a major change has occurred in the *Gazette*.

Increased advertising was an important factor of change. Immediately after the war ended, demand for advertising, which had remained relatively constant during the war years, began to increase dramatically.[17]

In his *Autobiography* White noted this influx of advertising in the twenties:

> The advertising patronage of the paper was growing rapidly, crowding extra pages in every day. . . . Merchants were spending their

money freely to attract buyers. And from the East came thousands of dollars in advertising, calling attention to national products — automobiles, radios, phonographs, tobacco, oil, transportation — a long list of things which once were luxuries and were becoming the common comforts of the people.[18]

Thus he attributed increased advertising largely to so-called foreign advertising, that is, ads placed by agencies for nationally marketed items. However, the proportions of advertising origins actually remained fairly constant, with local firms continuing to do the bulk of advertising (see Table 2).

Local merchants, facing increased competition with urban areas because of the spread of automobiles, were receptive to the improved advertising offered by professional agencies. A significant feature of the period is the increased use of well-planned, multifaceted advertising campaigns orchestrated nationwide by manufacturers or agencies. Using the local newspaperman as intermediary, with increased advertising revenues as his incentive, manufacturers marshalled the participation of all local merchants in drives to push their brand products. Retailers were asked to place ads featuring the product in question, and all ads were grouped on a newspaper page with a larger one paid for by the manufacturer. Merchants were also supplied with posters and displays with which to remind customers that they carried the product which was being extolled in many media. Although they seemed to welcome this increased promotional aid, individual retailers were ultimately made more dependent upon manufacturers and upon changing styles originating in urban centers.

In mounting these campaigns advertisers seem to have drawn upon Progressive and war preparedness experiences insofar as their ads showed the effectivness of unified large-scale drives. They made heavy emphasis upon the war-time ethic of "cooperation." While organizing a campaign for the California Fruit Growers Exchange, the Lord and Thomas Agency reminded the *Gazette* "that the papers getting the largest amount of co-operation will of course be the first considered on future advertising on this account."[19]

During the twenties urban advertising agencies turned out increasingly well-designed copy, which made locally produced ads seem correspondingly old fashioned.[20] Local merchants therefore relied much more upon advertising designed by agencies and supplied by brand-name manufacturers as standarized mats. Only the local merchant's name and address was added at the bottom. Increased use of mats in the twenties, for features and photographs as well as advertising, resulted in much wider distribution of urban trends in fashion and decorative styles than ever before. To keep in step, even non-brand local advertisers used general purpose commercially designed mat illustrations.

By far the most striking change between 1916 and the mid-twenties in the *Gazette*'s advertising occurred in the movie ads. The modest all-type announcements were replaced by energetic and arresting designs that made the most innovative use of typography and illustration in the newspaper. Such liveliness was mirrored by the use of peppier copy. Where previously movie ads had if anything underplayed their products — "emotional" isn't the most arresting adjective one can imagine for Theda Bara — these ads were often more titillating than the movies themselves. An ad for "His Secretary" with Norma Shearer promised revelations of "the temptations, the romance, the adventure" found by "the millions of young girls who seek to get ahead in the world of business. . . . Here is the drama of our sisters and daughters who offer themselves on the altar of business."[21]

Whatever the visual effect of the more sophisticated advertising, the impact of increased advertising volume is emphatically clear. First, it caused a significant increase in the size of the newspaper (see Table 1). This and the increasing sophistication of advertising and public relations practices of American business led to the use of special interest pages. Far more than in 1916 the *Gazette* by the mid-twenties was divided into sections such as sports, homemaking, entertainment, society, and even automobiles and real estate. These pages were clearly motivated by advertising needs. Each contained ads appropriate to the tastes of a particular consumer audience: barber shops, tobacco, and sporting goods in the sports section; clothing in society; groceries in homemaking; and movies and vaudeville in entertainment.

Much of the news on these pages was promotional material for the products advertised. While this was nothing new, the arts of public relations made great advances in technique and organization in the twenties. Advertisers flooded small newspapers with news releases and mats that could conveniently fill their additional space.[22] Since the Gazette elected to print some of these releases, there was a more obvious correlation between advertising and news in the *Gazette* by the mid-twenties as well as a heightened emphasis upon advertising at the expense of the less visually attractive news.

In many cases advertising contracts were followed by publicity releases informing consumers of the newest products and the care taken to develop them. For example, when the new car models were introduced in 1927, three of the *Gazette*'s eight pages that day carried highly illustrated ads by Emporia agencies for Hudsons, Chryslers, Oldsmobiles, Chevrolets, Fords, Studebakers, Nashes, Oaklands, and Willys-Knights.[23] These were surrounded by feature articles with such headlines as "Manufacturer Says Two Cars Save Family Money," "Give New Oakland 100,000 Mile Test," and "Chevrolet Trucks Lead Their Field." Similarly, the homemaking tips and recipes offered on the Friday evening Market Basket Page were often provided by corporate publicity departments. On June 17, 1927, the page was filled by mat ads for Mazola, Karo, and Argo Corn Starch as part of "Corn Products Day." The only non-advertising copy on the page was a recipe column, "Modern Method of Preparing Delightful Foods," in which all the recipes specifically called for Mazola corn oil and Karo syrup.

The compartmentalization of the *Gazette* and increased visibility of advertising and publicity combined to upset the delicate balance between Emporia and the outside world. Local news continued to appear but was overwhelmed by more visually arresting aspects of the paper. Stories about normal life-cycle events no longer stood on their own as news but were relegated to appropriate columns. Weddings appeared in short notices on the society page. Lists of housing starts were published in a column on the real estage page, accompanied by advertising for local lumber yards.

What was lost in the departmentalization of the newspaper was the sense, at least as it had been conveyed by the *Gazette*, that Emporians shared a common interest in the details of their neighbor's lives. No longer was it assumed that everyone was interested in all the news of the community. The *Gazette* was now divided into sections defined according to categories of consumption, in the interests of advertisers. While many readers may have found the paper easier to read, the new fragmentation nonetheless diminished the extent to which Emporia readers could be assumed to share a common experience. At least as reflected in their newspaper, Emporians were no longer so much community members as consumers.[24]

In addition to publicity releases, the preponderance of the *Gazette*'s increased space was filled with material bought from one or another of the flourishing wire services and feature agencies. As discussed above, the *Gazette* had its share of outside material in 1916; White was not above using boiler plate on occasion. But these sorts of materials had possessed of necessity a certain timeless, placeless quality, enabling them to blend in with the surrounding stories. They often had been items of historical interest, such as an item on Eleazar Williams, Wisconsin's pretender to the French throne in the mid-nineteenth century, or one on Mark Twain's financial fiascos.[25] These were worlds apart from the Central Press and United Press materials appearing in the *Gazette* ten years later. Photographs and features about the latest celebrities were now distributed in mats with stylish layout and headlines already provided.[26]

As early as 1908 White had denounced illustrations in newspapers: "The big newspapers have gone mad on the 'art' business since the half tone process made engravings cheap. . . . It will be a glad day when newspapers are once more newspapers, in fact as well as in name and not abominations in color."[27] He particularly detested comics, and refused to have them in the *Gazette* until, in 1920, he finally gave in. He editorialized: "The boss is whipped . . . the force has beat him. He thinks that they [comics] make a low appeal; that their humor is broad, and their level of intelligence negligible. But the force maintains that they sell papers."[28]

By the mid-twenties the *Gazette* carried "The Gumps," "Bringing Up Father," and "The Figgers Family" daily and a full-page version of "The Gumps" on Saturday evenings, since it did not publish a Sunday edition. In fact, the *Gazette* had put aside its former prejudice to the extent of running a mat ad in January 1927 calling attention to "National Laugh Month" and advising its readers to "Laugh and Grow Fit every day by following the fun elements in *The Emporia Gazette*."[29] The paper also published political cartoons and syndicated political columns on the editorial page, and photographs of sports heroes on the sports page and of striking new fashions on the society page. There was often a full-page montage of "The Day's News in Pictures" provided by the Central Press Agency.[30] And, of course, the omnipresent publicity photographs of Hollywood starlets. While the *Gazette* still published few photographs of Emporians, its pages glittered with the faces of Hollywood's citizens.

Like White, the Associated Press had long resisted pressures to l News Service, Central Press Agency and the United Press Agency. But AP members other than White increasingly supplemented their AP news with materials from these agencies. UP, well known for its sprightly and sometimes sensational coverage, grew rapidly in the twenties, and in 1928 it had 1150 clients to AP's membership of 1246.[31] Kent Cooper, AP's chief of traffic until he became general manager in 1925, had long urged that the cooperative must make its coverage more lively and interesting and expand its services to include features and photographs. But he had been consistently overruled by more conservative leadership. When he became general manager he quickly moved to change editorial policy and institute a new feature service. Soon thereafter a photograph service was added.[32]

In early 1927, White wrote Cooper:

> Let me say here and now that I appreciate this [feature mat] service. I have been buying Central Press stuff and United Press stuff for a year or two, and if the Associated Press service continues I shall be glad to drop them both. As it is I've dropped the red letter mail service which I have been buying from the United Press. Personally as between two newspaper men, I loathe the whole business, the U.P. service and the

Central News Service. But I run a paper in a town without competition
and I have to give the morons and nitwits something for their money.[33]

Loathe them or not, White used a considerable amount of Central Press
and UP material in the *Gazette,* even after the AP feature service began.

It was through these services that the *Gazette* registered the journalistic shock waves originating with the new urban tabloids. Brash,
irreverent and risqué, tabloids like the *New York Daily News* altered
journalism in America by enlarging the boundaries of what was considered
legitimate news.[34] However much newsmen like White might lament over-
use of screamer headlines, large photographs, and the exploitation of sex
and murder subjects, they felt compelled to offer at least a mild form of
competition.[35] Consequently, the trial of "statuesque blonde" Ruth
Snyder and "her corset salesman paramour" Henry Judd Gray for the
murder of her husband received extensive attention in the *Gazette* via AP
and Central Press. Running accounts of the New York City trial, verdict,
sentencing, and execution were accompanied by large, austere photographs and drawings of the grim couple.[36]

This case had barely ended when another sensational trial opened
in Los Angeles in which film actor Paul Kelly was tried for the murder of
musical comedy star Ray Raymond over the love of actress Dorothy
MacKaye. While giving the trial ample space, the *Gazette* felt called upon
to comment editorially upon this rash of murders: "Today the American
press is getting its new murder from the Pacific coast in a nice juicy tale of
slaughter that comes buzzing over the wires, just as the last click of the
grisly horror from the Snyder case is slowly ticking into the long silence.
Every week the press of the land is soaked with blood. . . . Murder will not
only out but it will soak its blood into the consciousness of the American
people."[37]

The editorial did not consider whether this impression of slaughter might not be the result of the press's scramble to exploit such "juicy"
tales. Rather, in a parody of those calling for repeal of prohibition, it
advocated that laws against murder be abolished because they only tempted
human frailty to break them.

During the heyday of "ballyhoo" in the mid-twenties, the *Gazette*
reflected all the sensations: the "Peaches" Browning marriage and separation, the Rhinelander annulment suit, and, of course, the Lindbergh flight
were all followed in day-by-day detail through AP dispatches and Central
Press photographs.[38] The generally colorless front page sported an
uncommon banner headline the day Lindy landed in Paris, along with a
large photograph of the "Flying Fool."[39] In succeeding days an illustrated
installment traced the life of Lindbergh "as told exclusively to Miss Bonita

Witt of Central Press" by his mother.[40] His return to America was cheered with an oversized decorative banner, "Welcome Lindbergh!," probably from a Central Press mat, complete with stars and bunting, soaring airplanes, and photos of Lindbergh and Coolidge. In the center of the page was a large sketch of Lindbergh over a spread American eagle.[41]

In comparison to these excitements the stories that had been the staples of the *Gazette*, the daily comings and goings of Emporians, their marriages and deaths, seemed pale indeed. One reason, of course, was that they were not illustrated as were the wire service stories. In fact, one of the few local photographs to appear in the *Gazette* showed College of Emporia students concentrating upon their catechism studies, which, while not the sort of thing to rival Central Press offerings, ought to remind contemporary readers to be wary about generalizations concerning "flaming youth."[42] For fashion Emporia no longer looked to descriptions of gowns worn at local society events, but instead to Central Press photographs and reports by "Mme Lisbeth" of what was current in the great cities.[43] No photographs appeared of newlywed Emporia couples, but readers could see "one of the first photos," of the daughter of the American ambassador in Berlin and her new groom, thanks to Central Press.[44]

This disparity no doubt resulted partly from the greater interest some readers had in far-off news, as White seemed to believe. But it also stemmed from improvements in communications and printing technology. Because of the large numbers of subscribers, services could provide mats for stories and photographs at prices far below the cost of filling a comparable amount of space with local news.[45] Improved wire service technology made it possible to send larger amounts of news over an increasingly wider network.[46] A good deal of this news concerned significant political developments, albeit sometimes reflecting a conservative bias on the part of the Associated Press.[47]

Nevertheless, much of this increased news was of a purely human interest nature. As Helen MacGill Hughes would note, human interest stories derived their attraction not from their importance but from universal human qualities.[48] Looked at from this perspective, the "sweet, intimate stories" that White extolled in 1916 did resemble in some aspects the scandals of the mid-twenties. Yet there are significant differences. Stories about weddings and divorces may appeal to like interests, but they convey very different messages about human society.

For example, there was continuity in terms of human interest between the twenties and earlier periods in stories about the frailties of woman. From the beginning of White's editorship there appeared lively pieces like this: "The west side girls are working a partnership game that is

making half of the boys in town go wild. They each get a fellow in a sisterly
sort of anxious way that completely disarms suspicion and tell him how
much the other girl likes him. One dose is usually enough and the way the
boys are biting is scandalous. The boys pay the livery and candy bills.
These girls ought to go into politics."[49]

Such items brought White criticisms from some local quarters for
"sensationalism."[50] In later years the *Gazett* was more circumspect, but it
could not refrain from commenting in 1916 about woman's weakness for a
uniform: "Last Sunday, a body of Pennsylvania troops came through
Emporia, and Emporia girls by the dozens flocked to the train, and scraped
up acquaintance with men whom they never had seen before, and who, in
all probability, they never will see again. It has been the same in Emporia
on other days, and it has been the same in other towns. Women fall for
brass buttons."[51]

In the twenties this particular human interest formula reached its
apotheosis with the flapper, and the *Gazette* reflected the trend, as in this
AP story:

> Charleston is too Tame
> Addicts Try Parachute Jumping
> Charleston enthusiasts here are turning to parachute jumping
> to obtain an added kick. Matching her life against the luck she believed
> attached to her, Teresa M. Kirshe, 18-year-old stenographer, yesterday
> crawled onto the wing of a plane bucking a strong wind at 2,160 feet and
> leaped clear. Her luck held. Now her sister Mary wants to borrow the
> parachute.[52]

However, with increased attention to crime in the mid-twenties
the flapper assumed a more threatening demeanor. When she was not
jumping from airplanes in search of thrills, the flapper as portrayed in
many wire service stories appeared to be running completely amok. Thus
we find Central Press photos of 17-year-old Dorothy Perkins of New
York, on trial for the murder of the man her father had chosen to be her
husband. She was said to have killed him because "she preferred the
attentions of a 35-year-old man."[53] Hard-faced Maxine Spangler was
pictured, cigarette in hand, in a wire release, following sentencing for check
forgery. The headline read "Must Have Her 'Smokes.'" Describing her as a
"16-year-old flapper," the caption quoted her as saying "I'd as soon be in
the pen as any place if they'll just give me plenty to smoke." It concluded,
"her aged father spent his all trying to make good the checks."[54]

Compared to the behavior of these flappers, the transgressions of
the Emporia girls seemed the innocent flings of adolescents who would
likely soon settle down. Such flappers denied traditional values in a more

fundamental way by smoking and drinking, by refusing to be ruled by patriarchal authority, and by committing adultery and even murder. They seemed to threaten the very continuity of society. A revealing photograph appeared in the *Gazette* above the caption: "The More Dolls the Fewer Flappers — Acting on this theory the Professional Women's League is encouraging interest in dolls for very young ladies. Miss Martha Hogan appears both interested and interesting."[55] In the photograph the aforementioned young woman, fetching in a short skirt, sits surrounded by baby dolls.

Such symbols of disruption and discontinuity conflicted markedly with other aspects of the *Gazette,* which continued to document the cyclic continuities of its community: births, marriages, the building of homes, and deaths. While local news continued to appear, it was now overwhelmed by the variety of more lively wire service materials. In the twenties the normal pecadillos of small-town youth hardly commanded national attention, and so they missed even local notice. Instead the *Gazette* published photographs of Cincinnati schoolboys Albert Rosenberg and William Straus who, "deciding that life was not worth the effort," made a suicide pact and shot themselves.[56]

The net effect, then, of the *Gazette*'s increased advertising and greater access to syndicated materials was to diminish the very centrality of its community. Emporians could no longer gain the impression from reading their local newspaper that Emporia — or their own lives — mattered much in the scheme of things. While many no doubt welcomed the *Gazette*'s more fashionable appearance in the twenties, they may also have been aware of a concomitant waning of a sense of the legitimacy of their day-to-day lives. For, rather than focusing on local events, the paper dramatized far-away people and places. Instead of recording the life passages of their neighbors, it reported the abnormality of strangers.

White had written in his *Harper's* article: "It is the country newspaper, bringing together daily the threads of the town's life, weaving them into something rich and strange, and setting the pattern as it weaves, directing the loom, and giving the cloth its color by mixing the lives of all the people in its color-pot — it is this country newspaper that reveals us to ourselves."[57]

In 1926 the *Gazette,* with its more stylish advertising, celebrity photographs and "livelier" news, no longer could be said to reveal Emporia to Emporians. Rather, the paper's overall impression was of an increasing divergence between an exciting but dangerous outside world and the day-to-day life of Emporians. Unexpectedly, the result of more news available to small town newspapers seemed to be the greater marginality of small town life.

Notes

1. "The Country Newspaper," *Harper's Monthly Magazine* 132 (1915-16): 888.
2. *Ibid.*, p. 890.
3. *Ibid.*, p. 891.
4. According to the Kansas decennial censuses, Emporia's population was 10,664 in 1915 and 12,243 in 1925. See *Emporia Gazette*, 16 November 1925.
5. The *Gazette* received an Associated Press telegraphic report, but because AP did not require members to use its logotype or otherwise identify its news until 1917, it is impossible to distinguish which agencies provided particular news stories. From internal evidence it is clear that the *Gazette* used a variety of sources, such as clippings, boiler plate and other agencies such as Reuters, but AP material predominated. Averages from a random sample of the front pages of ten issues in 1916 are: National, 55 percent; State, 10 percent; Local, 35 percent.
6. For a description of the development and use of dry mats, see George A. Kubler, *A New History of Stereotyping* (New York: privately printed, 1941).
7. *Emporia Gazette*, 17 August 1916; *ibid.*, 5 September 1916. September 1916.
8. For details of the coverage see Oliver Gramling, *AP: The Story of New* (New York: Farrar and Rinehart, Inc., 1940), pp. 245-246.
9. *Emporia Gazette*, 4 March 1916.
10. See *Emporia Gazette*, 7 January 1916; *ibid.*, 27 March 1916.
11. Advertising comprised about 43% of space in 1916.
12. See Daniel A. Pope, "The Development of National Advertising 1865-1920" (Ph.D. dissertation, Columbia, 1973) and Glenn Porter and Harold C. Livesay, *Merchants and Manufacturers* (Baltimore: John Hopkins University Press, 1971), pp. 223-225.
13. See *Emporia Gazette*, 17 February 1916.
14. *Emporia Gazette*, 1 May 1916.
15. *Emporia Gazette*, 7 January 1916; *ibid.*, 11 June 1918.
16. A random sample of 10 issues from 1926 averages 49 percent National and International, 12 percent State, and 39 percent Local. However, this includes one issue in which virtually all the front page was devoted to a local flood disaster. If that issue is left out, the averages are 55 percent, 12 percent, and 33 percent, practically the same as in 1916.
17. See Walter E. Hughes (*Gazette* business manager) to Arthur Wilson, 23 July 1919, Series D, Box 10, William Allen White Papers, Library of Congress, Washington D.C.
18. *The Autobiography of William Allen White* (New York: Macmillan, 1946), p. 625.
19. Lord and Thomas to *Gazette*, 2 November 1916, Series D, Box 8, White Papers.
20. Hower points particularly to the more effective integration of illustrations after World War I in his study of the N. W. Ayer agency. Ralph M. Hower, *The History of An Advertising Agency* (Cambridge, Mass.: Harvard University Press, 1939), pp. 329-38. See Stevens chapter in this volume.
21. *Emporia Gazette*, 3 May 1926.
22. A contemporary publicity guide noted that a mat service "is especially welcome to the editors of the country press, for it obviates the necessity of setting up the type, and has the added advantage of carrying its own illustrations. . . . Much of the material in the country press is printed from type impressions obtained from mats." Glenn C. Quiett and Ralph D. Casey, *Principles of Publicity* (New York: D. Appleton, 1926), p. 347.
23. *Emporia Gazette*, 28 February 1927.
24. Of course, this process of fragmentation would continue for another half century, as is well described by Anthony Smith in *Goodbye Gutenberg: The Newspaper Revolution of the 1980's* (New York: Oxford University Press, 1980), especially Chapter 4.

25. *Emporia Gazette*, 11 January 1916; *ibid*, 12 October 1916.

26. Gramling, *AP*, p. 328.

27. *Emporia Gazette*, 22 January 1908.

28. *Emporia Gazette*, 4 October 1920, quoted in Walter Johnson, *William Allen White's America* (New York: Henry Holt, 1947), pp. 490-91.

29. *Emporia Gazette*, 3 January 1927.

30. *Emporia Gazette*, 30 November 1925.

31. Richard A. Schwarzlose, *The American Wire Services: A Study of Their Development as a Social Institution* (New York: Arno Press, 1979), p. 396.

32. See Cooper's own account in *Kent Cooper and the Associated Press: An Autobiography* (New York: Random House, 1959), pp. 92-140.

33. White to Cooper, 3 February 1927, Series C, White Papers.

34. Discussions of the tabloids, varying in sympathy, can be found in Silas Bent, *Ballyhoo: The Voice of the Press* (New York: Boni and Liveright, 1927), pp. 180-98; and Simon Bessie, *Jazz Journalism* (New York: Dutton, 1938). See Murphy chapter in this volume.

35. Bent notes that 120 reporters covered the Snyder-Gray trial, not counting the celebrity commentators such as D.W. Griffith and Billy Sunday. He confessed, "this author himself was one of the 'trained seals' who helped overcrowd the press of the United States with balderdash about the Snyder-Gray trial." Bent, *Ballyhoo*, p. 194.

36. See *Emporia Gazette*, 9, 10 and 23 May 1927, for a sampling.

37. *Emporia Gazette*, 12 May 1925.

38. For a sampling of the first two, see *Emporia Gazette*, 8 January 1927; *ibid.*, 5 December 1925.

39. *Emporia Gazette*, 21 May 1927. A similar banner head greeted news that Captain Nungesser's plane was nearing New York, on 9 May 1927.

40. *Emporia Gazette*, 27 May 1927.

41. *Emporia Gazette*, 11 June 1927.

42. *Emporia Gazette*, 21 April 1927.

43. *Emporia Gazette*, 7 February 1927.

44. *Emporia Gazette*, 30 November 1925.

45. The new AP mat service cost the *Gazette* only $1.50 a week. N. A. Huse to White, 31 January 1927, Series C, White Papers.

46. Alfred McClung Lee, The Daily Newspaper in America (1937; reprint ed., New York: Octagon Books, 1973), pp. 526-28.

47. On this subject see Oswald Garrison Villard, *The Disappearing Daily: Chapters in American Newspaper Evolution* (New York: Alfred A. Knopf, 1944), pp. 40-50. White also criticized Cooper on AP's handling of the issue of "Bolshevik tactics" in Central America. See White to Cooper, 25 February 1927, Series C, White Papers.

48. Helen MacGill Hughes, *News and the Human Interest Story* (Chicago: University of Chicago Press, 1940).

49. *Emporia Gazette*, 7 May 1898.

50. William W. Cuthbertson, "William Allen White and the *Emporia Gazette*, 1895-1944" (Ph.D. dissertation, University of Rochester, 1962), pp. 89-90.

51. *Emporia Gazette*, 12 October 1916.

52. *Emporia Gazette*, 17 May 1926.

53. *Emporia Gazette*, 15 June 1926.

54. *Emporia Gazette*, 30 November 1925.

55. *Emporia Gazette*, 8 January 1927.

56. *Emporia Gazette*, 30 November 1925.

57. "The Country Newspaper," p. 890.

Section III
Resurgence

The deepest problems of modern life derive from the claim of the individual to preserve the autonomy and individuality of his existence in the face of overwhelming social forces, of historical heritage, of external culture, and of the technique of life. . . . The person resists being leveled down and worn out by a social-technological mechanism.

Georg Simmel, "The Metropolis and
Mental Life" (1902)

F ocusing on developing situations when mass media seemed to be failing and people felt themselves or their values threatened, essayists in this section see some people adopting distinctive strategies to make the mass media more responsive to human needs.

These were both lay people and media professionals. In the face of the unexpected, they did not remain passive. Instead, they moved to revive intitiative, exercise creativity, reassert command. Out of strains in the culture—literary, political, philosophic, ethical—came the shape of their response—new literary forms, new patterning of social organization, new levels of consciousness.

Picturing the old newspaper reporting style of the 1920s as bankrupt in the face of depression realities, James Boylan perceives the emergence of a new literary form of magazine reportage which not only defined the crisis more sharply, but helped to create a style of journalism fitting for a time out of joint.

Mark Fackler traces the interest groups offended by movie content who responded by proposing moralistic codes to control content in the 1920s and 1930s; challenging the traditional view of such movements as reprehensible, Fackler links their arguments to intellectual currents out of which came the social responsiblity theory of the Hutchins Commission on press freedom.

Catherine L. Covert discerns an affront to sensibility posed by early radio, undermining an older sense of mastery over communication and of connection to other individuals and to society more generally; some individuals responded, she argues, by challenging the idea that technology could inevitably shape lives.

More general questions suggested by the above essays are these: What shocks to thought or feeling did mass communications afford in this period? What specific values did they threaten? What expected functions did they fail to perform? How did individuals, professionals or consumers, combat or adapt to these threats and disappointments? What more general tides in the culture seemed to prompt people to respond as they did?

10 Publicity for the Great Depression
Newspaper Default and Literary Reportage

James Boylan

So deep is the gulf cut in the history of this century by the Great Depression that it may be difficult for later generations to realize that in its own time the depression gained widespread and public recognition only slowly and belatedly. Irving Bernstein has observed in *The Lean Years* that "Americans were hardly aware of the problem in the first year or two." Polls of opinion leaders placed the major symptom of the depression, unemployment, far down the list of national problems as late as 1932.[1]

Some of the reasons for this misperception, or non-perception, were circumstantial, rising from the very character of a depression. The federal government also contributed, with its stuat society had charged with reporting such malfunctions, the newspaper, did not itself function well in sizing up the depression. Rather, it fell to a small band of litterateurs turned journalists to produce reporting that helped define the crisis more sharply in the American mind. In doing so, they created a style of journalism that drew on such predecessors as the sociological style of the muckrakers and anticipated many of the characteristics of the New Journalism of the 1960s.

Obstacles to Perceiving a Depression

Americans were ill-prepared for the hard times that came with the 1930s. Little in their collective experience had alerted them to the possibility of a prolonged depression. In 1929 only about one person in six was old enough to have more than a distant childhood memory of the last prolonged crisis, that of 1893 and the years following. The slumps centering on 1908 and 1921 had left rather the opposite message — that recovery could be swift and not excessively painful.[2]

Neither did the depression offer much to see, even to the searching eye. Many writers have commented since on its invisibility. It has sometimes been characterized in fact as things not happening — business not transacted, factories not producing, stores not open, workers not going to jobs. Even the victims, the jobless and the hungry, seemed to drift out of sight to the fringes of civilization — the dumps, the railroad sidings, the highways. Or they stayed at home, if they still had a home. Moreover, at first most of the victims tended to be those of marginal visibility, those who had already been poor in the 1920s. Only later did the "cold bay fog" of fear drift up into the middle class.[3]

News events offered far from unambiguous clues. To us, looking back with foreshortened vision across fifty years, the stock-market crash may appear to have announced the Great Depression as certainly as the attack on Pearl Harbor signaled war with Japan. But the depression was more elusive than a war. Americans could be excused for having viewed the panic as a momentary phenomenon, for within five months the market had rallied to within points of its boom levels of a year before. After the crash, few economic events gained national attention; only bank closings were conceded to have "an alarming effect upon the public mind."[4]

Possibly most important, the crisis remained in limbo for three years for lack of a strong voice to define it. The Hoover administration attempted to dissipate the depression (a word that Hoover chose for it in preference to, say, "panic")[5] by failing to concede that it existed or by suggesting that it had passed or by denying that it was a concern of government. Such a policy encouraged the natural tendency of business to pretend that things were not so bad, that upbeat sales psychology would ultimately pull the nation out of the trough. It was primarily at government and business that one of the depression's first historians, Gilbert Seldes, directed his charge that "we were not permitted for many months to confront the reality of our situation."[6]

Newspapers and the Depression

But what had become of the institution that society had entrusted with a major share of the task of portraying "the reality of our situation?" Newspapers were still the dominant news medium in 1929; radio, an amusing supplement. Even during the pit of the depression, newspapers remained a daily staple for millions. But critics of the time and critics since have charged that newspapers repaid the faith of their readers badly — that they played the tune of Hoover and the business community. Hoover called that tune early when he appealed to the press not to overexert itself:

"If we overdo our job we may create a sense that the situation is more serious than it really is . . . if you could confine yourselves merely to the statement of things that actually happen . . . that would be the most helpful form of news on the subject."[7]

Newspapers probably did not need the nudge. Most appeared ready to maintain discreet silence until the depression blew over. Malcolm Cowley summed up the indictment years later: "In those years the press was afflicted with a lofty sense of its own responsibilities. Its function of telling people what happened was being subordinated to the apparently greater function of saving the nation's business . . . most of the newspapers were trying to make their readers confident again and abolish the depression by printing very little news about it."

The evidence supporting this accusation is scattered but fairly plentiful. For example, the Lynds, who returned to Muncie, Indiana, in the early 1930s for their second study of "Middletown," found: "The papers did not stress the depression. Hopeful statements by local bankers and industrialists, increases in work forces, and similar items tended to make the front page, while shrink-ages in plant forces and related unhappy news commanded small space on inside pages or were omitted entirely."

Mauritz Hallgren of *The Nation,* visiting South Bend in the same state, observed that the local press in 1931 took "for granted, as do almost all of South Bend's leading citizens, that good times are now returning."[8]

Such emphases were not confined to the small-city press. The New York *Times* repeatedly lifted to the front page momentary good news from the stock market, while leaving at the back of the paper most of Wall Street's slide into the depths of 1932. In addition, as could be expected of a newspaper of the *Times*'s quasi-official character, the president's reassurances were given dominant positions on page one, so much so that Elmer Davis, a former staff member and historian of the *Times,* chided the paper for wasting its space. And the *Times* was careful to air the reassurances of the press establishment when the publishers came to New York for their annual meeting; the headline on April 25, 1932, was "Publishers Report Business Is Reviving."[9]

For the most part the press revealed little consciousness that it had left anything undone. Several hundred newspapers, in fact, cooperated enthusiastically in a survey of "newspaper leadership" in the depression, which noted, among other things, that editors had been proud to receive the encomiums of bankers' associations for "steadying the social, economic and business structures of the communities they serve" and for their "refusal to become vehicles for hysteria." The survey also indicated that much of the volume of depression coverage by these papers was "informational publicity" — that is, promotional material presented in the interests of "patriotic cooperation."[10]

Well into the depression some big-city editors began to have second thoughts, quickly subdued. At the 1933 meeting of the American Society of Newspaper Editors, a dissident, Grove Patterson of the Toledo *Blade,* introduced a resolution charging that newspapers had lulled the public into an "unreal and false economic security" and had "tended to keep from readers the truth about the economic and financial status in various local situations." The resolution sparked a sharp discussion in which several editors defended their withholding of news, notably on potential bank failures. Fred Fuller Shedd of the Philadelphia *Bulletin* praised editors because "they had used discretion and had not told people all the facts that they know." Ultimately, the Patterson resolution was tabled and, apparently uneasy about the whole debate, the body authorized its board of directors to censor the transcript. (The directors did not.[11])

Although there is no definitive historical verdict on newspaper performance in the depression, one important study has concluded: "What the newspapers did not print was undoubtedly as important as what they did print." It is certain at least that the press did not much outstrip business or government in facing up to the depression. Like government and business, it ultimately had depression forced upon it; coverage markedly improved in 1932 and 1933. But it is still startling to find one historian contending, as William E. Leuchtenburg does, that the appearance of a story in *Fortune* magazine in the fall of 1932, three full years into the slump, was "a milestone in national acceptance of the reality."[12]

One circumstance that sharpens the indictment of newspapers is that they appear to have missed much that historians of the depression have uncovered rather readily — the effects of the mass unemployment that Irving Bernstein has called "the saddest proletarian episode in American history"; the "fear and shame" that Warren Susman finds to have drained the middle class; the panoply of disruption — erosion of families, loss of homes, transiency, apathy. It could be argued that news values carried over from the 1920s, particularly the showmanship that Silas Bent anatomized in his *Ballyhoo,* may have been ill adapted to presenting the depression's miseries. But this possibility seems nowhere near so substantial as the institutional barriers that lay between newspapers and frank coverage of the depression — the fear of making things worse, the assumption that the business community *was* the community, past hostility to those who seemed most concerned with the depression — labor and radicals. The press seemed curiously passive. Until other institutions in society, notably business and government, were ready to define the depression, it appeared to be unready to attempt to assert its own definitions.[13]

An Alternative Journalism

So it was that the depression became in a sense an increasingly unwieldy client in need of publicity; more precisely, the victims and potential victims of the depression became a clientele, for whom little could be done until there was national acceptance of the existence of the presence and permanence of the depression.

The first means available was protest, the forcing-open of news channels by disruption. Although street theater did not have the potential scope that it gained in the age of television, it could at least reach the front pages. The Communists led the way on March 6, 1930, with an International Unemployment Day that produced a crowd in New York City of 35,000 and a violent clash. The *Times's* lead headline was: "REDS BATTLE POLICE IN UNION SQUARE." But success was nowhere near so simple as Bernstein has suggested in writing that "bleeding heads converted unemployment from a little-noticed to a page-one problem in every important city in the United States." The press managed to place a heavy discount on radical protest; three days after the Union Square confrontation, the *Times* was promoting a Red Scare set afloat by the city's police commissioner, Grover C. Whalen.[14]

Protest had other limitations, most notably the lack of protesters. Although Bernard Sternsher tabulates a "sampling" of seventeen disruptive incidents between February 1930 and July 1932, he finds that these were too small and few to upset the conclusion that the depression produced "apathy rather than rebellion." Moreover, in the long run protests were discouraged by the country's response, which was as indifferent as repressive. The press helped to underwrite that indifference with censorship of news of disruptions that it considered dangerous. Bernstein writes that most of the instances of what he calls "illegal self-help," such as raids on food stores, "are lost to history; the press in many communities refused to publish the news in fear of stimulating similar action."[15]

With conventional news channels blocked or restricted, a wide field was left to those who wanted to seek out and publicize the depression by other means. There were a good many such, acting out of political, social, or artistic motives. Some were of high literary standing, others one-time writers eager to tell their own experience. They had in common a desire to provide testimony about the depression. For better or worse, and partly by default, these writers became agents for the publicity that the depression so badly required and, for later generations, the first among its definers. This group of volunteers is hardly being rescued here from obscurity, for their paths have been visible in much of the political, literary, and cultural history of the time. This is inevitably the case, for the most eminent among them are still counted among the major American literary figures of this century.

Political history views them primarily as writers who were, in that time at least, radicals. Daniel Aaron has tracked them through the labyrinth of literary communism. Murray Kempton designated them "votaries" of the "social myth of the thirties" — the replacement, he wrote, for the individualist myth of the twenties.[16]

Culturally, they have been viewed as castaways from the old business civilization, looking on with grim satisfaction as its wreckage slipped beneath the surface. One of their number, Edmund Wilson, later wrote of the depression era: "to the writers and artists in my generation who had grown up in the Big Business era and had always resented its barbarism, its crowding-out of everything they cared about, these years were not depressing but stimulating. One couldn't help being exhilarated at the sudden unexpected collapse of that stupid, gigantic fraud." Leslie Fiedler wrote bluntly that these writers sought "a vision of disaster and a pleasuring in it."[17]

The easily donned radicalism and the alienation from what they saw as the culture of the 1920s contributed to the determination of these writers to seek out the depression rather than simply holing up. More important, these predispositions made it easy for them to interpret the depression almost at once as a collapse, not merely a crisis. Besides radicalism and alienation, there remained a third important element in what they did — their choice of form, which proved to be journalism.

Not much of the discussion of this body of depression writing has called it "journalism" outright. The preference, first adopted by Alfred Kazin in 1942, has been for "documentary." In describing this "literature of fact" in *On Native Ground,* he elaborately developed the metaphor of the camera to describe the documentary approach; like cameras, the depression writers were "always trying to catch reality on the run; . . . to identify the object by etching it sharply on the mind; to give it a kind of wry objective bitterness." These effects were achieved, Kazin implied, at the cost of "a certain enforced simplicity and passivity of mind."[18]

William Stott, who has given the documentary forms of the 1930s their most extended exposition, defines the work of the depression writers by placing them in categories, sub-categories, and sub-sub-categories. First, they are put under the heading of nonfiction documentary writing, then under "first-hand reportage that tried to convey the texture of actuality as well as the facts," and finally under "*radical* reportage" (emphasis added), which he condemns as "characteristically primitive in its emotionalism, and distortive and reductive in its vision of the world." Where Kazin

saw passivity, Stott finds tendentiousness. These are not really contradictory views, for while the seeming passivity took the picture, the tendentiousness generally selected what would be shot.[19]

Even while skirting the name "journalism," Stott and Kazin have
acknowledged covertly that this body of work was indeed journalism, for
they both describe the one act that is inseparable from journalism —
reporting. "Many writers," Kazin noted, "seemed bent on reporting,
reporting." Elsewhere, he called it "reportage," the term commonly used
by Stott. Why "reportage" rather than plain "reporting?" Apparently the
term became popular in the 1930s to denote a kind of journalism that was
different from what appeared in newspapers and from the ancient notion
of reporting as literal transcription. Although practitioners did not appear
to use the terms much themselves, it was often attached to them as a
compliment. Joseph North, editor of *New Masses,* attempted a definition
at the American Writers' Congress of 1935: "Reportage is three-dimensional
reporting. The writer not only condenses reality, he helps the reader feel
the fact. The finest writers of reportage are artists in the fullest sense of the
term. They do their editorializing through their imagery."

Although inelegant, North's definition at least isolated two elements of reportage — personal observation and personal sensibility — and
implied a third, an editorial goal.[20]

One major treatment of this body of work — that of Richard H.
Pells — designates it as journalism. He too emphasizes purposefulness
over passivity:

> Journalism tried to deal with whatever was concrete, specific,
> and essential. Unlike art, it valued substance over images, experience
> over ideas, situations over symbols. Consequently it gave writers an
> opportunity to anchor their ideals and ambitions in definite places,
> people, and events; it permitted them to re-establish communication with
> their society; it helped them understand their relationship to the "facts"
> they discovered; and it help out at least a limited sense of order and
> security in a time when little else seemed real or clear.

Unlike Stott, Pells finds the choice of journalism as a form implied for
these writers a commitment to "truth, honesty, and objectivity [that]
forced them to confront America as it was."[21]

It is a little harder to infer that these writers were motivated by the
deficiencies in newspaper journalism, although there is evidence of awareness that little they considered true was being published. Malcolm Cowley,
as noted, was retrospectively critical of newspapers: "People . . . did not
find answers to the questions they were asking. When they turned to the

daily press, they hardly even found the questions: 'But why?' and "How much longer?' and 'What should be done?'" Mauritz Hallgren of *The Nation* concluded: "We cannot depend on the public record." John Dos Passos put it sharply in a letter to Edmund Wilson: "I'm beginning to think that every printed publication ought to be required by law to print at the bottom of each page: NB: THIS IS ALL BULLSHIT."[22]

The medium these writers chose was the natural one for them — the quality magazine (and often, subsequently, the book). Although *New Masses* has sometimes been credited with stimulating this kind of journalism, the most important host was *The New Republic,* partly for its adequate circulation, partly for the breadth of its hospitality. In the late 1920s its younger editors had felt increasingly restive under the founder and editor-in-chief, Herbert Croly. Wilson recalled in particular his disappointment when Croly balked effective coverage of the bitter Gastonia textile strike because he considered the two reporters nominated, John Dos Passos and Mary Heaton Vorse, too far to the left. Croly, after a series of strokes, died in May 1930 and the group suddenly had, in Cowley's words, the "sort of opportunity journalists dream of having" — a going magazine, theirs in the midst of a growing national crisis. They operated as a kind of collective, listing themselves as equals on the masthead.[23]

The instinct of the editors of *The New Republic* was almost the reverse of that of the newspapers. They sought, rather than shunned, the depression, and saw themselves as providing a kind of open line to its victims. How did magazines remain free of the restrictions that seemed to dampen the newspaper press? Obviously, their sense that they were operating "outside the American business system" was borne out in reality. With five-figure circulations and scratchy advertising revenue, they had no powerful business community looking over their shoulder; on the contrary, they could count on addressing a largely sympathetic audience when they provided evidence the country was going to hell. They were free, too, of the obligations of daily journalism to give respectful attention to official statements and actions and to package even the bad news in standard, impersonalized forms.

Thus *The New Republic* and to a lesser degree *The Nation,* as well as the serious monthlies such as *Harper's, Scribner's,* and *The Atlantic,* became the focus of writing about the depression. *The New Republic* in particular attracted a variety of contributors — some obscure, some famous, some disguised. The editors themselves contributed a good share — among them, George Soule, the economics analyst; Cowley, the new literary editor; Bruce Bliven, who eventually subordinated his writing to the duties of managing editor; and Wilson, the former literary editor, who was now embarking on period of reporting. In addition, the magazine called on such liberal-to-radical journalists as Louis Adamic, Mary Heaton Vorse, and, most important, Sherwood Anderson and John Dos Passos.

Anderson was one of the earliest to respond. Fifty-three years old in 1929, he had settled a few years before in southwest Virginia and had become the proprietor there of two weekly newspapers. His base lay at the edge of the great Piedmont textile-mill region, afflicted by a recession since 1924 and, starting early in 1929, troubled by a series of desperate and ultimately fruitless strikes. Half a year before the crash, he wrote a story for *The Nation* about the first strike, at Elizabethon, Tennessee. The Anderson of journalism was readily recognizable to the reader of Anderson fiction; the story was studiedly simple, seemingly bumbling, curiously mild and indirect, almost writing away from the strike instead of into it. His "Factory Town" appeared in *The New Republic* early in 1930; it not only displayed Anderson's fascination with industrial machinery but offered an early glimpse of a setting destined to become a powerful symbol of the depression:

> Have you ever visited a soup kitchen? I saw one recently in a Southern industrial town. Some seven hundred people were fed on the day I was there.
>
> They were Americans, such people as you and I. I stood watching them. I was ashamed of my warm overcoat, my stout shoes.
>
> I made men ashamed standing there.
>
> There was a man approached the soup kitchen three times. Each time his eyes met mine. . . . He stopped beside me. He lied. I had said nothing about his wanting hot soup. "I am not here for soup," he said defiantly. "I came here to meet a friend."

These vignettes of the mill towns formed the core of his depression writing, which was collected in a book, *Puzzled America,* in 1935.[24]

Through the depression years, John Dos Passos, who was thirty-three in 1929, was engaged in writing the trilogy, *U.S.A.,* that made him the era's pre-eminent political novelist. But he still managed bursts of journalism. He was in the first expedition, led by Theodore Dreiser, of left-wing writers who went to investigate the Harlan County coal fields, and wrote a substantial part of its report, *Harlan Miners Speak;* he also wrote an extended account for *The New Republic.* He did one effective close-up of Detroit, a frequent stop for depression writers. Dos Passos sketched the life of the unemployed:

> They are everywhere, all over the vast unfinished city, the more thrifty living in shacks and shelters along the waterfront, in the back rooms of

unoccupied houses, the others just sleeping any place. In one back lot they have burrowed out rooms in a huge abandoned sandpile. Their stovepipes stick out at the top. All along the waterfront you can see them toasting themselves in the sun, or else patiently fishing. A sluggish, drowsy, grimy life, of which Grand Circus Park is the social center and the One Cent Restaurant operated by some anonymous philanthropist is the Delmonico's.

For the most part he made his "beat" national political events and pseudo-events, the depression's carnivals — a hunger march on Washington, the Republican and Democratic national conventions, the Bonus Army encampment. His journalism lacks the gadgetry of *U.S.A.* — there is no equivalent of "The Camera Eye" or "Newsreel" — but it still has the novels' texture:

> Two elderly laboring men are looking out of a cigar-store door at a bunch of Reds, young Jewish boys from New York or Chicago, with the white armbands of the hunger marchers. "Won't get nutten that a-way," one of them says. "Whose payin' for it anyway, hirin' them trucks and the gasoline. . . . Somebody's payin' for it," barks the clerk from behind the cash register. "Better'd spend it on grub or to buy 'emselves overcoats," says the older man. "Never get nutten that a-way."

Some of Dos Passos' depression reporting was included in a 1935 collection, *In All Countries*.[25]

Edmund Wilson, thirty-four in 1929, surpassed all the others in the duration and continuity of his reporting. Up to this point, his reputation was that of a critic, but one versatile enough to write in any form he pleased — play, novel, sketch, even now and again journalism. When he turned definitively toward reporting as his approach to the depression, both his versatility and his dawning radicalism served him well. Early efforts, such as his turgid "Foster and Fish" (William Z. against Hamilton) did not show his new politics to good advantage, as he acknowledged in later years. But early in 1931 his work took a new turn in "Communists and Cops," an almost film-script treatment of a hunger march on New York's city hall. His "Detroit Motors" was more complex — a depiction of the automobile industry, an oral history of some of its workers, and a subtly withering portrait of Henry Ford as a false humanitarian: "The idea that Ford is adored by his men has certainly never existed except outside Detroit." Wilson went into the coal country before the writers' committees, tracked rural poverty in the Kentucky hills, and paused to do an article on the case of the Scottsboro boys. In the West, he exposed the wretched, federally sanctioned, working conditions at Boulder (Hoover) Dam, then made his way to southern California, which inspired him to word play: "From the heart of thriving Los Angeles rise the groves of gorgeous business cathedrals; the blue Avocado Building, bawdy as the peacock's tail, with its frieze of cute little pukids; the golden Lubrication Building . . . the regal and greenish Citrus Building, made throughout of the purest lime candy, which has gone just a little sugary from the heat."[26]

He ended at San Diego, which he designated "The Jumping-Off Place." He had already turned repeatedly to suicide as a symptom of the depression. Here, in the city with the country's highest rate of self-destruction, he elevated it to a metaphor:

> These coroner's records in San Diego are melancholy reading. You seem to see the last blind feeble futile effervescence of the great burst of American adventure. Here this people, so long told to "go West," to escape from poverty, ill health, maladjustment, industrialism and oppression, discover that, having come West, their problems and their diseases still remain and there is no further to go. . . . Brokers and bankers, architects and citrus ranchers, farmers, housewives, building contractors, salesmen of groceries and real estate, proprietors of pool-rooms, rustic stores and hotels, marines and supply-corps lieutenants, molders, machinists, oil-well drillers, auto mechanics, carpenters, tailors, soft-drink merchants, cooks and barbers, teamsters, stage drivers, long-shoremen, laborers . . . ill, retired or down on their luck — they stuff up the cracks of their doors in the little boarding-houses that take in invalids, and turn on the gas; they go into their back sheds or back kitchens and swallow Lysol or eat ant-paste; they drive their cars into dark alleys and shoot themselves in the back seat; they hang themselves in hotel bed-rooms, take overdoses of sulphanol or barbitol, stab themselves with carving-knives on the municipal golf-course; or they throw themselves into the placid blue bay, where the gray battleships and cruisers of the government guard the limits of their enormous nation.

The articles through the fall of 1931 were collected in a volume, *The American Jitters,* published in April 1932. When Wilson resumed reporting, a few months after the accidental death of his wife, he went to Chicago and gathered material for "Hull House in 1932," which appeared in three parts in *The New Republic* early in 1933. A few weeks later, he stood in chill, gray Washington for Roosevelt's inaugural parade: "Comic lodges and marching clubs . . . curled-up shoes and fezzes . . . hideous green, purples and reds . . . Tom Mix." He looked back instead of forward: "The America of the boom definitely died today, and this is the ghost it just gave up."[27]

What Depression Reportage Achieved

How well did Anderson, Dos Passos, Wilson, and their fellows achieve the goal — however they might have stated it — of publicizing the depression, of changing the way people thought about it? They were scarcely competing with newspapers for the mass audience or even for influence on public policy, for the means they chose were so indirect, so fragmentary, so gradual that they could scarcely be translated into recommendations. Rather, they seemed to have engaged themselves in an act of faith — that telling about the depression as they saw it might somehow dent American indifference.

But how was what they saw different? The answer does not appear to lie in depth of investigation, for the range of subject matter that depression reportage covered is not imposing and indeed often seemed to be rather casually chosen. A fair amount of it dealt with topics that were not only obligatory for writers on the left but often constituted news events that had appeared in the general press — Harlan County, hunger marches, the Bonus Army, strikes. Nor can it be said that the reportage systematically documented the suffering of the depression in the sense that, say, the Farm Security Administration photographs later documented rural poverty. Rather than intensive, the observation tends to be fleeting, the work of writers in transit, peering through a windshield or a train window — as Wilson did, literally, in the opening paragraphs of his Hull House series. The "road" book later became a standard genre of the 1930s, but in this early reportage the road was not yet the object but a condition.[28]

Given such limitations of system of scope, what then did the reportagists have to offer? Themselves, of course — that is, the application of what they had learned as workers in other forms of literature to their journalism, and of their own sensibilities. As Alfred Kazin put it in an appreciation of *The American Jitters* "Wilson's chronicle is so unflinchingly personal, it presents so dramatically the confrontation of the period by a mind unused to social ugliness, that it catches perfectly the revolutionary and unsettling impact of the 1930s on those who were least suited to it."[29]

Yet saying that this journalism was personal and literary does not go far toward explaining its strategy as journalism. One characteristic is immediately apparent, which it shares with much other journalism of dissent or agitation — that is, the use of the specific example for its own sake where conventional journalism uses it to affirm a more general point. This point can perhaps be more clearly made by example, in stories that were written about one incident by a New York *Times* reporter and by Edmund Wilson.

This was the demonstration in New York's city-hall area on January 20, 1931. An unsigned account appeared in the *Times* the next morning under the headline, "2,000 REDS ATTACK POLICE AT CITY HALL." Wilson's "Communists and Cops" was published in *The New Republic* for February 11. The stories were of roughly the same length, and contain no obvious disagreements in facts. (Wilson, of course, had the benefit of reading the *Times* story before he wrote.) Yet the differences are striking, beyond the superficial differences in format and organization. The distinction lies in the use made of parallel facts. Compare these passages about an identical observation:

> Sympathy was obviously with the police. Small articles and bags of water were cast on the rioters' heads from the windows of nearby buildings. [Times]

> Somebody from a high floor of the Sun Building drops a paper bag full of water down into the swarm around the statue. The bag comes apart in the air and people watch the whirls of water fall. [Wilson]

The key difference here is not quantity (one bag or more?) but the effect. The *Times* reporter saw the falling bag(s) and locked up their meaning securely with a conclusion about political sentiment in the upper floors. Wilson let the bag fall bearing only its own message, but one that is somehow infinitely richer.[30]

This was not merely a difference between newspaper and magazine journalism, however, or between overt political objectives. Instead two different models of journalism are implied. This can be seen in a pair of articles that appeared a few weeks apart in *The New Republic*. Both Louis Adamic and Sherwood Anderson, as it happened, wrote articles on the strike in Danville, Virginia. Adamic's account was informative, in the literal sense that it provided statistics, chronology, quotations, conclusions — all the marshaling of fact that educated Americans have learned to take as authentication. By contrast, Anderson's article was shambling, almost incompetent by Adamic's standards, an illustration of Anderson's statement in his memoirs: "Facts elude me. . . . When I try to deal in facts at once I begin to lie." Instead, Anderson told an allusive tale about a writer who drove to Danville in the rain, spoke to strikers in a hall recently vacated by the Ku Klux Klan and still incongruously decorated with an electric-lighted cross:

> A thousand eyes looking up at you. . . . They so believe in you, or in someone like you, some talker, some writer, some leader, some poet who is to come and make what they want understood to their boss, to all bosses.

Well. you do nothing. You say a few words. You go away. You go back to
your hotel. Some man comes in and offers you a drink. That's that.
Adamic's article, read now, offers accurate enough data, but it is dead;
Anderson evokes states of mind.[31]

Yet another comparison — between Wilson's Hull House series
and the work of Mauritz A. Hallgren, a former newspaper reporter and
foreign correspondent, and *The Nation*'s national correspondent during
the depression. Hallgren's seven-part series on hunger was one of the era's
major reporting efforts; it abounds in information and has been frequently
cited by historians. Yet most of it, too, is dormant for today's reader, for, in
the newspaper tradition, Hallgren largely removed his own presence and
offered a disembodied, impersonal report. In his Chicago article, he supplied elements of the situation that Wilson entirely omitted — the city's
upper-class tax revolt, the shadow government of wealth behind the
elected officials, the policies that had made misery worse. At the same time,
Hallgren missed most of the sense of desperation that Wilson caught so
well — the stink of the flophouses, the deadly midwinter cold in condemned tenements.[32]

Such comparisons are not necessarily invidious. In theory at least,
there should be ways to combine informative with evocative elements; the
more skillful muckrakers appeared able to do so. But in depression reportage, the combination rarely occurred; indeed, even individual writers
slipped from one mode to the other in different stories. On the one hand
there was generalizing journalism, which always faced the danger of the
distorting, obscuring conclusion deteriorating ultimately into Orwellian
euphemism. On the other there was particularizing journalism, which
faced a counterpart danger — that of the distorting specification, the
possibility that the given detail might not represent all it was intended to or
might suggest more than it ought. (Was the collapse of American society
really inherent in the suicide rate in San Diego? Or was that really what
Wilson was implying?)

In a way reminiscent of, but not really analogous to, Dos Passos'
famous assertion that "we are two countries," we have had two journalisms. Michael Schudson has divided them into "information" journalism,
for those whose lives are somewhat structured and predictable, and "story-
telling" journalism, for those whose destinies are less certain. His partition
depends somewhat on differing audiences. But it is also possible to look at
the two journalisms as divided less by class or politics than by use —
whether the underlying purpose is to confirm or dissipate standing perceptions of society. Information journalism, even when it advocates social
change, appeals to acceptable generalizations. Story-telling or, more nar-

rowly, reportage seeks to set forth contrary examples, which defy social generalizations — that in effect remove the frame from the picture.[33]

Although the depression writers apparently chose their journalistic methods without much premeditation, their strategy was similar to those adopted in other eras of social tension and agitation. In searching for antecedents the depression writers themselves generally looked back no farther than the 1920s; Wilson, for example, acknowledged a debt to H. L. Mencken, but he set himself apart from the "Menckenian gentleman . . . enjoying the debauchment of American life as a burlesque show." Other parallels may be stronger, particularly those with two periods in which journalism, weighted with social purposes, took forms resembling those of depression reportage. As a predecessor, there is muckraking of a certain type. As a successor, there is a school of the New Journalism of the late 1960s.[34]

, The comparison with muckraking rests largely on the similarity of means used to show social injustice. Although categorizing muckraking is a slippery business, it can at least be said that its first phase, before 1906, tended to expose major social institutions — municipal, state, and national government; corporations; labor unions. The later phases concentrated on afflicted classes of people. As in the Great Depression, genteel radicals — in that era, converts to socialism — did much to publicize poverty, child labor, prostitution, slums, and oppression in factory and mills. By far the most celebrated of these works was a novel, *The Jungle.* But there were more: Robert Hunter's *Poverty,* John Spargo's *The Bitter Cry of the Children,* Charles Edward Russell's study of the Trinity Church tenements in New York, Lewis Hine's photographs for the National Child Labor Committee, Ray Stannard Baker's coverage of the 1912 Lawrence textile strike.[35]

Although such work was of lesser literary caliber than that of the depression writers, it shared both function and to an extent technique with it. The aim of the second-wave, socialist muckraking — much in the vein of the depression reportage — was to publicize the suffering of the underclasses, for they had scarcely been noted in the first round, which had concentrated on the harm corruption had done the middle class. In many of these works, the presence of the writer is important. Spargo wrote of his visit to the night shift in a glass factory where the lives of boys were consumed in grueling, dangerous work. Hunter, although he made use of official investigations, also provided personal observations. Baker, who had deplored the power of the unions in a 1903 series, became a partisan eyewitness to the strikers' ordeal in 1912. Many of these articles were directed in a general way toward reform; but as Richard Hofstadter has pointed out, the greatest impact of muckraking was that it changed "the thinking of the country" by providing "a fresh mode of criticism that grew out of journalistic observation." Such, too, was the implied mission of depression reportage.[36]

The parallels with New Journalism are, if anything, stronger. As some depression reportage preceded the depression, forms of the New Journalism began to emerge before the crisis that produced the work most analogous to that of publicizing the depression — that is, of depicting the Vietnam war as a national catastrophe. Again, American consciousness, shielded by government and the press, resisted coming to grips with what radicals saw as reality. Again, a major avenue of dissent was the magazines, and again writers of the left provided much of the journalism. A particularly close parallel with depression reportage can be seen in Norman Mailer's *The Armies of the Night*, which can be said to stand in relation to the war much as *The American Jitters* stood to the depression. Neither seemed to be about the crisis, exactly, yet each was devoted to changing perceptions of it.[37]

There are journalistic similarities as well. In David L. Eason's useful discussion of the New Journalism, he separates strains of "ethnographic realism" and "cultural phenomenology." He sees the former as maintaining the conventional observer's distance in reconstructing reality. The latter, in essence, "explores the reality which actor and spectator create in their interaction" — that is, concedes the presence of the writer. Eason's prime example of ethnographic realism is the work of Tom Wolfe, and of cultural phenomenology *The Armies of the Night*, which he sees as aimed at undercutting "the realm of appearances constituted in the mass media." The depression writers seem to have characteristics of both types. Dos Passos and Wilson in particular seemed to take the traditional observer's role, yet their presence seems always strongly implied. Occasionally Wilson did pop up: "The trouble is that neither the politicians nor the intellectuals have really been hit by the depression . . . I've done unusually well this winter myself." Anderson, of course, was baldly phenomenological: he told the story and told the story of how he found the story. But possibly the key element that links their journalism with that of Mailer is that goal of destabilization, the dissipation of the media's "realm of appearances."[38]

But what about the apparently more obvious links between depression reportage and the mélange of documentary work in the New Deal period? Most treatments have not even distinguished between the rather thin stream of journalism before 1933 and the broad output of the later 1930s. Stott, however, recognizes the importance of the division: The documentary of the early 1930s, he wrote, was designed to upset the status quo, but "when the New Deal came to power, it institutionalized documentary; it made the weapon that undermined the establishment part of the establishment." By extension, the New Deal institutionalized the whole depression crisis, making it the basis of its agenda and the mainspring of its actions.[39]

This was a critical change, for the depression journalism derived its special character by, in effect, swimming upstream. It was not a journalism of affirmation, as much of what followed tended to become. It was by definition negative, tendentious, and unfair in that it gave its attention only to the wounds in the system. It did not cease abruptly with Roosevelt, of course, for many of those on the left initially regarded the New Deal as a continuation of Hooverism. But by the end of the 1930s, as Stott and Kazin have made clear, the sting had long since gone out of the reportage of hardship and social injustice.

In an essay on Edmund Wilson's journalism written in the 1950s, Alfred Kazin wrote a little wistfully that he missed "the frankly 'literary' reportage of national events that used to be done by writers like Theodore Dreiser, H. L. Mencken, John Dos Passos, Edmund Wilson," and wondered why it was "that the literary man on a news story belongs only to a blazing time of troubles." The implied question contains the implied answer — that such journalism becomes important only in a time so out of joint that conventional journalism defaults. So it was with the depression and depression reportage.[40]

Notes

1. Irving Bernstein, *The Lean Years: A History of the American Worker 1920-1933* (Boston: Houghton Mifflin, 1960), p. 257. Polls are cited in Bernard Sternsher, "Introduction," in Sternsher, ed., *Hitting Home: The Great Depression in Town and Country* (Chicago: Quadrangle, 1970), p. 19.

2. One in six: U.S. Bureau of the Census, *Historical Statistics of the United States 1789-1945* (Washington, D.C.: USGPO, 1949), p. 26.

3. Invisibility: Frederick Lewis Allen, *Since Yesterday: The Nineteen-Thirties in America* (New York: Bantam, 1961; first published in 1940), pp. 45-52; Caroline Bird, *The Invisible Scar* (New York: David McKay, 1966), p. 22; and William Stott, *Documentary Expression and Thirties America* (New York: Oxford, 1973), p. 71. "Cold bay fog": William E. Leuchtenburg, *The Perils of Prosperity 1914-1932* (Chicago: University of Chicago Press, 1958), p. 248.

4. *Historical Statistics of the United States*, p. 345. "Alarming effect": John D. Hicks, *Republican Ascendancy 1921-1933* (New York: Harper, 1960), p. 268 (quoting administration supporters).

5. Stott, *Documentary Expression and Thirties America*, p. 68.

6. On Hoover's depression actions, see Hicks, *Republican Ascendancy*, pp. 223 ff.; Arthur M. Schlesinger, Jr., *The Crisis of the Old Order 1919-1933* (Boston: Houghton Mifflin, 1957); and Leuchtenburg, *The Perils of Prosperity*. Seldes: *The Years of the Locust (America, 1929-1932)* (Boston: Little, Brown, 1933), p. 11.

7. On the press in the 1920s, see Silas Bent, *Ballyhoo: The Voice of the Press* (New York: Boni & Liveright, 1927); and Catherine L. Covert, "A View of the Press in the Twenties," *Journalism History* 2 (Autumn 1975): 66-67, 92-96. Hoover caution: news conference of November 29, 1929, *Public Papers . . . 1929* (Washington, D.C.: USGPO, 1974), pp. 401-402. In January 1933, Hoover asked Kent Cooper, general manager of The Associated Press, to suppress speeches by members of Congress that he considered "alarmist." Cooper wrote that he disregarded the request but that the Washington staff had considered the speeches "repetitious, therefore not newsworthy and not reported." Cooper, *Kent Cooper and the Associated Press* (New York: Random House, 1959), pp. 156-57.

8. Cowley, *The Dream of the Golden Mountains: Remembering the 1930s* (New York: Viking, 1980), p. 3; Robert S. Lynd and Helen Merrell Lynd, *Middletown in Transition: A Study in Cultural Conflicts* (New York: Harcourt, Brace, 1937), pp. 15-16; Hallgren, "Easy Times in Middletown," *The Nation*, 6 May 1931, p. 497.

9. Analysis based on front pages printed in Arleen Keylin, ed., *The Depression Years as Reported by The New York Times* (New York: Arno Press, 1976). Davis is quoted in Bernstein, *The Lean Years*, p. 258.

10. Thomas F. Barnhart, "Newspaper Leadership in Times of Depression," *Journalism Quarterly* 10 (March 1933): 1-13.

11. *Editor & Publisher*, 6 May 1933, pp. 3-4. Some in the press believed that it had given the depression too much attention. Earlier in 1933, an upstate New York weekly charged that the newspapers had "sold" the depression and said it would never again mention it. *Editor & Publisher*, the industry weekly, called this an "ostrich sentiment," *ibid.*, 11 February 1933, p. 18. A similar reaction on the part of the old mercantile press to the panic of 1857 is noted in James L. Crouthamel, "The Newspaper Revolution in New York 1830-1860," *New York History* 45 (April 1964): 91-113.

12. Sternsher in *Hitting Home*, p. 20; Leuchtenburg, introduction to Leuchtenburgh ed., *The New Deal: A Documentary History* (Columbia: University of South Carolina Press, 1968), p. xiv; cited in Stott, Documentary *Expression in Thirties America*, p. 69. A compilation from *Reader's Guide* showed an abrupt rise in articles on business conditions and unemployment in 1932-33, after relatively little attention in the two preceding years. Hornell Hart, "Changing Social Attitudes and Interests," in *Recent Social Trends in the United States* (New York: McGraw-Hill, 1933), p. 434.

13. Bernstein, *The Lean Years* p. 316; Susman, "Introduction," in Susman, ed., *Culture and Commitment 1929-1945* (New York: George Braziller, 1973), p. 24. On news values in the 1920s, see not only Bent, *Ballyhoo*, but Covert, "A View of the Press in the Twenties." Covert sees the press of the 1920s as "romantic," and concerned with the inner life of the individual, and by implication in contrast with the concern of the 1930s for the fate of the individual in society.

14. The idea of the potential benefits of publicity is adapted from Sternsher, in *Hitting Home*, pp. 19-20. Note John Kenneth Galbraith's comment: "when the misfortune struck, the attitudes of the time kept anything from being done about it. . . . Nothing, it seemed could be done. And given the ideas which controlled policy, nothing would be done," *The Great Crash 1929* (Boston: Houghton Mifflin, 1955), p. 192. Protests: Bernstein, *The Lean Years*, p. 427, and Keylin, ed., *The Depression Years as Reported by The New York Times*, at the dates specified.

15. Sternsher, *Hitting Home*, pp. 9-10, 17-18. Sternsher in fact finds rather more repression than indifference as the direct response to protests; I refer here to the apparent general public and official attitude. "Illegal self-help": Bernstein, *The Lean Years*, p. 422. John Dos Passos came across a newspaperman in Detroit who told him about "a story that keeps coming in that we don't dare touch" — crowds that came to grocery stores, intimidated the employees, and walked out with food. "Detroit: City of Leisure," *The New Republic*, 27 July 1932, pp. 280-82.

16. Daniel Aaron, *Writers on the Left: Episodes in American Literary Communism* (New York: Harcourt, Brace & World, 1961), especially pp. 173 ff.; Murray Kempton, *Part of Our Time: Some Monuments and Ruins of the Thirties* (New York: Delta, 1967; first published in 1955) pp. 105, 2.

17. Edmund Wilson, "The Literary Consequences of the Crash," in *The Shores of Light: A Literary Chronicle of the Twenties and Thirties* (New York: Farrar Straus Giroux, 1952), p. 498; Fiedler, "The Two Memories: Reflections on Writers and Writing in the Thirties," in David Madden, ed., *Proletarian Writers of the Thirties* (Carbondale and Edwardsville: Southern Illinois University Press, 1968), p. 14. Arthur M. Schlesinger, Jr. wrote of intellectuals of this time: "Mencken had armed them with contempt for American culture, Veblen had exposed the economic system for them, Beard had exhibited the sordid motives behind official ideas. And depression now liquidated their margin of emotional security." *The Crisis of the Old Order*, p. 205. See also Frederick J. Hoffman, *The Twenties: American Writing in the Postwar Decade* (rev. ed., New York: Collier, 1962), pp. 420-21.

18. Kazin, *On Native Ground: An Interpretation of Modern American Prose Literature* (New York: Harcourt, Brace & World, 1942), pp. 490-91, 494-95.

19. Stott, *Documentary Expression and Thirties America*, pp. 143, 171, 189.

20. "Reporting, reporting": *On Native Ground*, p. 491. North, "Reportage," in Henry Hart, ed., *American Writers' Congress* (New York: International, 1935), pp. 120-21. Between Webster II (1934) and Webster III (1962), the Merriam-Webster definition of *reportage* changed from "writing of a journalistic character; reportorial or gossipy style of writing" to "writing intended to give a factual and detailed account of directly observed or carefully documented events."

21. Pells, *Radical Visions and American Dreams: Culture and Social Thought in the Depression Years* (New York: Harper & Row, 1973) p. 197.

22. Cowley, *The Dream of the Golden Mountains*, p. 3; Hallgren, *Seeds of Revolt* (1933), p. 5, quoted in Stott, *Documentary Expression and Thirties America*, p. 71; Dos Passos in Townsend Ludington, ed., *The Fourteenth Chronicle: Letters and Diaries of John Dos Passos* (Boston: Gambit, 1973), p. 397.

23. For emphasis on *New Masses*, see Aaron, *Writers on the Left*. Gastonia incident: Wilson, "The Literary Consequences of the Crash," p. 498. See also Cowley, *The Dream of the Golden Mountains*, pp. 4, 9. Vorse article: "Gastonia," *Harper's* 159 (November 1929): 700-10.

24. "Elizabethton, Tennessee": *The Nation*, 1 May 1929, pp. 526-27. "Factory Town": *The New Republic*, 26 March 1930, pp. 143-44. "Danville, Virginia": *ibid.*, 21 January 1931, pp. 266-68. *Puzzled America* (New York: Charles Scribner's Sons). In general, only the first place of publication of articles will be cited here. Many of the *New Republic* articles were reprinted in Groff Conklin, ed., *The New Republic Anthology 1915-1935* (New York: Dodge, 1936). Anderson's depression writing has been reprinted in part not only in *Puzzled America* but in Jack Salzman et al., eds. *Sherwood Anderson: The Writer at His Craft* (Mamaroneck, N.Y.: Paul P. Appel, 1979). On Anderson's activities, see Irving Howe, *Sherwood Anderson* (New York: William Sloane Associates, 1951), pp. 206 ff.; and Howard

Mumford Jones and Walter B. Rideout, eds., *Letters of Sherwood Anderson* (Boston: Little, Brown, 1953), pp. 204-33.

25. "Detroit: City of Leisure"; "Red Day on Capitol Hill," *The New Republic*, 23 December 1931, pp. 153-55. *In All Countries* (New York: Harcourt, Brace). For details of Dos Passos' activities, see Ludington, *John Dos Passos: A Twentieth Century Odyssey* (New York: Dutton, 1980), pp. 286-310; and Melvin Landsberg, *Dos Passos' Path to U.S.A.* (Boulder: The Colorado Associated University Press, 1972), pp. 168 ff. and bibliography, pp. 260 ff.

26. "Foster and Fish": *The New Republic*, 24 December 1930, pp. 158-62. When the article was republished in Wilson's *The American Earthquake*, Wilson admitted to the "kind of thing that is to be sedulously avoided by honest reporters" — that is, characterizing a witness by physical impression and personal bias (p. 194). Robert Cantwell later insisted that Marxist bias sent Wilson's journalism into a downward spiral that lasted three decades. Few agree. See Cantwell, "Wilson as Journalist," *The Nation*, 22 February 1958, pp. 166-70. "Communists and Cops": *The New Republic*, 11 February 1931, pp. 344-47. "Detroit Motors": *ibid.*, 25 March 1931, pp. 145-50. Coal country: "Frank Keeney's Coal Diggers," *ibid.*, 8, 15 July 1931, pp. 195-99, 229-31. Kentucky poverty: "Red Cross and County Agent," *Scribner's* 90 (September 1931): 249-58. Scottsboro: "The Freight-Car Case," *The New Republic*, 26 August 1931, pp. 38-43. "Hoover Dam": *ibid.*, 26 September 1931, pp. 66-69. Los Angeles: "City of Our Lady Queen of the Angels," *ibid.*, 2, 9 December 1931, pp. 67-8, 89-93.

27. "The Jumping-Off Place," *The New Republic*, 23 December 1931, pp. 156-58. The earlier portrayals of suicide were in "A Bad Day in Brooklyn," *ibid.*, 22 April 1931, pp. 263-66; and "The First of May," which appeared first in *The American Jitters* (Freeport, N.Y.: Books for Libraries Press, 1968; first published in 1932), pp. 132-43. "Hull-House in 1932," *The New Republic*, 18 January, 25 January, 31 January 1933, pp. 260-62, 287-90, 317-22. "Inaugural Parade": *ibid.*, 22 March 1933, pp. 154-56. Wilson's depression reporting appeared not only in *The American Jitters* but in *The American Earthquake* (Garden City, N.Y.: Doubleday, 1958). Book-length studies include Sherman Paul, *Edmund Wilson: A Study of Literary Vocation in Our Time* (Urbana: University of Illinois Press, 1967); and Leonard Kriegel, *Edmund Wilson* (Carbondale and Edwardsville: Southern Illinois University Press, 1971). For a recent discussion, see George H. Douglas, "Edmund Wilson: The Man of Letters as Journalist," *Journal of Popular Culture* 15 (Fall 1981): 78-85.

28. Kazin, *On Native Ground*; Stott, *Documentary Expression and Thirties America*; and Pells, *Radical Visions and American Dreams*, all have discussions of the "road" books.

29. Kazin, "Edmund Wilson on the Thirties," in *Contemporaries* (Boston: Little, Brown, 1962), p. 408.

30. New York *Times*, January 20, 1931; Wilson, "Communists and Cops," pp. 344-47.

31. Adamic, "Virginians on Strike," *The New Republic*, 24 December 1930, pp. 163-64; Anderson, "Danville, Virginia." "Facts elude me": quoted in Brom Weber, review of *Sherwood Anderson's Memories*, *Saturday Review*, 23 August 1969, p. 39.

32. Hallgren's series began with "How Many Hungry?," *The Nation*, 10 February 1932, pp. 159-61; and concluded with "Help Wanted — For Chicago," *ibid.*, 11 May 1932, pp. 534-36. For Wilson's descriptions, see the third part of "Hull-House in 1932."

33. Michael Schudson, *Discovering the News: A Social History of American Newspapers* (New York: Basic Books, 1978), pp. 88-120.

34. Wilson, "The Literary Consequences of the Crash," p. 492. Murray Kempton also distinguished Wilson from Mencken, who "sat in Baltimore all through Edmund

Wilson's rootless, desperate voyage into the storm." *Part of Our Time*, p. 114. Alfred Kazin suggested an interesting parallel between Wilson and Henry Adams, each of them, he proposed, "not a reporter but a literary artist driven by historical imagination." Kazin, "Edmund Wilson on the Thirties," p. 409.

35. For background on sociological muckraking, see in particular Robert H. Bremner, *From the Depths: The Discovery of Poverty in the United States* (New York: New York University Press, 1956); Upton Sinclair's *The Jungle* (New York: Doubleday-Page, 1906); Hunter's *Poverty* (New York: Macmillan, 1904); Spargo's *The Bitter Cry of the Children* (New York: Macmillan, 1906) and Russell's "The Tenements of Trinity Church" in *Everybody's* 19 (July 1908): 47-57. Lewis Hine began his work for the National Child Labor Committee in 1907; and Baker's "The Revolutionary Strike . . . at Lawrence, Massachusetts" appeared in *American Magazine* 74 (May 1912): 19-30, censored over Baker's objections.

36. Hofstadter, *The Age of Reform from Bryan to F. D. R.* (New York: Knopf, 1955), p. 198. On the effects of muckraking, see also Kazin, *On Native Ground*, pp. 82-83; and Jay Martin, "The Literature of Argument and the Arguments of Literature: The Aesthetics of Muckraking," in John M. Harrison and Harry H. Stein, eds., *Muckraking Past Present and Future* (University Park: Pennsylvania State University Press, 1973), pp. 100-15.

37. *The Armies of the Night: History as a Novel; The Novel as History* was published in 1968.

38. Eason, "New Journalism and the Image-World: Two Modes of Organizing Experience," in Jack Salzman, ed., *Prospects: An Annual of American Cultural Studies* 8 (1983), in press. "Unusually well": Wilson, "Still — ; Meditations of a Progressive," *The New Republic*, 8 April 1931, pp. 198-200.

39. Stott, *Documentary Expression and Thirties America*, p. 92.

40. Kazin, "Edmund Wilson on the Thirties," p. 405.

11 Moral Guardians of the Movies and Social Responsibility of the Press

Two Movements toward a Moral Center

Mark Fackler

Orestes A. Brownson, the Unitarian transcendentalist who would later become a Catholic, was incensed. Guardians of culture lurked everywhere. "Matters have come to such a pass, that a peaceable man can hardly venture to eat or drink, or to go to bed or get up, to correct his children or to kiss his wife, without obtaining the permission and direction of some moral . . . society."[1]

The year was 1838, but the sentiments of this nineteenth century writer-editor could easily fit a full century later. The moral guardians of mass media, particularly of film, had demonstrated so effectively on behalf of their constituents that Hollywood producers could not afford to ignore them.[2] Indeed, by 1938 producers had submitted to self-regulation, giving temporary stability to the industry and a reprieve from trumpeted claims that movies were wrecking the country's moral fabric. At the same time, producers chaffed under these self-imposed irritations — false fences to creativity which members of any creative industry, squatting like captives behind them, must agitate to break down.

In 1938, however, the guardians were as influential as ever an "interest group" unaffiliated with government and dependent on mass appeal could be. A hundred years after Brownson decried the stultifying influence of his era's guardians, those concerned with the new movie medium could claim a remarkable share of influence, a moral victory in no small measure. Hollywood's big event — called by Westbrook Pegler the "happiest thing that has happened in this world since the armistice" — would be a 1938 Disney fantasy made to the moral prescription: *Snow White.*

Censorship, one of the ugly words of the English language, speaks of repression and bigotry; it warns of tyranny through state power, corporation power, church power — the strong arm of any bureacracy silencing the dissenting voice. The "guardians" of motion picture morals, principally the Legion of Decency, would be typically regarded as censors pure and simple, backward-thinking conservatives struggling to impose on others the restrictions of their narrowly moralistic codes.

Such a critique missed what was frequently perceived as the dilemma of democratic theory: liberty, that elusive ideal, could never be absolute; censorship could never be absent. Liberty required constraints at every level — from speech to sex, business practice to religious practice. That which was prized moste tribe. Psychologists given to the new psychoanalysis were explaining that any lines were subject to quizzical subconscious forces. Philosophers given to scientific naturalism were drawing lines behind the pragmatic creed: if efficient, then right.[3] World views were changing; for media owners and moral guardians, the rumpus over liberty's lines was played out in codes of ethics, professional reviews, and public pressure — all fundamentally democratic processes, and all, suprisingly, to be given sanction and respectability by the Hutchins Commission on Freedom of the Press, author in 1947 of the "social responsibility" theory of the press.[4]

The Guardians Grow

As early as 1895. one year after the first commercial film was shown in New York, the fires of reform began to glow. Wilbur Fisk Crafts established the International Reform Bureau to lobby in Washington against drugs, alcohol, and motion pictures. When actor John C. Rice gave a prolonged kiss to May Irwin in *The Widow Jones* in 1896, one viewer expressed publicly his wish to "smash the vitascope." To the family magazine *Chap Book* he wrote: "The spectacle of their prolonged pasturing on each other's lips was hard to bear. When only life-size, it was beastly. Magnified to gargantuan proportions and repeated three times over, it is absolutely disgusting. . . . The Irwin kiss is no more than a lyric of the stock yards. Such things call for police interference."[5] Such interference came in 1907 when the Chicago chief of police was granted authority to issue mandatory licenses to films. State boards of censorship and various film review boards proliferated during the next decade, aided in large measure by the 1915 Supreme Court *Mutual Film* decision which called the exhibition of motion pictures a "business pure and simple, originated and conducted for profit, like other spectacles, not to be regarded . . . we think, as part of the press . . . or as organs of public opinion."[6] Thus were films cast beyond the protective pale of the First Amendment.

The 1920s saw several disjointed efforts to bring moral pressure against the filmmakers. Six proposals for federal film regulation were presented to Congress in the decade; none passed. John Phelan's "Toledo Study," published in 1919, established that films were the preferred entertainment for most urban dwellers, especially the young, a finding that fueled much of the ensuing debate.[7] Church agencies reacted strongly to Hollywood scandals, such as Mary Pickford's divorce in 1920 and Fatty Arbuckle's manslaughter charge in 1921, but film content was the guardians' chief concern.

At century's turn, films were made to appeal to the working man, and even lurid titles such as *Old Man's Darling* and *Gaieties of Divorce* offered only a restrained eroticism. *Traffic in Souls* (1913) opened the way for the use of sex as a major ingredient in movie plots, and after World War I, when the middle-class audience became Hollywood's target, sex and crime became prominent. Title such as *Forbidden Fruit* and *Why Women Sin* were now a more realistic clue to a film's graphic daring. Advertisements as well told the explicit tale: "The scarlet truth about a reign of terror broken by a night of love." Gangster films — *Little Caesar* (1930), *The Public Enemy* (1931), *Scarface* (1932) — glorified crime and criminals. Mae West's *She Done Him Wrong* (1933) and *I'm No Angel* (1933) were ammunition for the guardians' campaigns. Said William de Mille about the new visual boldness: "The bath became a mystic shrine . . . and the art of bathing was shown as a lovely ceremony. . . . Undressing was not just the taking off of clothes; it was a progressive revelation of entrancing beauty."[8]

An indication of the guardians' grievances is found in the "Thirteen Points" issued by the National Association of the Motion Picture Industry in 1921. The Points expressly prohibited a film's depicting sexual exploitation, white slavery, nudity, prolonged kissing, excessive violence, favorable portrayal of crime figures and the Mafia, and unfavorable depiction of the armed forces.

Against such content the guardians made their appeal. The Catholic *Standard and Times* (Philadelphia) ventured that "no elevating influences can come from the movies. . . . Insidious and evil influences will reach out from the screen as long as moral corruption holds sway behind the camera."[9] Resolutions favoring supervision and regulation of film content by some kind of extra-industry authority were debated and passed by the Protestant Episcopal Church, Methodist Episcopal General Conference, Northern Baptist Convention, and Worldwide Christian Endeavor. In 1922 the General Assembly of the Presbyterian Church instructed its Board of Temperance and Moral Welfare to unite all concerned moral agencies in a coordinated movement for congressional action, specifically for federal censorship.[10] Board director Charles Scanlon organized national conferences for the purpose in 1922, 1924, and 1925. Representatives from the three conferences organized the Federal Motion Picture Council in 1925 with a policy both straightforward and threatening: "Nothing short of intervention by a centralized power outside the motion picture industry can bring about fundamental and permanent changes."[11] The Social Service Commission of the Federal Council of Churches directed a series of studies in 1921 concluding that federal and community measures were necessary to tame the production and distribution companies. Unless decisive action were taken, youth crime would continue to mount, and a generation of impressionable children would be sidetracked from the basics of reading and math.[12]

Along with church action came the state censor boards, which reached their strongest influence in the early 1920s. By 1921 more than 100 motion picture bills were before thirty-seven state legislatures.[13]

The reorganization of the National Association of the Motion Picture Industry in 1922, the establishment of the Hays Office, the cooperative efforts of "interest groups" and the industry in the Committee on Public Relations, and the various industry codes of the 1920s all helped quiet the guardians, at least for a time. The Hays Office was Hollywood's effort to slow the momentum of the various state censorship efforts. In March 1922 the National Association of the Motion Picture Industry was allowed to fade away, and the Motion Picture Producers and Distributors of America (MPPDA) was born with promises to improve the industry's less than stellar reputation for wholesome content. Postmaster General Will H. Hays — a Presbyterian elder, nondrinker, and nonsmoker — was recruited to head the new agency, and indeed he did begin to turn the tide of reform toward self-regulation. Hays won a dramatic victory in Massachusetts when a referendum calling for censorship of films was defeated by a two-to-one margin. Quickly he established the Committee on Public Relations, which included representatives from four Catholic, five Protestant, five Jewish, and forty-three civic and fraternal organizations.[14]

Capping the movie industry's efforts at self-regulation was the Motion Picture Production Code of 1930, written by Martin Quigley, a Catholic layman and owner of motion picture trade publications, and Daniel A. Lord, S.J., professor of dramatics at St. Louis University.[15] Enforcement of the Code was given to the Studio Relations Committee of the MPPDA and later to the Production Code Administration headed by another Catholic, Joseph I. Breen.[16]

Reaction to the Code was mixed. Catholics took some comfort in the reliability of the Code's authors. Protestants were skeptical. The *Chris-*

tian Century editorialized: "If pious resolutions and vows of chastity could have saved the motion picture industry, it would have been saved long ago. The big producers have given us a plethora of promises, but a dearth of deeds. They get converted too often."[17]

Supporters of the Code would insist that it reflected the growing sense of social responsibility in the motion picture business. Geoffrey Shurlock, who succeeded Breen as the PCA chief, wrote: "The innate Americanism of the code operation is underlined by the fact that the industry adopted it quite voluntarily, and out of its own innate sense of responsibility. . . . It is in fact as near to a purely democratic system of industry control as can be found operating anywhere today."[18] By the early 1930s, however, the guardians were ready to abandon any illusions concerning the strength of the Code's influence. Promises by the industry of self-reform were unkept. To many guardians the Code and its enforcement procedures seemed porous and ineffective. The Payne Fund Studies of 1929-33 had underscored popular intuitions that motion pictures were "not good" for children (too much sex and crime). Only a year after the Code was adopted, forty national religious and educational groups were sounding the call for federal regulation.[19]

The threat of government intrusion came at an inauspicious time. Motion pictures had been the nation's fourth largest industry in the 1920s, and the coming of sound helped bridge the box-office crisis that followed in the wake of Wall Street's collapse. By 1933, however, about a third of the country's movie houses were closed. Just as box-office revenues were at their lowest, guardian agencies were forging a loosely organized consensus: something must be done to counter the power and prurience of a major culture industry; the absence of enforced accountability would destroy the country. On the other hand, liberals and libertarians were charging that imposition of narrow moralism would destroy the arts.

In November 1933, six weeks after Vatican spokesman Amleto Cicognani called for a "united and vigorous campaign for the purification of the cinema," the nation's Catholic bishops appointed an Episcopal Committee on Motion Pictures to plan and execute a national campaign, not for federal intervention, but to conform industry practice to its own Code. A 196-word pledge was read in parishes across the country on April 11, 1934, and the Legion of Decency was born. Catholics in each of the 103 U.S. dioceses were encouraged (though not coerced on pain of sin) to commit themselves to the fight against "vile and unwholesome" pictures, to condemn "suggestive advertisements," and to "remain away" from films which offended "decency and Christian morality." Seven to nine million Catholics took the pledge; many from outside the Catholic fold applauded.[20]

During the Legion's first six months, fifty-four non-Catholic agencies lent support. Among them was the Federal Council of Churches (forerunner of the National Council of Churches) which set October 21, 1934, as its day for film criticism, and the announcement of a pledge for Protestants.[21]

While the Legion's immediate goal was the support of a movie code that would eliminate profanity, brutality, and sex, the crusade was symbol of a much more powerful spirit that *Commonweal* perceived when it noted that the vigor of the Legion may "enable the Catholic Church in America to infuse its redemptive life-force into the whole body of our society."[22] Part of the meaning of that life-force was the recovery of community values, the integrity of social groups living prophetically in the midst of a larger society. Against commercial interests in undifferentiated mass audiences, the church primarily, and civic groups also, insisted that their distinctive values ought to be taken seriously, not regarded as obscure or sectarian, by producers of mass media. The guardians' legitimate concerns would be echoed later by such social commentators as C. Wright Mills, lamenting the decline of "voluntary associations" as a "genuine instrument of the public." He would call for "intermediate associations" to negotiate the interests of primary social institutions (family and community) and bureaucracies (media corporations).[23] Jacques Ellul would call this process of authenticating group values a key to cultural survival.[24]

Major themes of the campaign from the Catholic perspective were "redemption," "responsibility," and "guardianship," not the "censorship" or "coercion" that became catchwords for the Legion's critics. Against efforts for federal legislation, the Legion counselled self-regulation by film makers. "The Legion is not an appeal to state action," wrote *Commonweal* in late 1934, "but to the individual conscience. Censorship is prescribed by natural law, by one's own common sense."[25] Catholics did not deny that their efforts involved some form of control, but like the Index of Books, the control was restricted only to films which transgressed the boundaries of a canon law openly negotiated and deeply rooted in the Church's history. Said a church official in 1934: "It is not our business to destroy any industry or business. It is our purpose to protect the souls of the children committed to our keeping. Legitimate recreation is necessary . . . but it must be wholesome and good."[26]

Pope Pius XI's encyclical *Vigilanti cura* (1936), the first major papal statement on cinema, called the movie industry to reckon with its influential place in the social matrix. "The force of a power of such universality as the cinema can be directed with great utility to the highest ends of individual and social improvement. Why, indeed, should the motion picture simply be a means of diversion and light relaxation to occupy an idle hour? With its magnificent power, it can and must be a right and positive guide to what is good."[27] Pius concluded that recreation must be "worthy of the rational nature of man and therefore must be morally healthy."[28]

A year after the Legion was organized, Quigley wrote his position paper in support of industry self-regulation and the role of the Legion in encouraging enforcement of the MPPDA Code. With interests in both the Legion and the Code, he was in a unique position to offer a rationale for "pressure group" influence: "The system proposed has its essence in the freely accepted responsibility of the producer properly to govern his activities. . . . Regulatory methods are not imposed by an external force but rather are voluntarily set up by, for and within the industry."[29]

How close was this concept and strategy of moral guardianship to the "social responsibility of the press" thesis fermenting in the 1930s and finally articulated by the Hutchins Commission in 1947?

The Crisis of Democratic Theory

The Thirties saw no sterner critic of the guardians than the noted civil liberties attorney Morris Ernst. On the eve of 1930 he and Pare Lorentz noted the "serious and unhealthy condition" of American liberty and warned that another world war might result from state control of media. The unknowing perpetrators of that holocaust, he thought, were the industrial, legislative, and social-institutional censors. The two authors wrote: "Fanaticism reaches an epitome of organization in movie censorship. The movie censor is a curious exhibit, not only because he has flagellated life and courage from a promising craft, but because he has gained strength and has the dignity of law, salary, mother and churches by his side."[30]

On the surface, Ernst's claim that controlled media leads to war seems exaggerated and irresponsible. It reflects, however, one of the chief intellectual battles of the interwar years. Moral absolutism, which many intellectuals perceived to be the thrust of the guardians' campaigns, favors totalitarian government, they maintained. Only an open universe of relativism and moral skepticism is conducive to the process of democratic compromise and concession. During the 1930s most American intellectuals were committed to a scientific naturalism that perceived itself the true champion of democracy. The enemies were those who advocated a revival of moral absolutes, of whom the Catholics "were the most powerful and therefore the most dangerous."[31]

Nonetheless a vigorous reaction to the naturalistic world view arose in the Thirties. Around Harvard professors Paul Elmer More and Babbitt Irving gathered a movement to resist the breakdown in the duality of man and nature, to object to naturalism's "ostensible abnegation of spiritual values, its concentration on the coarse, irrational aspects of human existence."[32] The New Humanists looked to tradition for their timeless truths and regarded human nature as unchanging in its essence.[33] The Southern Agrarians called for a return to the best of the past as a way to secure the humanitarian future. *I'll Take My Stand*, written by Twelve Southerners in 1930, observed how thoroughly accepted were the theories and practices of pure and applied science, but runaway investment in them "has enslaved our human energies to a degree now clearly felt to be burdensome."[34] To rectify bankrupt social theory Pitirim Sorokin was collecting mountains of data, proving, he thought, that the twentieth century was the most violent and wicked century ever. That decade's sensate world view he considered the most ominous threat to civilization faced by man.[35] In Catholic circles the writings of Thomas Aquinas were being revived, and liberal Protestants were beginning to abandon their optimistic platitudes for some old doctrine, albeit in new garments, which took more seriously man's capacity for evil.[36] At the University of Chicago a revival of classicism was challenging the positivistic biases of pragmatism and cultural relativism. Unless values could be demonstrated and the "civilization of the Dialogue" recovered,[37] the foundations of democratic theory — human freedom and moral order — would be lost to nihilism or fascism. Western culture was vulnerable to both, argued leaders of the resurgence in metaphysics — scholars and writers such as Robert Hutchins, Reinhold Niebuhr, William Ernest Hocking, Archibald MacLeish, and George Shuster. Even empiricists Harold Lasswell, Charles Merriam, and Robert Redfield were swayed to relinquish hard-line positivism for a humanism that allowed for moral discourse and conviction. These spokesmen were, of course, the intellectual leaders of the Commission that in 1947 issued *A Free and Responsible Press* and that called the media, including motion pictures, to a new sense of social responsibility.

The Commission on Freedom of the Press was instigated by publisher Henry Luce in late 1942. With a sizable grant from Time, Inc., University of Chicago president Robert M. Hutchins gathered twelve distinguished scholars and several foreign advisers for two years of meetings and hearings. Several books were the result, but the Commission's joint conclusions were published in a thin volume in 1947. The Report, as the book has come to be called, was roundly criticized by most media professionals, for in it the Commission took issue with the traditional liberal notion of the laissez-faire marketplace of ideas.[38]

Protestant and Catholic pressure groups had long extolled the virtues of cooperation between industry and guardian agency, claiming that the long-range interests of each were the same: "making human life richer."[39] The findings of the Hutchins Commission were strikingly parallel. Basically the commission recognized the need to extend constitutional protection to motion pictures while at the same time creating a recognized and accessible forum for public feedback.[40] The latter, the commission suggested, might take the form of citizens' committees "not to further narrow purposes, but to encourage worthy achievement."[41] The commission proposed a national advisory board as its version of the movement toward federal control. It endorsed government efforts to break monopolistic practices in the industry, perhaps its bow to federal-control pressure groups. But in the final analysis, the commission placed responsibility for house-cleaning and civic benevolence in the hands of the house owners and occupants, the producers. Guardian agencies had always maintained that the end product of their effort was a higher industrial consciousness, and to this notion the commission gave its third-party approbation. "We take the view that the long-range self-interest of the movies and the public interest coincide in large part. . . . Ultimately, progress depends upon the enlightenment and public spirit of those who control the movie industry."[42]

The commission was much more inclined toward the theoretical claims of guardian agencies than they were toward the anti-agency libertarians. Freedom "is not synonymous with complete lack of control," the report on film claimed. "Defining the basis and extent of control, not the existence of any controls whatsoever, is the question."[43] Concerning the social legitimacy of guardian agencies, the commission was not insensitive: "How can the public will prevail and order be maintained," it questioned, "and at the same time, dissident minorities have their proper influence for change?"[44] An on-going citizens' review board was the commission's formal answer, but toward that goal the Legion itself was accorded a measure of approval: "To liberals the Legion of Decency is anathema; yet the Legion is completely within its rights. It merely reviews pictures and publicizes its recommendations to its own constituency. The Legion does not attempt to dictate what all movie-goers are to see. Only because of its size and the faithfulness of its followers does the industry pay attention to its ratings. Any other similar group would receive equal consideration."[45]

Harvard philosopher William Ernest Hocking wrote the apologia for the Hutchins Commission. He rooted his argument firmly in the Western tradition of free expression, yet Hocking was no more an absolutist than was Milton. He recognized the responsibility of value-conscious groups to participate in the commerce of ideas, and acknowledged that the

state had an interest in legally restricting the outer moral fringes of entertainment media content. Participation by guardian agencies in the criticism of media fare was part of the fundamental process of democracy. The
"utterer of ideas" should expect and welcome "the type of pressure we may
call moral," so long as those pressures refrain from coercive forms such as
"bribes or loss of basic rights or needs."46 The industry had positive
responsibilities to the culture; if the industry wished the freedom to draw
its own guidelines of decency, let it take those positive public responsibilities seriously.

> The agencies of amusement and art touch the most potent springs of the
> emotional unity in which alone, through the meeting of minds, public
> discussion can be fruitful. This is why degradation of the arts through
> commercialized vulgarity, claiming the cover of freedom, stands out as so
> vital a blow to freedom. What men decide to enjoy is not purely a private
> concern. A vulgarized art elicits disintegrating rather than uniting emo-
> tions. If the agencies of amusement and art recover a sense of the dignity
> of their social function . . . the instinct of regulation . . . would be put to
> rest.47

Prior to their gathering as a commission, Hutchins and Niebuhr,
Hocking and Chafee, Ruml, MacLeish, Shuster, and Schlesinger had been
independently sorting through the remnants of the 1930s to assist in the
recovery of democratic values.

Hutchins, controversial president of the University of Chicago,
was urging that democracy required belief in the difference between "truth
and falsity, good and bad, right and wrong, and that truth, goodness, and
right are objective standards even though they cannot be experimentally
verified."48 All his life, Hutchins claimed, had been a search for standards
and a search for community.49 The search had turned up obvious cultural
differences between human communities, but a deeper unity — a universal
human nature — was the guarantor of human solidarity and the measuring
rod of freedom. "No matter how environments differ human nature is,
always has been, and always will be the same everywhere. Above all
nations is humanity; and beneath all human law and custom lies the
natural moral law which is the same for all men."50

Fullfillment for human beings, Hutchins thought, comes in the
"fullest exercise of their highest powers; that is, in living in accordance with
virtue and intelligence."51 Rhetoric closer to that employed by the guardians (especially in Catholic circles) can hardly be imagined.

MacLeish, while strongly opposed to the particulars of the Movie
Code and the Legion's pledge, did acknowledge a general moral obligation
borne by the movie industry:

> It is necessary now for the motion picture industry . . . to face the fact that an attempt of the industry to evade responsibility for the formation of American opinion by protesting that it had no relation to the formation of opinion . . . is a protest without truth or merit. . . . The motion-picture industry bears a primary and inescapable responsibility . . . for the failure of the American people to understand . . . the nature of the world they lived in and the dangers which that world presented.[52]

The source of the modern crisis, wrote MacLeish, was the loss of a moral center. "The crisis of our time . . . is a failure of the spirit to imagine and desire. . . . Actually the issue, the one issue we should talk about is this: What do we love? What truly do we love? To what do we desire to be loyal?"[53]

Schlesinger, another ardent liberal who would never surrender traditional media freedoms, applauded the work of voluntary organizations as "one of the strongest taproots of the nation's well-being." Far from posing an anti-democratic threat, "self-constituted bodies have seldom been a divisive factor and never for long. Reaching out with interlocking membership to all parts of the country, embracing all ages, classes, creeds, and ethnic groups, they have constantly demonstrated the underlying unity that warrants diversity. They have served as a great cementing force for national integration."[54]

The diffusion of power through society via moral agencies was a theme in the writings of Merriam, Ruml, Clark, and Lasswell. Merriam saw moral agencies as "non-legal courts of appeal and centers of resistance against the absolutism of political authority."[55] Clark urged balance between various decision-making groups in an economy so that no one will overpower or control any of the others.[56] Ruml considered family, trade union, and church as "private governments within whose pluralistic rule-making and rule-enforcement the individual must find his dignity and freedom."[57] The key task, he wrote, was generating "homefulness," a society in which the traditions and culture of all groups are respected.[58] Lasswell spoke up for the notion of non-governmental specialists exerting leadership in social planning.[59] During commission deliberations, Lasswell argued that "informal groups" rather than courts of law could settle disputes over the truthfulness of media reports. "No one government or private agency can be trusted to get at the truth. . . . The determination by private processes has the advantage that people can take it or leave it — no police back the statements of authority. The role of the state is kept at a minimum."[60]

Chafee severely criticized the Legion, but nearly in the same breath advocated the principle of "wisely constituted private groups" providing affirmative guidance to the media: "The press will not serve a democratic society adequately without affirmative action to make the press do a better job. Not that all of this action has to be governmental. Part, at least, of the guidance desired will come from self-regulation within the communications industries and from wisely constituted private groups."[61]

Niebuhr, critical of Catholic absolutism and institutionalism, nevertheless praised the Church's provision of an "integral community in the cold technical togetherness of an urban culture."[62] He called city dwellers people held together by common productive processes, not by "human bonds." Spiritually isolated though dependent on common mechanical devices, the modern person struggled to maintain "the moral and cultural traditions [needed] to save his life from anarchy."[63] In his introduction to Schramm's *Responsibility in Mass Communication,* Niebuhr still viewed the guardians' influence as negative, but accorded them the privilege of organizing as a more powerful form of protest than the lone customer refusing to buy.[64]

Hocking admonished the "free arts" to "regain their rootage in the universal . . . in religion" as a proper situation in which to explore human feeling.[65] The arts have been conducted at times during the liberal era as if freedom from churchly limitations gave warrant for the rejection "of all standards, trying to live experimentally with none at all," an independence that has blinded art to the "sense of its own message to mankind."[66] "Freedom is not enough . . . repentence is due. Without standard, no art, no right, no truth, no joy in living, no civilization to transmit."[67]

The working out of personal moral character is the goal of the "cosmic process," wrote Hocking,[68] and in that quest, the influence of Catholic thinking on the arts is an expression of the Church's recovery of a holistic world view.[69]

Virtue-bound freedom was central to Hocking's philosophy of communication. Speech and artistic expression must be free, but not unrestrained. "To the hideous perils and absurdities of the Censorship, we must join the equally hideous perils, hypocrisies and humbugs of No-censorship. And so for all the items of the Liberal program. In every point, men must be free; and in every point they must be subject to a sobering objective judgment which checks that freedom."[70] Hocking's *Framework of Principle* would outline a theory of freedom that respected moral norms as it urged individual consciences to contribute to the human library of ideas.

Shuster, a devout Catholic, took issue at several points with his Church's social and political programs. Nowhere in his public writings did he specifically herald the Legion's campaign. While many Catholics were busy building optimism around a revival of Thomism, Shuster steered from the universe of laws and abstract designs toward a recovery of "freshness of reality and confidence in experimental intuition."[71] Early Shuster had applauded the resurgent metaphysics and noted the limited role of science in resolving the moral crisis.[72] In view of the cultural malaise, he would restore "moral balance" by banning relativism "as if it were the plague, and insist that discernment of the good has been the rigorous business of all the rigorous philosophies."[73] Though the media did not figure significantly in Shuster's writings, he did acknowledge the press's responsibility to "build community" through its educational function.[74]

In this fashion did spokesmen for social responsiblity theory of the press share common ground with the guardians of motion picture content. On policy and program they would differ, but on fundamental issues they were remarkably alike. Against the parade of changing intellectual paradigms — Newton to Einstein, Locke to Freud, Aristotle to Wittgenstein — the guardians and the leaders of social responsibility theory argued for a recovery of man as unique, rational, and free (however morally fragile and susceptible to the corruptions of a prevailing materialist ethos). Society might be an experiment, but one incorporating moral parameters and responsibilities that applied as much to the present as the past and upon which the future could be successfully planned. The centralizing, bureaucratic direction of technology and scientific naturalism was ably counterbalanced by voluntary associations representing value-conscious groups within the social whole. Beneficient social progress would require each person contributing a responsible share to the commonweal, not coerced or oppressed, but freely joined with others for the promotion and preservation of the moral givens of Western heritage. Specifically, owners of media could no longer regard their channels as purely private property. A new awareness of the interdependency of the postwar world urged media owners toward a wider vision of their role, in essence, toward a moral vision.

Perhaps the milieu of the thirties was especially ripe for the guardians and the responsibility theorists. Oppression loomed heavily in Europe; economic chaos tore at the nation's internal stability. Then, as a half century later, "value-conscious publics" and the notion of freedom bounded by virtue were regarded by the media with considerable suspicion. Then, as later, persons outside media institutions sought a voice in the quality of the cultural products offered them. If the guardians' policies were time-bound and flawed, the broader perspectives of social responsibility theory might still hold pathfinding powers.

Notes

1. Orestes A. Brownson, "Ultraism," *Boston Quarterly Review* 1 (July 1838): 379.

2. Moral guardians refer to the non-governmental agencies which tried through chiefly non-legal means to bring change to the content of media fare. This "interactional" change is a basic form of democratic social dialogue, since it depends on public opinion and moral suasion, not on the powers of courts or the military.

3. For a cogent review of the conflict in moral reasoning during the interwar years, see Edward A. Purcell, Jr., *The Crisis of Democratic Theory: Scientific Naturalism and the Problem of Value* (Lexington: The University Press of Kentucky, 1973).

4. The Commission met from February 1944 to September 1946 and included Robert M. Hutchins, Zechariah Chafee, Jr., John M. Clark, John Dickinson, William Ernest Hocking, Harold D. Lasswell, Archibald MacLeish, Charles E. Merriam, Reinhold Niebuhr, Robert Redfield, Beardsley Ruml, Arthur M. Schlesinger, and George N. Shuster.

5. Quoted in Geoffrey Shurlock, "The Film Industry and Self-Regulation," in *The Responsibility of Press,* ed. Gerald Gross (New York: Fleet, 1966), p. 338.

6. *Mutual Film Corporation* v. *Industiral Commission of Ohio,* 236 U.S. 230, 35 S. Ct. 287 (1915). That decision was not rectified until 1952 when the Supreme Court would hold that a New York law banning sacrilegious films was an abridgement of free speech. In *Joseph Burstyn, Inc.* v. *Wilson,* 343 U.S. 495, 96 L. Ed. 1098, 72 S. Ct. 777 (1952). Nearly a decade later the Court would be called upon to further define the nature of First Amendment protection for motion pictures. In a 5-4 decision, the Court would rule that prior censorship of motion pictures was not in itself unconstitutional. In *Times Film Corp.* v. *City of Chicago,* 365 U.S. 43, 5 L. Ed. 2d 403, 81 S. Ct. 391 (1961).

7. Garth Jowett, *Film: The Democratic Art* (Boston: Little, Brown, 1976), p. 215.

8. Quoted in *ibid.,* p. 188. Also see Jowett for a summary of film content during the era.

9. "Time to Clean Up Movie Morals," *Literary Digest,* 15 October 1921, pp. 28-29.

10. For a review of censorship action, see Ruth Inglis, *Freedom of the Movies* (Chicago: University of Chicago Press, 1947), and the *Annals of the American Academy of Political and Social Science* 128 (November 1926).

11. Catheryne Cooke Gilman, "Government Regulations for the Movies," *Christian Century,* 26 August 1931, pp. 1066-68.

12. Dean Charles N. Lathrop, "Motion Pictures and the Churches," *The Playground* 16 (October 1922): 308, 342.

13. The Federal Council of Churches' Social Science Commission reported in 1922 that thirty-two state legislatures considered censorship bills in 1921. See Lathrop, "Motion Pictures," p. 364. Howard T. Lewis sets the number at thirty-six in *The Motion Picture Industry* (New York: Van Nostrand, 1933), p. 367. Inglis reports thirty-seven in *Freedom of the Movies,* p. 71.

14. Inglis, *Freedom of the Movies,* (pp. 101-102), lists the groups represented. Such members as the National Association of Book Publishers, the National Education Association, and the Woodcraft League of America indicate that "moral guardians" were not all affiliated with organized religion.

15. The 1930 Code recited a long list of prohibitions, adding to previous lists such things as the depiction of revenge, the finger (gesture), dances suggestive of sexual actions, and articulation of such vulgarisms as "madam," "slut," "broad," "tom cat," "whore," "fanny," traveling salesman or farmer's daughter jokes, and "hell" (except with certain prescribed qualifications). The entire Code is reprinted in Inglis, *Freedom of the Movies,* pp. 205-219.

16. The Production Code Administration, a part of the Hays Office, became a serious force in movie content after the Legion of Decency was organized by Catholics in 1934. The PCA label was thereafter required on all films released by MPPDA member studios, and a $25,000 fine was the penalty for noncompliance. It is a tribute to Hays's acumen that he put Breen in charge. The latter had helped organize the Legion of Decency, was a tough negotiator, yet mediated successfully between competing interest groups. Breen developed the concept of "compensating moral values" to save the Code from casuistry.

17. "The Movies are Converted Again," *Christian Century*, 9 April 1930, p. 455.

18. Shurlock, "Film Industry and Self-Regulation," p. 344.

19. W. W. Charters, *Motion Pictures and Youth* (New York: Macmillan, 1933), pp. 60-63; and *Christian Century*, 21 October 1931, p. 1301.

20. The two important studies on the founding of the Legion are Gerald Kelly, S.J., and John C. Ford, S.J., "The Legion of Decency," *Theological Studies* 18 (September 1957): 387-433; and Paul W. Facey, S.J., "The Legion of Decency: A Sociological Analysis of the Emergence and Development of a Social Pressure Group" (Ph.D. dissertation, Fordham University, 1945). A recent study has added some significant details; see William M. Halsey, *The Survival of American Innocence* (Notre Dame: University of Notre Dame Press, 1980), pp. 119-21.

21. Federal Council of Churches of Christ in America *Biennial Report* (1934), p. 73.

22. "Progress of the Legion of Decency," *Commonweal*, 17 August 1934, p. 375.

23. C. Wright Mills, *The Power Elite* (New York: Oxford University Press, 1956; Galaxy Books, 1959), pp. 306-11.

24. Jacques Ellul, *The Political Illusion*, trans. Konrad Kellar (New York: Vintage Books, 1967), p. 217.

25. T. O'R. Boyle, "We Are All Censors," *Commonweal*, 21 December 1934, p. 227.

26. Quote by the Most Rev. John T. McNichols, O.P., archbishop of Cincinnati, at the National Catholic Education Association meeting in Chicago, 1934. In "Campaign Against Objectionable Motion Pictures," *Catholic World* 139 (August 1934): 617.

27. Quoted in Murray Schumach, *The Face on the Cutting Room Floor* (New York: William Marrow, 1964), p. 88.

28. Quoted in *Catholic World* 143 (August 1936): 618.

29. Martin Quigley, *Decency in Motion Pictures* (New York: Macmillan, 1937), p. 51.

30. Morris L. Ernst and Pare Lorentz, *Censored: The Private Life of the Movies* (New York: Jonathan Cape and Harrison Smith, 1930), p. 199.

31. Purcell, *Crisis of Democratic Theory*, p. 208.

32. Charles C. Alexander, *Nationalism in American Thought, 1930-1945* (Chicago: Rand McNally, 1969), p. 27.

33. *Ibid.* Also see Clarence J. Karier, *Man, Society, and Education* (Chicago: Scott, Foresman, 1967), p. 186.

34. Andrew Nelson Lytle, "The Hind Tit," in *I'll Take My Stand* (New York: Harper and Brothers, 1930; reprint ed., Harper Torchbooks, 1962), p. 205.

35. For insights into Sorokin's work, see his autobiography, *A Long Journey* (New Haven, Conn.: College and University Press, 1963).

36. Neo-Thomism arose in reaction to sociological jurisprudence and legal realism. Catholic legal scholars led by Dean Clarence Manion at Notre Dame argued that natural law is a guide to the validity of the claims of positive law. Neo-orthodoxy was a Protestant reaction to liberal notions of man's perfectability and historical progress. Neo-orthodox theologians, among whom Niebuhr was pre-eminent, argued the necessity of divine grace, the validity of divine revelation, and the evil of human sin, without, of course, taking Scripture with the same literalness as did the Reformers.

37. This was Robert M. Hutchins' term for the heritage of Western culture. See his *The Higher Learning in America* (New Haven, Conn.: Yale University Press, 1936), and *Great Books: The Foundation of a Liberal Education* (New York: Simon and Shuster, 1954).

38. The Commission on Freedom of the Press, *A Free and Responsible Press* (Chicago: University of Chicago Press, 1947). Also see Fred S. Siebert, *et al., Four Theories of the Press* (Urbana: University of Illinois Press, 1956), pp. 39-104.

39. "The Movies: Entertainment Plus Education," *Christian Century* 55 (27 April 1938): 521.

40. *A Free and Responsible Press,* p. 100.

41. Inglis, *Freedom of the Movies,* p. v.

42. *Ibid.,* pp. 23-24.

43. *Ibid.,* p. 172.

44. *Ibid.,* p. 173.

45. *Ibid.,* p. 190.

46. William Ernest Hocking, *Freedom of the Press: A Framework of Principle* (Chicago: University of Chicago Press, 1947), pp. 137-38.

47. *Ibid.,* pp. 206-207.

48. Robert M. Hutchins, "What Shall We Defend?" *Vital Speeches,* 1 July 1940, p. 548.

49. Robert M. Hutchins, "First Glimpses of a New World," *Saturday Review,* 4 December 1965, p. 33.

50. Robert M. Hutchins, "Toward a Durable Society," *Fortune* 27 (June 1943): 201.

51. *Ibid.,* p. 159.

52. Archibald MacLeish, *A Time to Act* (Boston: Houghton Mifflin, 1943), p. 150.

53. Archibald MacLeish, *A Time to Speak* (Boston: Houghton Mifflin, 1940), pp. 2-3, 6.

54. Arthur M. Schlesinger, "Biography of a Nation of Joiners," *American Historical Review* 50 (October 1944): 25.

55. Charles E. Merriam, *Systematic Politics* (Chicago: University of Chicago Press, 1945), p. 40.

56. Edward James Powers, "The Social Economics of John Maurice Clark" (Ph.D. dissertation, Boston College Graduate School, 1967), p. 66.

57. Beardsley Ruml, *Government, Business and Values* (New York: Harper and Brothers, 1943), p. 31.

58. *Ibid.,* p. 48.

59. Larry Robert Matheny, "Harold D. Lasswell and the Crisis of Liberalism" (Ph.D. dissertation, University of Virginia, 1969), p. 198.

60. Chicago, University of Chicago, Commission on Freedom of the Press Papers, Document 17.

61. Zechariah Chafee, Jr., *Government and Mass Communication* (Chicago: University of Chicago Press, 1947), p. 686.

62. Reinhold Niebuhr and Alan Heimart, *A Nation So Conceived* (New York: Charles Scribner's Sons, 1963), p. 59.

63. Reinhold Niebuhr, *Leaves from the Notebook of a Tamed Cynic* (Cleveland: Meridian Books, 1929), p. 139.

64. Reinhold Neibuhr, Introduction to *Responsibility in Mass Communication,* by Wilbur Schramm (New York: Harper and Row, 1957), p. xv.

65. William Ernest Hocking, *The Coming World Civilization* (New York: Harper and Brothers, 1956), p. 84.

66. *Ibid.*

67. *Ibid.*

68. William Ernest Hocking, "This Is My Faith," in *This Is My Faith*, ed. Steward G. Cole (New York: Harper and Brothers, 1956), p. 143.

69. Hocking, *Coming*, p. 135.

70. William Ernest Hocking, *The Lasting Elements of Individualism* (New Haven: Yale University Press, 1937), p. 175.

71. Halsey, *Survival of American Innocence*, p.96.

72. George N. Shuster, *Catholic Education in a Changing World* (New York: Holt, Rinehart and Winston, 1967), p. 210.

73. George N. Shuster, *Education and Moral Wisdom* (New York: Harper and Brothers, 1960), p. 38.

74. George N. Shuster, *The Ground I Walked On*, 2nd ed. (South Bend, Ind.: University of Notre Dame Press, 1969), p. 94.

12 "We May Hear Too Much"

American Sensibility and the Response to Radio, 1919-1924

Catherine L. Covert

I have always dodged this radio question," Chief Justice William Howard Taft is reported to have said during the early years of broadcasting. "Interpreting the law on this subject is something like trying to interpret the law of the occult. It seems like dealing with something supernatural. I want to put it off as long as possible."[1]

Taft could not be considered an innocent. His public life encompassed both the Radio Act of 1912 when he was president and the Radio Act of 1927 when he was chief justice. Yet here he expressed quite simply the bafflement many people felt when confronted with something so new, so incomprehensible as radio. All he could do was to reach for an old metaphor; invoking the "supernatural" was an ancient way of comprehending the new and making it accessible to the understanding.

This chapter focuses on such organizing ideas and images that Americans used to make sense — either intellectual or emotional sense out of what they saw and heard as they experienced radio's startling impact on sensibility after the Great War.[2]

Americans talked enthusiastically of the new radio in these years, borrowing prewar images of heroism and venture to describe their experiments with batteries and headsets. Most historians of radio have also focused primarily on the wonder, joy, and excitement radio produced.[3]

Barnouw would entitle an entire section of his first volume on radio history, "The Euphoria of 1922."[4] Radio did represent a remarkable expansion of powers over time and distance; "euphoria" was appropriate. But this heady sense was tinged by an uneasy impression that radio was also ominous and somehow foreboding. Some individuals could also, of course, project on any new cultural element all their dominant fears. Henry Ford's *Dearborn Independent* instantly saw in radio the frightful new weapon of Communists and Jews.[5] Such warnings are evidence to the extremes of sensibility in the period. Amid their din more contained voices sounded, those of observers who sensed the psychic costs this new technology was beginning to exact.

These pessimistic comments tended to be fleeting, atypical, and cloaked in denial of one sort or another. Nevertheless they were significant fore-runners of common apprehensions that would develop as electronic communications pervaded American life.[6]

One of the costs suffered in confronting such new technology — indeed in confronting anything new — was that of a sense of loss; loss of old behavior, old values, old relationships, old senses of the self. An argument can be advanced that such a loss resembled bereavement. The bereaved suffers not only the loss of the old but the meaninglessness of the new, and the grieving process can be successfully completed only by attaching the meanings of the lost object to the new. (Widows, for example, have to find some new person or activity which revives the old sense of themselves as valuable persons.[7])

This process of assimilating the new to the old involved moving back and forth between the two, accommodating one to the other, until finally a synthesis was achieved. Only then could genuine new meaning evolve, and with it a new sensibility.

The people of the twenties experienced some such process of grief as they learned to attach old meanings to experience with new technology, reweaving patterns of imagination and behavior to encompass radio in the new fabric of their lives.[8]

This chapter focuses on a five-year transitional period, 1919-24, between the lifting of controls on amateur radio experimenters after World War I and David Sarnoff's proposal for a "chain" of high-powered stations across the country in 1924. In this period corporations fixed their hold on radio receiver manufacturing. They and would shortly expand to control broadcasting, but the rationalizing effect of the networks and the radio legislation of 1927 were still to come. By 1922 some 500 transmitting stations had been set up under the auspices of such organizations as churches, newspapers, educational institutions, department stores, and equipment manufacturers. Programming was chaotic, built at first around speakers and performers who volunteered. Advertising developed only slowly; listening and transmitting were in a wildly experimental state. In this fluid period would be shaped the nature of radio impact on American sensibility.[9]

My primary sources for this study are selected from popular print media because I wish to argue that the press in this transitional time played a crucial conservative role in the process of confronting the new.[10] Serving as a cultural storehouse of images and metaphors, the press helped make it possible for people to imagine the new in terms of the old. This process took place with radio. Only after experiences with radio had been clothed with meaning according to old systems of images and explanations could this new technology become really "available to the imagination" — Fussell's phrase — on its own terms.[11]

Inherited Images

Leonard Smith, Jr., reporter for the *New York Times,* put on a pair of ear phones in 1922 and was "fascinated . . . awestruck" by "sounds that surely were never intended to be heard by a human being . . . noises that roar in the space between the worlds."[12]

"'What are those noises?' you ask the operator. . . . He shrugs his shoulders. 'You know as much as I do,' he says."

The mysterious sounds proved difficult to describe. In mustering an analogy in order to domesticate the experience, Smith succeeded almost too well, comparing the "noises that roar in space" to the sound of frying eggs. Others found more trenchant analogies.

From deep in cultural memory came Taft's concept of the supernatural, primitive and powerful as an explanation of the unknown. Post-war readers appeared to conceive of radio most easily in images inherited from wireless. Some might carry in their imaginations the aura of the famous Kipling story published by *Scribner's* in 1902, a haunted thing about a night experimental wireless signals across England were blocked by transmissions from the beyond, the voice of the long-dead poet Keats.[13]

The two decades after the Kipling story had seen arguments among scientists and the laity as to whether electric "waves" relayed by wireless telegraphy provided evidence for the existence of thought "waves" relayed by telepathy.[14] In 1919 an essayist for *Harper's* sensed "something uncanny, something savoring of telepathy" in wireless, "something which did not obey the recognized laws that have been derived from experience in other fields" even though he promptly smothered such indiscretion in stolid arithmetic about sound waves.[15]

Almost all such excursions were immediately demystified by scientific explanation. These "magic powers," as Smith of the *New York Times* put it, had been "harnessed" by science.[16] The sentence would become a formula for science writers, a ritual transition from alluring "mystery" headlines to the more mundane account that followed.

Even the *Harper's* exercise had climaxed somewhat ambiguously, however, in speculation about voices from "spheres other than our own."[17] Such hearing of a disembodied voice was a shock to sensibility difficult to imagine a half-century later. But it struck ancient chords in the Protestant imagination, steeped in Old Testament imagery, resonating to the voice from the burning bush. Future movie makers and lyricists would apply old story to new technology, turning out film and song in which the voice from the radio was the voice of God.[18]

Much of the inherited language science used in discussing radio still bore religious or spiritual connotation. Mentions of the "ether" and the "heavens" had always invoked other-worldly associations.[19] And wireless shared its designation as a "medium" with the spiritualist practitioner, an individual of increasing prominence in the troubled years following the Great War.[20] A striking essay by W. H. Worrell appeared in the November 1922 issue of *Radio Broadcast*, a handsome new Doubleday publication whose contributors seemed particularly sensitive to the subtle implications of the new technology. Invoking radio as "apparently supernatural . . . affording a change from the regularity of nature and of average human experience," Worrell found that radio appeared to be "transmission and reception of pure form, without substance. . . . This form, this exchange of thought, is constantly passing about us — *passing through us — from countless transmitting stations, at this very instant!*" Radio possessed all the fascination of a link between the physical and the spiritual; one felt at the threshold of fundamental truths.[21]

Adding lustre to this complex strand of associations was identification of wireless telephony with psychoanalysis, often linked in this period to the occult.[22] By 1922 the *New York Tribune*, published a fantasy about a novelist who played golf while his unconscious dictated his latest work to his secretary by a mysterious kind of interpersonal radio.[23]

Altogether the experience of radio seemed to invoke a different sensibility. In contrast to the printing press or the motion picture, radio broadcasting "harks back to the primitive," said one Scribner's critic in 1923, "giving it new power as yet unmeasured."[24] In a period when fears rose and confidence in rationality grew increasingly fragile, the ancient comforts of the non-rational seemed appealing. Taft's intuitive remark floated on a strong under-current of the time.[25]

Contrary to this supernatural explanation, and existing in comfortable contradiction with it, was the quite worldly experience of Americans with the telephone — as a direct connection between real human beings. In fact the new radiophone behaved in the American imagination as a sort of eccentric telephone without wires.

The old long-distance phone had moved signals dependably along wires between two people. Its primary purpose, as a turn-of-the-century telephone executive had assured his customers, had been to provide "confidential" conversations. Indeed a chief triumph for Angus S. Hibbard, general manager of the Chicago Telephone Company, had been to persuade late-Victorian businessmen that they were not "talking into a hole in the end of an iron arm," but "speaking into the ear of a man." Women had posed no such problem, Hibbard observed, being keen to "grasp the personality" of the invisible conversationalist, smiling and bowing into the telephone and even stopping to touch up their hair before taking a call in their own rooms. The whole effect had been that of intimate connection — private, personal, and direct.[26]

It seemed reasonable to expect that the new wireless telephony would also serve as a device for interpersonal communication. Veteran telephone users were affronted, then, to discover that radiophone signals connecting two people also radiated indiscriminately through the air, allowing other individuals with radiophones to listen or wantonly to interrupt. Writers spoke resentfully of "leakage of signals" into the hands of "unauthorized persons." The factor of "non-secrecy" was also deplored through the teens as a vital commercial defect. (The idea of deliberately using this unfortunate radiating quality to enable one person to communicate with many, i.e., to "broadcast," occurred only to a few before World War I. There seemed nothing in the technology to shape inevitably the mass form radio "broadcasting" would eventually take.[27])

At the same time the growing tribe of amateur experimenters shared the telephonic model, smirking about "eavesdropping" on others' signals. As late as 1923, radio fans would still talk of "listening in," language evoking the clandestine pleasures of the rural party line.[28]

When the American Telephone and Telegraph Company set out to exploit wireless telephony, it intended to facilitate private conversation from persons abroad, from moving vehicles, from ship to shore. Even its ground-breaking experiment of 1922 in setting up a station to send signals only one way, the famous Station WEAF, was conceived as a sort of open-ended telephone. Anyone who wanted to talk to the public could step up to the microphone and pay a toll for the time. Senders proved distressingly few, musical intervals had to be improvised, corporations began to buy time, and paid commercial "broadcasting" was willy-nilly under way.

The expectation of private communication betweeen individuals died slowly as the idea of a medium controlled by institutions and broadcasting to masses came to dominate American consciousness.[29]

Radio also entered the national consciousness on a wave of fantasy about wireless operators. At hand were all the formulas lovingly compounded by writers over the years — romance, melodrama, heroism, self-sacrifice. "Never yet has a wireless operator failed in his duty to humanity on land or sea!"[30] There was a vital sense of connection, of responsibility.

Such images had crested on a wave of news stories about the operator on the liner "Carpathia" who clung to his key, speeding rescue to the sinking "Titanic" in 1912.[31] They surfaced in the enlistment propaganda of 1917. Whether the choice would be trench or radio shack, "You can be heroic and manly in either."[32] The "Romance of the Wireless" became almost a cliché in both headline and magazine title.

It was not surprising that the journalists assembling the first issue of the magazine *Radio Broadcast* in 1922 invoked that lovely sense of excitement in experimenting with radio, a pursuit endowed with a "romance" and a "spirit of adventure" that "no other branch of science enjoys!"[33]

The mention of science here invoked the notion of dominance. Images of power and control had frequently surfaced in both scientific journals and the magazines of lay science during the teens, reporting new dominion over trains, weather, crime, steamships, railroads, warfare, and indeed over time itself — all made possible by ever-expanding forays with radio-telephony.[34]

Thus when the amateur experimenter of the early twenties sat down in his garage, shack, or attic bedroom to assemble his mystifying array of wires, coils, and batteries, he could inhabit a world of excitement, drama, and power. He could choose to exert his will over time and distance. He could send his voice across the miles. In those precious hours of the imagination, there was symbolic expansion, aggression, responsibility, and action. "Manly" was indeed the word.

Transition

It is historically accurate for masculine terminology to have dominated the preceding paragraphs. Amateur radio was almost exclusively a male affair; a fraternal brotherhood pursued it.[35] Small boys bought parts and assembled crystal sets; fathers ventured into the complexities of the super-heterodyne. Mothers, sisters, daughters rarely participated. They were cast — at best — in popular periodical accounts on radio as mildly tolerant, so long as the venture did not intrude on their domain.[36]

In the early twenties articles began to appear in popular magazines describing devious ways of sneaking the radio apparatus into the living room. Females would object. There would be noise, mess, and battery acid on the rug. Therefore Mother must be lured from home and the radio installed in her absence. In some fashion the unreliable apparatus must be persuaded to emit enticing music as she was introduced back onto the scene. She would smile, and the battle would be won. In various forms this drama was re-enacted in contemporary print.[37] Radio appeared gradually to inhabit the living room, not the garage. Installed in a modishly designed cabinet, it was transformed from a laboratory apparatus into a piece of furniture. It began to be thought of as a family pastime, not a lone flight of the imagination. It meant listening, not transmitting; consuming, not creating. A once venturesome pursuit appeared to have become domesticated and passive.[38]

Indeed the notions of domestication and passivity would characterize much of the new imagery of radio listening. "Having my after-dinner coffee in the den," reflected one listener, "I couldn't help but think how comfortable I was, seated in my easy chair with the earphones in place." By 1924 a new symbolic triad of masculine satisfactions had emerged — radio, slippers, and cigar.[39]

There were many such expressions of delight over the new luxury and ease of access to distant events. But there was also dismay. The most cutting comments came from the cultists of true manhood. It was simply effete to lounge at home, listening to the ball game rather than shouting from the stands. Amateur radio experimenters also joined in the derision. Restricted by 1922 to transmitting on no more than a 200-meter wave length, amateurs saw themselves as an embattled elite of activists. Threatening them they saw a growing mass of sluggish "proletarians" who thought amateur signals interfered with living-room reception, a mass which could only listen, not transmit.[40] And keening from the edges of the battle were those critics who deplored radio as typical of all technology, transforming man into passive consumer or man into machine.[41]

Such loss of mastery and loss of connection were perhaps most effectively evoked by the magazine essayist, Bruce Bliven. In 1924 he made a fancied visit to the "Legion" family whose lives centered on radio. A once-dominant father now quails before a domineering wife — whose favorite radio listening is a fundamentalist preacher — and petulant children bent on the new jazz. Father will be banished to a portable in the basement if he persists in "debauching" himself with a prize fight. The teenage children commandeer the set, turn on jazz for dancing, and Father subsides with the rug rolled up over his feet.[42]

The sense of conflict between gain and loss expressed so vividly in this satire seems akin to the feelings of any loss. Journalism such as this gave imaginative shape to the ambivalence and anxiety occasioned by the new technology. Its phrases helped to crystalize the conflict between hope for the new and pain over loss of the old.

The New Ambiguities

Popular language about radio became more ambiguous as post-war Americans submitted to the electronic experience. That experience appeared subtly to be altering consciousness; gone was the old world of sight as primary vehicle of sensual data. One must be prepared to live alternatively and intensively in a world constructed only of sound. "For centuries the ear has played a secondary role," announced the *Dearborn Independent*. "The eye with the aid of the printed page, supplanted it. . . . With radio the ear comes back."[43]

To many, indeed, the ear now appeared supreme.[44] Its language dominated reports of the new radio-induced sensibility. In an April 1923 essay in *Scribners,*' O. E. McMeans reproduced the sensations of a new instantaneous experience of environment. By a "slight crooking of the finger" one could elicit a locomotive whistle in Georgia, a Kansas City siren, "My Old Kentucky Home" from Louisville, or the police gongs and crowd yells at the scene of a robbery-in-progress, reported by an announcer from a station window across the street. Even the early studio broadcast reproduced a complete aural environment with startling impact. One heard all too clearly the rustle of papers in the speaker's hand, the taking of breath between the singer's phrases, "every sound made or uttered while the switch is turned on."[45]

The experience was a new blind-man's buff; the blind listener sat fascinated, wrapped completely in aural sensation, visual data replaced the eyes and imagine.[46] Earphones completed the sense of isolation. And yet one was not alone. Before long, predicted the *Literary Digest* in June of 1923, the radio would put every one on earth in the presence of every other, auditorily speaking.[47] The idea was staggering. This was not the old sound-world of the telephone with its sense of finite, personal exchange, nor yet the contrasting sound world of the phonograph with its impersonal performance available to all. Radio presented a new reality which trans-cended both — the immediate experience of the remote person or event, an experience in company with millions of others, yet strangely separate. Here were the ambiguities: the sense that one was participating, yet alone; in command, yet swept blindly along on the wave of sound. Prevalent images of mastery and connection, then, were punctuated by those suggest-ing intrusion into the intimate environment and alienation from social and personal relationship.

Extended Mastery Versus Intrusion

Prevailing descriptions of radio continued hearty and optimistic. The greatest new power seemed that of obliterating distance; the world appeared to shrink.[48] "DX fishing" became a ruling pastime; tuning in Cuba or California was the rage. For the Legion family it partook of a "sacrificial rite."[49] The new radio machine appeared also to be subtly altering consciousness; to some observers, listeners seemed to be developing a new imaginative mode. People had always envisioned themselves transported to distant vistas. Now listeners perceived the remote as though they had compelled it to appear in their own homes. "Pittsburgh and Newark are right here in the shack," exclaimed a correspondent from an Ontario mining camp.[50] The ability to command an experience to play itself out within one's own four walls was intoxicating — Melba singing next to one's own hearth, the Four Horsemen plunging through the door!

Having admitted radio and tuned to a station, however, one's sense of control weakened. Media language which presented radio's advent into the living room in sexual metaphor — male invasion of female space — also suggested invasion of personal boundaries for *all* members of a family — visual insult, aural trauma, perceptual disruption.[51]

The paraphernalia of radio, in the first place, was unaesthetic. Antennas were eyesores on rooftops. Lead-in wires dangled from fronts of houses. Inside, the necessary machinery seemed vulgar — so ironic, a box and a tangle of wires.[52]

The shock to hearing was even more universally observed. Articles and advertisements warned of "squawks, squeals, screams," and "enough howls and yells to make one think all Hell was let loose." In 1922, listeners were portrayed as victims of a hostile science:[53]

> From the huge phonograph horn . . . comes a sudden shrill whistle which rises and falls, a terrific volume of noise battering at our ears . . . made by some far-off world as it flees shrieking in agony across the firmament. . . . In a moment this celestial caterwauling is shouldered aside, so to speak, by the Sextette [from *Lucia*] being sung in our very ears and evidently by giants a hundred feet tall. . . . Still, science has conquered, the music is there . . . brought down and hurled upon us from the horn.

A sense of temporal disorientation, however, appeared the most significant source of distress. By the twenties, a sense of ever-accelerating time had been with Americans for a half-century. One had been able, however, to maintain a certain equilibrium, so long as time seemed a reliable linear flow.[54] Now, that vital sense of temporal continuity appeared threatened by radio's format — a succession of disparate elements, senselessly juxtaposed. One critic protested: "Busy as the average American is, he or she has not yet reached the point where either education or entertainment is absorbed in the five-minute installment plan. . . . yet the originators of the present style in radio programs multiply [the five-minute period] indefinitely."[55]

The jumble now included bands, orchestras, national rites, and public functions interspersed mindlessly with "explanations" by announcers. Radio broadcasting provided "the biggest crazy-quilt of audition" ever perceived by human ear. "Crazy-quilt" — a seemingly homely metaphor from the pioneer past — could also hint at fragmentation, disjunction, and consciousness pushed to the edges of sanity.

Modern science had split the older order into a thousand fragments, asserted sociologist E. C. Lindeman in a perceptive *New Republic* essay on radio. Increases in stimuli might result in increased difficulty in integrating behavior. "We may hear . . . too much for our capacities for experience." The stress seemed related to what the German sociologist, Georg Simmel, had called in 1903 the development of "urban perception." He had spoken of the "intensification of nervous stimulation" stemming from swift change of stimuli. Impressions from more regular experience "use up, so to speak, less consciousness than does the rapid crowding of changing images, the unexpectedness of onrushing impressions." In 1913, such discontinuity had been specifically associated with the new electronic experience by the Italian futurist, F. T. Marinetti, as he invoked the "confused medley of sensations and impressions" characteristic of what he called the "wireless imagination." Here then was a profound challenge to traditional consciousness posed by the new technology — the disruption of a sense of linear flow, of continuity, of unbroken time at one's command.[56]

To the modernist sensibility of the twenties, the "unexpected" in radio montage appeared a venture in surrealism, the method of *Ulysses* or *The Wasteland*. The sense of disconnection for the "modern" man would be forcefully put by Walter Lippmann in 1929, asserting that press, radio, and film compelled attention to elements "detached from their backgrounds, their causes, and their consequences . . . having no beginning, no middle, and no end, mere flashes of publicity playing fitfully on a dark tangle of circumstances."[57]

The disconcerting mosaic of radio did resemble the older make-up of the newspaper, to which citizens were accustomed.[58] And yet the visual mosaic of the newspaper seemed more under control than the temporal mosaic of radio. Once tuned to a particular station, radio provided a flow of impression like time itself which, as Bergson had said, permitted no repetition, no return. The radio listener was indeed helpless, concluded *Radio Broadcast* in 1922. "You turn on your switches and wait. . . . It may be a selection from 'Aida,' wonderfully executed, or it may be nothing but a scratchy, cracked phonograph record. You have nothing to say about it."[59]

"The newspaper can be read at one's convenience," aserted one radio reviewer, "it can be read to suit one's moods or interests, and selectivity therefore is at one's command. Radio's output must be caught at the hour it is scheduled, and if the auditor misses a few words, effectiveness is lost because it is not possible to go back."[60] Priority and rate of attention, reprise, and scanning — all had passed to others' control.

Accommodating both visual and auditory stimuli simultaneously appeared intolerable. Now the evening paper received short shrift, said one academic critic. Who could read while a loud speaker poured out the latest jazz?[61]

Such irritability over disruption of the newspaper ritual was amplified in a wave of periodical comment, comparing the impacts of newspaper and radio on society and the self.[62] Advantages were properly chronicled, but there remained a lingering sense of dis-ease. Americans had heavily invested themselves in the experience with newspaper; newspapers reflected not only exterior reality but the self. "We see ourselves in our newspapers," reflected one critic. "We *are* our newspapers."[63] Radio, with its raucous form, its demand for new behavior, and its seemingly erratic reflections of experience, meant a sharp break with the past. It appeared to threaten a traditional identification, an anchoring of self in what had been continuous relationship to a stable form.[64]

The importance of radio was scarcely to be overestimated, concluded the Dutch historian, Johan Huizinga, on visiting America in 1926. Farm families and invalids could share through radio some of the life of the city. "But no one who listens to it any longer chooses for himself the stuff upon which his mind feeds." Radio compelled a strong but "superficial" exercise of attention, "completely excluding reflection, or what I might call reflective assimilation." Huizinga's American colleagues amplified the observation, blaming radio for a national decay in concentration and predicting standardization of the American mind.[65]

One conflict thus emerging in the early twenties opposed a new sense of mastery to a newly discerned loss of control. On the one hand was the ability to command the remote event to occur within one's own hearing; on the other, the consequent threat to personal boundaries and familiar patterns of sensibility.

Connection Versus Alienation

With the advent of the radio age, the optimistic predicted the strengthening of international ties, enhancement of the democratic process, and the revival of the family. The magical new electric tie would surely bind. In conflict with such expectations came reports of individual alienation from social and personal involvement, an alienation which appeared to be encouraged by peculiar aspects of the process, content, and form of the new technology.

Though some could see in radio a potential for new social control over immigrants, criminals, and other non-conformists, a striking aspect of radio *process* seemed more apt to separate the ordinary individual from customary forms of authority.[66] Traditional mediators were circumvented. Children listened secretly at night under the covers, headphones over their ears, eluding parental authority. Women savored the forbidden male environment of the prize fight. Voters heard candidates without the filter of a partisan press.

Churchmen and politicians began to bewail lack of participation in their rites as individuals sensed the insulation radio could provide against community surveillance. "Why go to your parish church," came the ironic query from the Episcopal bishop, "when you can sit at ease in your parlor and hear a capable choir . . . a magnetic preacher?"[67]

The implications of this new escape from others' expectations appealed to the media columnists. As Heywood Broun remarked, one could listen to a sermon on the radio, throw in a few cuss words, and smoke a cigar all at the same time. If one disagreed with a political speaker, pointed out Mark Sullivan, no need to tip-toe, embarrassed, out of the auditorium. One just turned the dial.[68]

Oddly enough, however, freedom also meant loneliness. There came over individuals a new and strange sense, that of being one of an atomized mass. A distinctive impact of radio, said Eunice Fuller Barnard, lay in the unique position of auditors who were "of an audience, yet each alone in it." Though one addressed a million people at once, "he can count on no group response; his voice reaches them not as a mass but as isolated units. They do not, they cannot react on him or each other. He cannot sense their feeling. There is no mutuality, no give and take. . . . The listeners do not have to declare themselves. . . . They hear him practically alone."[69]

Radio could indeed separate one from all social activity. He was not going to the political meeting that night, a Middletown businessman told an interviewer in 1924, and he turned to his radio instead "for an evening's diversion." (More intimate connection was subject to the same strain. Most powerful symbol of interpersonal alienation was the "radio divorce," new to the headlines. One partner appeared to withdraw behind a wall of sound, leaving the spouse no recourse but the courts.[70])

The *process* of radio broadcasting was not the only alienating factor; some of its more unconventional *content* appeared to threaten traditional moral and political beliefs as well. The Tudors' sixteenth-century concern for the spread of sedition and heresy via the new technology of print was echoed four centuries later by those who viewed radio content as detrimental to government and dangerous to the immortal soul.

In the grip of paranoia over alien religious and political expression, the *Dearborn Independent* warned of Communist ideas beamed to innocent farm youth by "organized Jewry" from a radio station on the Sears, Roebuck building in Chicago. Borrowing the language of the Great War, the *Independent* saw radio as a new "poison gas." Liberals poked fun at such extremes. ("See grandmother being converted to Socialism as she knits of an evening with her earphones on.") But the problem remained, implicit in radio's most remarkable quality, the obliteration of time. No longer could an encounter with strange experience be delayed by its conversion into newsprint, while its language was tidied and its moral or political dangers removed. Now the listener was instantly present and vulnerable at the event[71]

The *Chicago Tribune* polled readers on its proposal to broadcast the sordid Leopold-Loeb trial in 1924, and implied that the shock would be discreetly cushioned by an approximation of the old editing process. "Sensation there will be," asserted the *Tribune*, "but no filth. The censor will be as discriminating with his push button as are the editors of the *Tribune* with their copy pencils. . . . Broadcasting of the trial will be as clean as the *Tribune*." Readers by the thousands voted against the promised "superlative experiment." Immediate exposure to such content was too threatening to the sensibilities; instant editing would not do. In Chicago, at least, time between such an event and its comprehension would stretch out for a comforting few more years.[72]

Probably the most intriguing questions were posed in connection with radio *form*. Could a reproduction provide an authentic experience of communication between individuals? Was the real, once reproduced, still real? Some observers saw in the adulation poured out on radio personalities a form of pseudo-encounter. Little Howard Legion, aged 8, did not suspect that the Uncle Charlie who told him bedtime stories was merely "pushing his personality through the ether at some thousands of children whom he has never seen, will never see, and cares rather less than nothing for."[73] More poignant must have been the plight of the hypothetical listener to a broadcast communion service who wondered whether the ritual was binding. Were the body and the blood truly hers?[74] "The presence of the original is the prerequisite to the concept of authenticity," the critic Walter Benjamin would declare on entering this debate, which ranged through the new technologies and across continents during the period. Reproduction, he said, would destroy both the uniqueness and the aura of the original.[75]

Perhaps a similar sense of inauthenticity, of lack of meaning, moved young Edmund Wilson to describe in his journal the "empty sonority," the "hollow yowling" of radio. The year was 1925, the same year T. S. Eliot published "The Hollow Men."[76]

Resolution and Transcendence

As Americans of the early twenties gave up their complete dependence on newspapers and wireless in order to cope with radio, they experienced an inevitable sense of loss — loss of the feelings of mastery and connection attached to the old means of communication. Print journalism seemed to reflect and respond to the ambiguity of a process like that of grief — providing familiar metaphors and analogies to make these contradictory new experiences more understandable. There were the images of romance and conquest that belonged to confidence, but also the crazy quilts and poison gas of fear and defensiveness.

Though this conflict appeared unresolved by the mid-twenties, a complex psychological process also seemed to be under way in which individuals were devising ways to barricade themselves against radio. Only gradually would they allow the barricade to become a kind of semiporous membrane, admitting desired aspects of the new radio-mediated world and rejecting others. This transcendent process would involve development of a new sensibility appropriate to an electronic environment, and its beginnings would be seen by 1924.[77]

In that year the *New York Times* reviewed the first American edition of *Beyond the Pleasure Principle*. In it the Viennese philosopher Sigmund Freud advanced speculatively the idea of consciousness as a "little fragment of living substance" threatened by a world charged with powerful energies. To avoid destruction, the organism developed what Freud called "a stimulus shield" allowing some stimuli to penetrate but excluding others. *Times* reviewer Mary Keyt Isham was reminded of the child's notion of a caterpillar, "all skin and squash." The skin was the rind against excessive stimuli; the squash, the inner consciousness.[78]

Freud intended to illustrate psychic process, but his language resembled that of others speculating on the problem of overwhelming stimuli in modern life. From Berlin two decades before, Simmel had suggested the "increased awareness" developed by the urban dweller to protect against environmental threat. And Walter Benjamin had specifically invoked Freud's stimulus shield in discussion of the "training" to which communications technology — newspaper or film —subjected the human sensorium.[79]

In his 1924 essay on radio Lindeman applied the model of the "postponed or delayed response to stimuli" specifically to the radio listener. Such secondary modes of communication as radio, he said, might well produce an environment so artificial that human adjustment would become impossible. Therefore their value depended on man's capacity to "control and appropriate" the resulting stimulus.[80]

In the first years of the decade, Americans seemed far from control. A great proportion were caught up in an infatuation with novelties of sound and distance. Those others who resisted engulfment by the new technology seemed to defend themselves either by denial or retreat. The usual prescription was to turn the switch. "If you have a radio," Will Rogers advised during the 1924 presidential campaign, "now is the time to get it out of fix." (Intellectuals, of course, had never taken up radio in the first place. They had not as yet, said one observer, come to grips with the typewriter.[81])

Some took aggressive action, advising stations to stop broadcasting when the supply of quality material ran out. Others talked censorship or legislation. A few took direct action. Secretary of State Charles Evans Hughes was entertaining distinguished guests in his own home when, in their full hearing on his own radio, a news commentator sharply criticized his State Department policy. The angry Hughes protested directly to the president of AT&T, owners of the offending station. The contract of the commentator, Hans von Kaltenborn, was not renewed.[82]

A bleak passivity, however, seemed more characteristic of the modernist reaction represented by Bliven, who sardonically predicted the world of 1930 in which "there will be only one orchestra left on earth, giving nightly world-wide concerts; when all the universities will be combined into one super-institution conducting courses by radio for students in Zanzibar, Kamchatka, and Oskaloosa; when instead of newspapers, trained orators will dictate the news of the world day and night . . . when every person will be instantly accessible day or night to all the bores he knows . . . when the last vestiges of privacy, solitude, and contemplation will have vanished into limbo."[83]

Such reactions — denial, rage, cynical despair — resembled the classic reactions to grief. Now came also, however, tangible indications of the fulfillment of Lindeman's prescription for adjustment to altered environment.

Looking back on the scene from 1931, the historian Frederick Lewis Allen would recollect that around 1923 people had begun to take their radio sets for granted, as background for a newer craze, Mah Jong. His recollection was faulty; radio was still very much in the foreground in 1923. What is significant in Lewis' statement is its embodiment of the consciousness that would develop by 1931 when radio would indeed have become psychically assimilated, a state which could be projected back onto the people of the early twenties.[84]

Perceptions and actions were reorganized around what once had been strange; as early as 1924 one writer could describe his habit, "to punctuate my space bar, as I typewrite, to whatever tempo radio sets for me."[85]

More importantly, an occasional observer perceived a new exercise of individual initiative. It became apparent that listeners, ventured one columnist, were no longer spellbound by a mediocre and haphazard succession of performers. A number now listened with discrimination, added another, instead of "swallowing all that they hear, whole and without thought."[86] Such individuals neither listened passively nor tuned out. They continued to engage with the new form. More selective reactions began to emerge — wariness, choice, control.

It would be impossible to recapture the old consciousness, so structured by the linear patterning and delayed timing of print. The new electric sensibility would range far more widely, but less contemplatively. It would accommodate the discontinuous more easily, but concentrate less effectively. It would extend relationships, but pursue them in less depth.

The unity of mankind was not to be sought in machines, Lindeman suggested in 1924, but in the human personality.[87] The way would be "complicated, difficult and conducive to sober reflection." An implication was there for an age troubled by dehumanizing forces: technology need not be destiny. Even in the face of such forces, the individual might reassert something of the old sense of communion and command, tempered by regret for what had gone. Such would be the kind of meaning and comfort future generations must find.

Notes

1. C. C. Dill, *Radio Law* (Washington, D.C.: National Law Book Co., 1938), pp. 1,2.

2. This essay uses "sensibility" to mean association and interaction of feeling and thought. Of major influence in shaping my thought have been Wolfgang Schivelbusch, *The*

Railway Journey: Trains and Travel in the 19th Century (New York: Urizen Books, 1979), and Marshall McLuhan, *Understanding Media: The Extensions of Man* (New York: 1964), both indispensable to study of sensibility in relation to technology. For particularly useful comment, I thank Michael Barkun, Seymour Fisher, and Andre Fontaine.

3. "Era of Expansion" is the title Gleason L. Archer gave to this early period in his classic work, *History of Radio to 1926* (New York: American Historical Society, 1938). By 1922 there were an estimated 600,000 "receiving stations," of which 678 were commercial. The overwhelming mood was astonishment and pleasure; as late as 1925, radio fan letters expressed primarily "enthusiastic surprise." "The March of Radio," *Radio Broadcast* (June 1922): 95; *New York Times*, 13 October 1925.

4. Erik Barnouw, *A Tower in Babel: A History of Broadcasting in the United States* (New York: Oxford University Press, 1966) I: 91. The separation of transmitting from receiving equipment, mass marketing of receiving equipment, and growth of "broadcasting" stations made living room listening possible for the general public in the early twenties. See also J. Fred MacDonald, *Don't Touch That Dial!* (Chicago: Nelson-Hall, 1979), pp. 1-23, and Philip T. Rosen, *The Modern Stentors: Radio Broadcasters and the Federal Government, 1920-1934* (Westport, Conn.: Greenwood Press, 1980), pp. 1-14.

5. "Shall the Youth of America be Exploited? A Brand of Communism Which Aims at Control of Junior Farm Centers," *Dearborn Independent*, 6 September 1924, p. 10.

6. The literature on culture and electronic technology is vast. See, for example, James Carey and John J. Quirk, "The Mythos of the Electronic Revolution," *American Scholar* 39 (Spring, Summer 1970): 219-41, 395-424. Harold A. Innis, *The Bias of Communications*, 2nd ed. (Toronto: University of Toronto Press, 1964); Barry N. Schwarz, ed., *Human Connection and the New Media* (Englewood Cliffs, N.J.: Prentice-Hall, 1973), and Raymond Williams, *Television: Technology and Cultural Form* (New York: Schocken Books, 1975).

7. "The working out of a severe bereavement represents . . . a general principle of adaption to change. . . . Change [involves] the need to re-establish continuity, to work out an interpretation of oneself and the world which preserves, despite estrangement, the thread of meaning. . . . The outcome of social changes, too, may depend on the management of the process of transition." Peter Maris, *Loss and Change* (New York: Pantheon, 1974), pp. 38, 42.

8. The language of the indexers to mass media — those of morgue-keepers for newspaper clippings or indexers to periodicals — is clues to the categories for organizing experience, which are available at any one time to culture. The *Readers' Guide* filed articles about wireless telephony under "WIRELESS" — a category indicating the loss of something, i.e., wires — until 1915. That year a new category, RADIO, merited one entry. By 1922 all articles about wireless were indexed under RADIO. The absence of wires as an organizing idea had been transcended by the presence of a new object, radio.

9. Barnouw, *Tower in Babel*, pp. 75-188. See Schwarzlose chapter in this volume.

10. Five sources have been particularly fruitful for comment on radio with regard to culture: the *New Republic* and the *New York Times*, appropriate to an urban, educated readership; the *Scientific American*, for a national audience of relatively sophisticated readers; *Radio Broadcast*, which appealed across class and geographic lines to a readership including children and the poor, and *Dearborn Independent*, calculated to suit small-town and rural Midwesterners.

11. Paul Fussell, *The Great-War and Modern Memory* (New York: Oxford University Press, 1975), pp. 74 and 137-39; also D. H. Hirsch, *Validity in Interpretation* (New Haven: Yale University Press, 1967), pp. 105.

12. "Broadcasting to Millions," *New York Times*, 19 February 1922.

13. Rudyard Kipling, "Wireless," *Scribners' Magazine* 32 (August 1902): 129-43. Kipling had a firm hold on the electronic imagination of the era. To Bruce Bliven in 1922 the

radio control switchboard with instruments, dials, and handles evoked the ray and its vigilant slave in Kipling's "With the Night Mail." See Bliven's "The Ether Will Now Oblige," *The New Republic*, 15 February 1922, p. 328.

14. "The Analogy between Wireless Telegraphy and Waves from Brain to Brain," *Current Opinion* 57 (October 1914): 253.

15. Buckner Speed, "Voices of the Universe," *Harper's* 138 (April 1919): 613.

16. "Broadcasting to Millions," *New York Times*, 19 February 1922.

17. Speed, "Voices of the Universe," p. 615. See Herwald chapter in this volume.

18. Before the advent of the microphone and radio, a disembodied voice figured in the human imagination most dramatically as the voice of God. Electronic technology made the voice an imaginable *thing* in its own right, separate from its bodily connection; see Schivelbusch, *Railway Journey*, p. 54. In the film, "The Next Voice You Hear" (1950), God would speak on the radio. The gospel song, "Turn Your Radio On," Barnaby Records, X30809, implored hearers to "listen to the Master's radio."

19. Scientific debates about wireless were marked by dispute as to the composition and function and indeed the very existence of the ether. See for example, the subhead to the article on brainwaves, "Subtlety of the Wave in the Ether," *Current Opinion* 57 (October 1914): 253; "Sir Oliver Defends the Ether," *Literary Digest*, 2 December 1922, p. 28.

20. "Spiritualism" was a substantial index category in the *New York Times* after the war. See R. Laurence Moore, *In Search of White Crows: Spiritualism, Parapsychology, and American Culture* (New York: Oxford University Press, 1977), p. 175. During the same years Edison was developing a "spiritual communications machine"; see Matthew Josephson, *Edison: A Biography* (New York: McGraw-Hill, 1959), p. 439.

21. W. H. Worrell, "Do Brains or Dollars Operate Your Set?" *Radio Broadcast* 2 (November 1922): 70.

22. This association was best preserved in the amber of the Dewey Decimal System which shelved Freud next to works on ghosts, spooks, and witches.

23. "Hitching the Wireless to Your Subconscious Mind," *New York Tribune*, 21 May 1922.

24. Orange Edward McMeans, "The Great Audience Invisible," *Scribners' Magazine* 72 (April 1923): 410.

25. Gilbert K. Chesterton in 1921 lectured in New York on "The Revolt Against Reason," discussing Christian Science, jazz, spiritualism, psychoanalysis, and associated phenomena; "Calls Psychoanalysis a Rival to Jazz," *New York Times*, 28 March 1921. See also Michael Schudson, *Discovering the News: A Social History of American Newspapers* (New York: Basic Books, 1978), pp. 126-27.

26. Angus S. Hibbard, "How to Use a Telephone," *Saturday Evening Post*, n.d., in Ray Brosseau, ed., *Looking Forward: Life in the Twentieth Century as Predicted in the Pages of American Magazines from 1895 to 1905* (New York: American Heritage Press, 1970), p. 81.

27. "The Persistent Mysteries of Wireless Telegraphy and Telephony," *Current Literature* 49 (December 1910): 636. See Schwarzlose chapter in this volume. See also William Peck Banning, *Commercial Broadcasting Pioneer: The WEAF Experiment, 1922-1926* (Cambridge, Mass.: Harvard University Press, 1946), pp. 41-61; David Sarnoff, writing his famous "Radio Music Box" memo in 1916, was among those who broke out of the telephonic model. His superiors at American Marconi ignored his suggestion. Eugene Lyons, *David Sarnoff* (New York: Pyramid, 1967), pp. 87-89; Laurence Bergreen, *Look Now, Pay Later: The Rise of Network Broadcasting* (Garden City, N.Y.: Doubleday, 1980), pp. 20-22.

28. " 'Listening In,' Our New National Pastime." *American Review of Reviews*, 19 January 1923, p. 52.

29. *New York Times*, 22 February 1922. Also see Richard Schwarzlose's chapter, this volume.

30. "75,000 American Boys Have This Enthusiasm," *American Magazine* 81 (June 1916): 104.

31. Guglielmo Marconi, "Wireless and the 'Titanic,'" *World's Work* 24 (June 1912): 225.

32. "Work for Wireless Amateurs," *Literary Digest*, 18 August 1917.

33. "Adventures in Radio," *Radio Broadcast* 1 (May 1922): 72-3. This article featured radio as a leading factor in the lives of gun-runners, smugglers, revolutionists, and international spies.

34. "Floods and Wireless," *Technological World* 23 (August 1915): 806-807; "How Wireless Helps the Mariner," *Scientific American*, 13 April 1918, p. 340; "Time by Wireless," *Harper's Weekly*, 28 June 1913, p. 19.

35. Making one's own crystal set became almost a ritual passage to manhood. See "Almost a Soldier is the Boy Who Understands Wireless Nowadays," *Woman's Home Companion* 43 (October 1916): 32. Women who assembled sets were so rare as to merit special articles: "How Two Girls Made a Receiving Radiophone," *Literary Digest*, 10 June 1922, p. 29.

36. "The first-class scout who . . . calls me 'dad,' worked manfully with me while we wound our coil of nights in the kitchen. . . . The good wife and scout-mother grew tired of our fussing around in the kitchen, so we retreated to the attic and kept on winding coils." McMeans, "Eavesdropping on the World," pp. 226-27.

37. A. R. Pinci, "This Is Radio-Casting Station 'H-O-M-E,'" *Dearborn Independent* 20 September 1924, p. 4. For feminine response see Alice R. Bourke, "O Woe! Radio," *Radio Broadcast* 2 (December 1922): 107: "Of course I am the boss, but it . . . is handy in many ways to let him think he is the Great Voice around this radio-devastated remainder of What Was."

38. The feminization of male experience with radio was exquisitely represented by an interior decorator's proposal for a special radio room. "Of masculine character, obviously," the room would be "developed" in the attic, that old male redoubt, with floors in two shades of slate, tinted plaster walls and chairs in dark blue corduroy. Alwyn T. Covell, "Decorating the Radio Room: A New Thought for the House in Town or Country Where 'Listening In' Is Getting to be One Serious Pastime," *House and Garden* 44 (August 1923): 50-1.

39. Ford A. Carpenter, "First Experiences of A Radio Broadcaster," *Atlantic Monthly* 132 (September 1923): 388.

40. "The Long Arm of Radio," *Current Opinion* 72 (May 1922): 684; "The March of Radio: Too Many Cooks Are Spoiling Our Broth," *Radio Broadcast* 2 (November 1922): 3; "Is The Radio Amateur Doomed?" *Literary Digest*, 2 December 1922, p. 28; Carl Dreher, "Is the Broadcast Listener at Fault?" *Radio Broadcast* 4 (March 1924): 424-25.

41. Some writers of the period saw passivity everywhere. They attributed it to a malign technology and to the growth of consumerism. Men were groveling before the machine, said Waldo Frank, because they had not the "consciousness" to master it; "The Machine and Metaphysics," *The New Republic*, 18 November 1925, pp. 330-31; Johan Huizinga bewailed the disappearance of "the active man, as embodiment of enterprise," in the wake of technological expansion, *America: A Dutch Historian's Vision from Afar and Near* (New York: Harper & Row, 1972), p. 234; Charles and Mary Beard ambivalently evoked masses listening "passively" to manufactured music, but also to a radio which permitted "buyers" to chose their music, in *The Rise of American Civilization* (1927; New York: Macmillan, 1930), p. 785.

42. Bliven, "The Legion Family and the Radio," *Century* (October 1924): 811-18.

43. "Radio To Supplant Press That Exploits It?" *Dearborn Independent*, 3 June 1922, p. 8.

44. The "presumed superiority of the radio over the newspaper," based on the assumption that "the sense of seeing is inferior to the sense of hearing," was hotly debated in a decade when psychology focused in comparative effects of sensual stimuli; e.g., E. C. Lindeman, "Radio Fallacies," *New Republic*, 19 March 1924, p. 228.

45. McMeans, "Great Audience Invisible."

46. *Ibid.*, p. 411.

47. "Wanted, A Radio Language," *Literary Digest*, 23 June 1923, p. 24.

48. Radio's ability to annihilate the time was frequently expressed in spatial metaphor. A tiny, dispirited globe was overshadowed in a *Chicago Daily News* cartoon by a gigantic radio listener, remarking, "Well, Well! Isn't he a cute little fellow?" The caption: GETTING SMALLER EVERY DAY; *Literary Digest*, 17 June 1922.

49. Bliven, "The Legion Family," pp. 814.

50. "A Wireless in Every Home," *Radio Broadcast* 1 (June 1922): 110.

51. The sense of physical invasion comes in a news account of a couple terrified by sounds of burglars apparently counting the family silver. The counting, it developed, came from a new radio, broadcasting setting-up exercises in the next room. *New York Times*, 3 August 1924.

52. Bliven, "The Legion Family," pp. 815; for some critics the machine created its own esthetic, to others it represented sheer vulgarity, the result of a desire for consumer goods. See Lewis Mumford, *American Taste* (San Francisco: Westgate, 1929), pp. 16-22, 27-31, 34; on life style in a machine age, see Warren Susman, *Culture and Commitment, 1929-1945* (New York: George Braziller, 1973), pp. 4-8.

53. *Radio Broadcast* (April 1923): 525; Bliven, "The Ether Will Now Oblige," p. 328.

54. Americans had always been people in a hurry. By the early years of the twentieth century, linear time itself seemed under seige — there was the relative time of the physicists, the simultaneity of the Cubists, and the rediscovery of "primitive" time by the anthropologists.

55. "Broadcasting or Outcasting," *Dearborn Independent*, 13 June 1925, p. 13.

56. Lindeman, "Radio Fallacies," pp. 227-28; Georg Simmel, "The Metropolis and Mental Life," in *The Sociology of Georg Simmel*, ed. Kurt H. Wolff (New York: The Free Press, 1950), p. 410; F. T. Marinetti, "Wireless Imagination and Words at Liberty: The New Futurist Manifesto," *Poetry and Drama* 1 (September 1913): 322.

57. Walter Lippmann, *Preface to Morals* (New York: Macmillan, 1929), p. 64.

58. McLuhan, *Understanding Media*, p. 188.

59. Review of *Time and Free Will: An Essay on the Immediate Data of Consciousness*, by Henri Bergson, *The Nation*, 24 November 1910, p. 499; *Radio Broadcast* 1 (May 1922): 1.

60. "The Lure of the World's Aerial Theater," *Dearborn Independent*, 30 August 1924, p. 3.

61. E. M. Johnson, "The Utilization of the Social Sciences," *The Journalism Bulletin* 4 (1927): 32.

62. See, for example, "Radio to Supplant Press," p. 8; McMeans, "Eavesdropping," p. 226; Eunice Fuller Barnard, "Radio Politics," *New Republic*, 19 March 1924, p. 91; "The Future of Radio," *New Republic*, 8 October 1924, p. 135; Mark Sullivan, "Will Radio Make the People the Government?" *Radio Broadcast* 6 (November 1924): 24-25.

63. Thomas L. Masson, "Well, What's All This About the Newspaper?" *Dearborn Independent*, 18 October 1924, p. 2.

64. The problem of relating the self to radio often surfaced in fantasy authors imagined themselves as incorporating radio's powers or *as* radio. The zenith of the form

probably came in *Argosy's* 1924 story in which the protagonist transmitted *himself* to Venus. Ralph Milne Farley, *The Radio Man* (Los Angeles: Fantasy, 1948).

65. Huizinga, *America*, p. 235; Jennie Irene Mix, "Is Radio Standardizing the American Mind?" *Radio Broadcast* 6 (November 1924): 49-50.

66. "Ether Waves Versus Crime Waves," *Literary Digest*, 7 October 1922, p. 25. J. M. McKibbin, Jr., "The New Way to Make Americans," *Radio Broadcast* 2 (January 1923): 238-39.

67. "The Effect of Broadcasting on the Churches," *Radio Broadcast* 2 (October 1923): 273.

68. "Listening In On The Radio," *New York Times*, 3 August 1924; Sullivan, "Will Radio Make the People the Government?" p. 23

69. Barnard, "Radio Politics," p. 92.

70. Robert S. Lynd and Helen Merrell Lynd, *Middletown: A Study in American Culture* (1929; New York: Harcourt, Brace, 1956), p. 416; "Wife Leaves Radio Fan: Judge Says She's Right," *New York Times*, 10 February 1924.

71. "Shall the Youth of America . . . ?" p. 10; "The *Tribune* Gets A Fast One," *Dearborn Independent*, 16 August 1924, p. 8; Barnard, "Radio Politics," p. 92.

72. Hal Higdon, *The Crime of the Century: The Leopold and Loeb Case* (New York: Putnam's, 1975), pp. 158-59, p. 167.

73. "The Legion Family," p. 812.

74. "Holy Communion by Radio," *Radio Broadcast* 5 (July 1924): 221-22.

75. Walter Benjamin, *Illuminations*, ed. Hannah Arendt (New York: Schocken, 1969), pp. 220-21.

76. Edmund Wilson, *The Twenties: From Notebooks and Diaries of the Period*, ed. Leon Edel (New York: Farrar, Straus and Giroux, 1975), p. 213. The sense of meaninglessness evoked by the content of electronic media would appear in 1961 in an echo of Eliot, the description of TV as "vast wasteland." Barnouw, *Tube of Plenty: The Evolution of American Television* (New York: Oxford University Press, 1975), pp. 299-300.

77. The structure of the following argument owes much to Schivelbusch, *Railway Journey*, pp. 152-60.

78. *The Standard Edition of the Complete Psychological Works of Sigmund Freud* (London: Hogarth Press, 1955-66) 12: 24-33; Mary Keyt Isham, "Freud's Imagination Flooding Wide and Obscure Areas," *New York Times*, 7 September 1924.

79. Wolf, *Sociology of Georg Simmel*, pp. 410-11; Benjamin, *Illuminations*, pp. 160-63; 175.

80. Lindeman, "Radio Fallacies," p. 228.

81. "Will Rogers, Humorist, . . ." *Radio Broadcast* 6 (November 1924): 39; Bliven, "The Legion Family," p. 811.

82. "And the sooner some stations curtail their programs, and go in for silent days and nights, the better," Pinci, "Broadcasting or Outcasting," p. 14; H. V. Kaltenborn, *Fifty Fabulous Years, 1900-1950* (New York: Putnam's, 1950), pp. 112-13.

83. Bliven, "The Ether Will Now Oblige," p. 328. Some historians would characterize such a reaction as Bliven's as "desperately resisting" mechanized culture, accepting alienation as the survival price. Evidence indicates, however, that a number of ordinary individuals, neither alienated nor despairing, found means to assert their own autonomy against mechanization of communication. Henry F. May, "Shifting Perspectives on the 1920's," *Mississippi Valley Historical Review* 43 (December 1954): 404.

84. Frederick Lewis Allen, *Only Yesterday* (1931; New York: Bantam Books, 1946), p. 101.

85. Pinci, "Station H-O-M-E," p. 4.

86. Edgar White Burrill, "Broadcasting the World's Best Literature," *Radio Broadcast* 2 (November 1922): 54; Mix, "Is Radio Standardizing?" p. 50.

87. Lindeman, "Radio Fallacies," p. 228.

Mass Media and
American Culture, 1918-1941
A Bibliographical Essay

Jennifer Tebbe

In his Introduction to *The Plastic Age, 1917-1930* (New York: Braziller, 1970), Robert Sklar wrote "American culture was born anew in the Twenties. It was a time for naming all things new, a task for language, to which novelists and poets, the critics and historians leaped as if predestined"(p. 1). Warren Susman concurred with this view in his Introduction to *Culture and Commitment, 1929-1945* (New York: Braziller, 1973), which assessed intellectuals' criticism of the period: "By the end of the 1920s there was general agreement : America had indeed brought forth upon this continent a new civilization." However, Susman also emphasized the tensions experienced by different kinds of Americans as they confronted new and old cultural forms in the interwar years: "As early as the 1920's there were those who were beginning to see that in a sense they were between two eras; they were in a machine age and yet somehow not completely of it; they were caught between an older order and older values and a new order with its new demands" (pp. 3,8).

This bibliographical essay focuses primarily on scholarship that illuminates the interaction between old and new cultural forms in the 1918-1941 period in America. It places less emphasis on more traditional intellectual history which has considered primarily the social thought of artists and intellectuals of the period. Rather, the intent is to explore the more recent scholarship of those who have "learned so much about the complexity, indeed the jarring discordance, of the thought patterns that have prevailed among large fractions of the population in America," as Lawrence Veysey notes in "Intellectual History and the New Social History," in *New Directions in American Intellectual History*, ed. John Higham and Paul K. Conkin (Baltimore: Johns Hopkins University Press,

1979), p. 22. In particular, work that reflects attempts to focus on the study of the consciousness of non-elites as well as elites and on the changing nature of communication between groups in America is highlighted. For further review of new approaches and methodologies in social, cultural, and intellectual history as practiced by American and European historians see Bernard Baily, "The Challenge of Modern Historiography," *American Historical Review* 87 (February 1982): 1-24; Robert Barnton, "Intellectual and Cultural History," in *The Past Before Us: Contemporary Historical Writings in the United States,* ed. Michael Kammen (Ithaca: Cornell University Press, 1980), pp. 327-49; James A. Henretta, "Social History as Lived and Written," *American Historical Review* 84 (December 1979): 1293-322; Gene Wise, "Some Elementary Axioms for an American Culture Studies," in *Prospects,* vol. 4, ed. Jack Salzman (New York: Burt Franklin, 1979), pp. 517-48; and Harry Stout, "Culture, Structure, and the 'New History,'" *Computer and the Humanities* 9 (1975): 213-30.

The essay surveys historical literature relevant to the interwar period in the following areas: socioeconomic and labor history; urban, ethnic, religious, and women's history; and the history of technology, material and popular culture. Secondly, history, American studies, and mass communication scholarship on the mass media of the period — print literature (newspapers, magazines, and books) and advertising, photography, film, and radio — are considered. Some of the most interesting studies of the social thought of artists and intellectuals in the interwar period are Daniel Aaron, *Writers on the Left* (New York: Harcourt Brace, 1961); Henry F. May, *The Discontent of the Intellectuals* (Chicago: Rand McNally, 1964); Christopher Lasch, *The New Radicalism in America, 1889-1963* (New York: Knopf, 1965); Charles C. Alexander, *Nationalism in American Thought, 1930-1945* (Chicago: Rand McNally, 1969); Donald Fleming and Bernard Bailyn, eds., *The Intellectual Migration: Europe and America, 1930-1960* (Cambridge, Mass.: Harvard University Press, 1969); Loren Baritz, "The Culture of the Twenties," in *The Development of an American Culture,* ed. Stanley Coben and Lorman Ratner (Englewood Cliffs, N.J.: Prentice-Hall, 1970); Roderick Nash, *The Nervous Generation, 1917-1930* (New York: Rand McNally, 1970); R. Alan Lawson, *The Failure of Independent Liberalism, 1930-1941* (New York: Putnam, 1971); Robert A. Skotheim, *Totalitarianism in American Social Thought* (New York: Holt, Rinehart and Winston, 1971); Robert M. Crunden, *From Self To Society, 1919-1941* (Englewood Cliffs, N.J.: Prentice-Hall, 1972); Edward A. Purcell, Jr., *The Crisis of Democratic Theory* (Lexington: University Press of Kentucky, 1973); Stow Persons, *The Decline of American Gentility* (New York: Columbia University Press, 1973); Richard H.

Pells, *Radical Visions and American Dreams* (New York: Harper and Row, 1973); Paul Fussell, *The Great War and Modern Memory* (New York: Oxford University Press, 1975); Paul A. Carter, *Another Part of the Twenties* (New York: Columbia University Press, 1977); Charles C. Alexander, *Here the Country Lies, Nationalism and the Arts in Twentieth-Century America* (Bloomington, Ind.: Indiana University Press, 1980); Paul Fussel, *Abroad: British Literary Traveling Between the Wars* (New York: Oxford University Press, 1980); and William Barrett, *The Truants: Adventures Among the Intellectuals* (New York: Anchor Books, 1982).

Socioeconomic and Labor History

The most significant new interpretation of the interwar period is Ellis W. Hawley's *The Great War and the Search for a Modern Order: A History of the American People and Their Institutions, 1917-1933* (New York: St. Martin's, 1979). His conceptual framework is organizational, emphasizing new technology and new managerial, bureaucratic, and voluntary government and business organizations. Hawley suggests that the elites' new structures failed to create their intended "common good" through cooperative efforts, and that social fragmentation increased as a consequence of the new economic and political connections. This insight is an especially valuable one for thinking about the creation and development of new mass media institutions and forms in relation to their preventing an integration of American thought and behavior. And Hawley's chapter on "Intellectual and Cultural Pursuits in a Modernizing Era" offers an especially interesting discussion of the "distances" between high culture and popular culture in science, literature, and the arts. Robert F. Berkhofer, Jr., in "The Organizational Interpretation of American History: A New Synthesis," in *Prospects,* vol. 4, ed. Jack Salzman (New York: Burt Franklin, 1979) also discusses the usefulness of an organizational framework.

Hawley also acknowledges the foundations of interwar events in the progressive and war years. Important for understanding the growth of a large scale organizational society in the early twentieth century are Arthur S. Link, "What Happened to the Progressive Movement in the 1920s" *American Historical Review* 64 (July 1959): 833-51; Gabriel Kolko, *The Triumph of Conservatism: A Reinterpretation of American History, 1900-1916* (New York: Free Press, 1963); Robert H. Wiebe, *The Search for Order, 1877-1920* (New York: Hill and Wang, 1967); James Weinstein, *The Corporate Ideal in the Liberal State, 1900-1918* (Boston: Beacon Press, 1968); Robert D. Cerff, *The War Industries Board: Business-Government Relations During World War I* (Baltimore: Johns Hopkins University Press, 1973); and John D.

Buenker, John C. Burnham, and Robert M. Crunden, *Progressivism* (Cambridge, Mass.: Schenkman, 1977).

The best social and economic examinations extending into the interwar years besides Hawley are Henry F. May, "Shifting Perspectives on the 1920s" *Mississippi Valley Historical Review* 43 (December 1956): 424-27; William E. Leuchtenberg, *The Perils of Prosperity, 1914-1932* (Chicago: University of Chicago Press, 1958); David A. Shannon, *Between the Wars, 1919-1941* (Boston: Houghton Mifflin, 1965, 2nd ed., 1979); Paul Conkin, *The New Deal* (New York: Crowell, 1967); Barton J. Bernstein, "The New Deal: The Conservative Achievements of Liberal Reform," in Barton Bernstein, ed., *Towards a New Past: Dissenting Essays in American History* (New York: Vintage, 1968), pp. 263-88; Morrell Heald, *The Social Responsibilities of Business: Company and Community, 1900-1969* (Cleveland: Case Western Reserve University Press, 1970); James Gilbert, *Designing the Industrial State: The Intellectual Pursuite of Collectivism in American, 1880-1940* (Chicago: Quadrangle, 1972); Joan Hoff Wilson, *The Twenties: Critical Issues* (Boston: Little, Brown, 1972); Louis Galambos, *The Public Image of Big Business in America, 1880-1940* (Baltimore: Johns Hopkins University Press, 1975); Burl Noggle, "Configurations of the Twenties," in *The Reinterpretation of American History and Culture,* ed. William M. Cartwright and Richard L. Watson, Jr., (Washington, D.C.: National Council for the Social Studies, 1973); Otis L. Graham, Jr., *Toward A Planned Society: From Roosevelt to Nixon* (New York: Oxford University Press, 1976); Robert H. Zieger, "Herbert Hoover, A Reinterpretation," *American Historical Review* 81 (October 1976): 800-10, and especially Alfred D. Chandler, Jr., *The Visible Hand: The Managerial Revolution in American Business* (Cambridge, Mass.: Harvard University Press, 1977).

An extensive literature on the history of labor "from the bottom up" began to appear during the 1970s. The most recent texts draw attention to the textures of life on the job and within the local community. They emphasize the everyday meanings of welfare capitalism and the uses of technology as social control mechanisms within and outside the factory. Especially helpful are Stuart D. Brandes, *American Welfare Capitalism, 1880-1940* (Chicago: University of Chicago Press, 1976); Herbert G. Gutman, *Work, Culture, and Society in Industrialized America* (New York: Vintage, 1977); John T. Cumbler, *Workingclass Community in Industrial America: Work, Leisure, and Struggle in Two Industrial Cities, 1880-1930* (Westport, Conn.: Greenwood Press, 1979); David Montgomery, *Workers' Control in America: Studies in the History of Work, Technology and Labor Struggles* (Cambridge: At the University Press, 1979); Gerald D. Nash, *The Great Depression and World War II: Organizing America: 1933-1945* (New

York: St. Martin's, 1979); David Brody, *Workers in Industrial America: Essays on the Twentieth Century Struggle* (New York: Oxford University Press, 1980); and James R. Green, *The World of the Worker: Labor in Twentieth Century America* (New York: Hill and Wang, 1981).

Some bibliographical and review essays that survey economic, social, or labor history are James R. Wason, "American Workers and American History," *American Studies International* 13 (Winter 1974): 10-36; James H. Soltow, "Recent Literature in American Economic History," *American Studies International* (Autumn 1978): 5-33; David Brody, "Labor History in the 1970's: Toward a History of the American Worker" in *The Past Before Us,* ed. Michael Kammen, pp. 252-69; and Melvyn Dubofsky, "Hold the Fort: The Dynamics of Twentieth-Century American Wormic History, Journal of Interdisciplinary History, Journal of Social History, Labor History, and *Radical History.*

Urban, Ethnic, Religious, and Women's History

A number of studies treating specific urban history issues of the interwar period have appeared since 1970. They elaborate on themes and events relating to national and state policies and local communities' concerns — their institutions, landscape, and environment, material culture, patterns of transportation, communication, and consumption. Significant surveys, anthologies, monographs, and articles include Don S. Kirschner, *City and Country: Rural Response to Urbanization in the 1920s* (Westport, Conn.: Greenwood Press, 1970); Neil Harris, "Four Stages of Cultural Growth: The American City," in *The History and Role of the City in American Life,* ed. Arthur Mann (Indianapolis: Indiana Historical Society, 1972); James E. Skideles, "Flappers and Philosophers and Farmers: Rural-Urban Tensions in the Twenties," *Agricultural History* 47 (October 1973): 283-300;Samuel P. Hayes, "The Changing Political Structure of the City in Industrial America," *Journal of Urban History* 1 (November 1974): 6-38; Blaine A. Brownell, *The Urban Ethos in the South, 1920-1930* (Baton Rouge: Louisiana State University Press, 1975); Sam Bass Warner, *The Way We Really Live: Social Change In Metropolitan Boston Since 1920* (Boston: Boston Public Library, 1977); Paul Boyer, *Urban Masses and Moral Order in America 1820-1920* (Cambridge, Mass.: Harvard University Press, 1978); David R. Goldfield and Blaine A. Brownell, *Urban America: From Downtown to No Town* (Boston: Houghton Mifflin, 1979); Morris J. Vogel, *The Invention of the Modern Hospital: Boston, 1870-1930* (Chicago: University of Chicago Press, 1980); Mark S. Foster, *From Streetcar to Superhighway: American City*

Planners and Urban Transportation (Philadelphia: Temple University Press, 1981); Eric H. Monkkonen, "A Disorderly People? Urban Order in the Nineteenth and Twentieth Centuries," *Journal of American History* 68 (December 1981): 539-59; and George E. Mowry and Blaine A. Brownell, *The Urban Nation: 1920-1980* (New York: Hill and Wang, 1981).

Finally, *In Community and Social Change in America* (New Brunswick: Rutgers University Press, 1978), Thomas Bender reviews definitions of "community" which historians and social scientists have assumed in studies of cities in the twentieth century and earlier periods. He argues for seeing community in relation to intense and close relationships built up by social groups within cities. And, in a focused case study of groups, "The Cultures of Intellectual Life: The City and the Professions," in John Higham and Paul Conkin, eds., *New Directions in American Intellectual History* (Baltimore: Johns Hopkins University Press, 1979), he examines the changing relationships between "particular cultures of intellectual life" and the local community as "context and audience for intellectual life" (pp. 181, 182). In her essay in this volume, Joan Shelley Rubin also explores these important issues in relation to understanding radio as a new medium of communication between different social groups in twenties America.

A good deal of recent work on ethnicity, race, religious, and women's history of the interwar period exists. Articles and books offering the most interesting insights into social tensions of the period include David A. Hollinger, "Ethnic Diversity, Cosmopolitanism and the Emergence of the American Liberal Intellegentsia," *American Quarterly* 27 (May 1975): 133-51; John Bodnar, *Immigration and Industrialization: Ethnicity in an American Mill Town, 1870-1940* (Pittsburgh: University of Pittsburgh Press, 1977); R. Fred Wacker, "Assimilation and Cultural Pluralism in American Social Thought," *Phylon* 40 (December 1979): 325-33; Richard Weiss, "Ethnicity and Reform: Minorities and the Ambience of the Depression Years," *Journal of American History* (December 1979): 566-85; James Borchert, *Alley Life in Washington: Family, Community, Religion and Folklife in the City, 1850-1970* (Urbana: University of Illinois Press, 1980); Elizabeth Rauh Bethel, *Promiseland: A Century of Life in a Negro Community* (Philadelphia: Temple University Press, 1981); William R. Hutchinson, *The Modernist Impulse in American Protestantism* (New York: Oxford University Press, 1976); Jack S. Blocher, *Retreat From Reform: The Prohibition Movement in the United States* (Westport, Conn.: Greenwood Press, 1977); William M. Halsey, *The Survival of American Innocence: Catholicism in the Era of Disillusionment, 1920-1940* (South Bend, Ind.: University of Notre Dame

Press, 1980); George M. Marsden, *Fundamentalism and American Culture: The Shaping of Twentieth Century Evangelicalism, 1879-1925* (New York: Oxford University Press, 1980); James McGovern, "The American Women's Pre-World War I Freedom in Manners and Morals," *Journal of American History* 55 (September 1968): 315-33; Margery Davies, "A Woman's Place Is at the Typewriter: The Feminization of the Clerical Labor Force," *Radical America* 8 (July-August 1974): 1-28; Estelle Freedman, "The New Woman: Changing Views of Women in the 1920s," *Journal of American History* 61 (September 1974): 372-93; Gerald E. Critoph, "The Flapper and Her Critics," in *Remember the Ladies: Essays in Honor of Nelson Manfred Blake*, ed. Carol R. George, (Syracuse, N.Y.: Syracuse University Press, 1975), pp. 145-60; Susan Porter Benson, "The Clerking Sisterhood: Rationalization and the Work Culture of Saleswomen in American Department Stores," *Radical America* 12 (March-April 1978): 41-55; Renate Brindenthal, "Something Old, Something New: Women Between the Two World Wars," in *Becoming Visible*, ed. Renate Brindenthal and Claudia Doonz (Boston: Houghton-Mifflin, 1977), pp. 422-44; Patricia Hammer, *Decade of Elusive Promise: Professional Women in the United States, 1920-1930* (Ann Arbor: University of Michigan Press, 1978); Catherine R. Stimpson, Elsa Dixler, Martha J. Nelson, and Kathryn B. Yatrakis, *Women and the American City* (Chicago: University of Chicago Press, 1981); Winifred Wandersee, *Women's Work and Family Values, 1920-1940* (Cambridge, Mass.: Harvard University Press, 1981); and Ruth Schwartz Cowan, "Two Washes in the Morning and a Bridge Party at Night: The American Housewife Between the Wars," in *Our American Sisters: Women in American Life and Thought*, ed. Jean E. Friedman and William G. Shade (Lexington, Mass.: Heath, 1982): 519-41.

Useful reference works, review, and bibliographical essays include Lina Mainiero and Langdon Lynn Faust, eds., *American Women Writers*, vols. 1-5 (New York: Frederick Ungar, 1979-82); Barbara Sicherman and Carol Hurd Green, eds., *Notable American Women: The Modern Period* (Cambridge, Mass.: Harvard University Press, 1980); Stephen Thernstrom, ed., *Harvard Encyclopedia of American Ethnic Groups* (Cambridge, Mass.: Harvard University Press, 1981); John Bodmar, "The Immigrant and the American City," Review Essay, *Journal of Urban History* 3 (1977): 241-49; Kathleen Neils Conzen, "Immigrants, Immigrant Neighborhoods, and Ethnic Identity: Historical Issues," *Journal of American History* 66 (December 1979): 603-15; Edwin S. Gaustad, Darline Miller and G. Allison Stokes, "Religion in America," *American Quarterly* 31 (Bibliography Issue 1979): 250-83; Rudolph J. Vecoli, "The Resurgence of American Immigration History," *American Studies International* 17

(Winter 1979): 46-66; Kathleen Neils Conzen, "Community Studies, Urban History and American Local History," in *The Past Before Us*, ed. Michael Kammen, pp. 270-91; Robert E. Bieder, "Anthropology and History of the American Indian," *American Quarterly* 33 (Bibliography Issue 1981): 309-36; Michael H. Ebner, "Urban History: Retrospect and Prospect," *Journal of American History* 8 (June 1981): 69-84; John Ibson, "Virgin Land or Virgin Mary? Studying The Ethnicity of White Americans," *American Quarterly* 33 (Bibliography Issue 1981): 284-308; L. Ling-chi Wang, "Asian American Studies," *American Quarterly* 33 (Bibliography Issue 1981): 339-54; Leila J. Rupp, "Reflections on Twentieth-Century American Women's History," *Reviews in American History* 9 (June 1981): 275-84; and Werner Sollors, "Theory of American Ethnicity, Or?" *American Quarterly* 33 (Bibliography Issue 1981): 257-83. Among specialized journals which publish articles and book reviews relevant to the interwar period are *Agricultural History, Ethnicity, Feminist Studies, Journal of American Ethnic History, Journal of Ethnic Studies, Journal of Urban History, Melus, Public Historian, Radical History Review, and Signs: Journal of Women in Culture and Society*.

History of Technology, Material, and Popular Culture

A number of American Studies scholars and historians who have been most successful in finding out how "people really lived" and what they "really" thought in the past have been those working within and around the fields of the history of technology and material and popular culture. The focus of their examinations has been the objects which people used in their everyday lives, or the events (e.g., recreational, work-related, political, criminal, religious) which ordinary people participated in or followed vicariously through the mass media. Scholars have pursued interdisciplinary methods to examine the things themselves, the individuals producing and distributing them and the consuming public. John William Ward's essay "The Meaning of Lindbergh's Flight," *American Quarterly* 10 (Spring 1958): 3-16, and Alan Trachtenberg's book *Brooklyn Bridge: Fact and Symbol* (Chicago: University of Chicago Press, 1965, 2nd ed., 1979) are classic examples of the scholar examining Americans' responses to the "machine" from the cultural perspective. In several essays on the twenties and thirties — especially "The Culture of the Thirties," in Stanly Coben and Lorman Ratner, eds., *The Development of American Culture* (Englewood Cliffs, N.J.: Prentice-Hall, 1971), pp. 179-218, and "Piety, Profits, & Play in the 1920's," in *Men, Women & Issues, American History*, ed. Howard H. Quint and Milton Cantor, (Homewood, Ill.: Dorsey, 1975), pp. 191-216. Warren Susman has also encouraged scholars to pay attention to the "meanings" of the decades' "cultural forms," their "Model A," "Machine Art," Williamsburg, the Pentagon, *How To Win Friends and Influence People*, "Monopoly," and *Let Us Now Praise Famous Men.* While in their work Ward, Trachtenberg, and Susman stay within the disciplinary bounds primarily of two fields, literature and intellectual history, other scholars are beginning to combine new methods and approaches within several diciplines: cultural and symbolic anthropology, philosophy, sociology, business history, social and labor history, art and architectural history, and the history of science, technology, material culture, and archaeology.

Further, in the close examination of machines and other things, commercial amusements and the arts, many of these scholars have continued to question even more closely the idea that twentieth century Americans broke sharply with the genteel cultural order of the nineteenth century. Rather, they see the simultaneous development of a self-conscious American aesthetic and international modernism as a culmination of events that began in the 1890s or even earlier. They find connecting links between Victorian America and the growth of twentieth century mass consumerism. The following studies offer the richest explanations of these cultural changes in the interwar period and the decades immediately preceding: James W. Carey and J. J. Quirk, "Mythos of the Electronic Revolution," Parts I, II, *The American Scholar* 39 (Spring and Summer 1970): 219-41 and 395-424; Daniel Walker Howe, "American Victorianism as a Culture," *American Quarterly* 27 (December 1975): 507-32; David Noble, *America by Design: Science, Technology, and the Rise of Corporate Capitalism* (New York: Knopf, 1977); John Kasson, *Amusing the Million: Coney Island at the Turn of the Century* (New York: Hill and Wang, 1978); Warren James Belasco, *Americans on the Road: From Autocamp to Motel, 1910-1945* (Cambridge, Mass.: MIT Press, 1979); Jeffrey L. Meikle, *Twentieth Century Limited: Industrial Design in America, 1925-1939* (Philadelphia: Temple University Press, 1979); Susan Porter Benson, "Palace of Consumption, Machine for Selling: The American Department Store, 1880-1940," *Radical History Review* 21 (Winter 1980): 199-221; Richard C. Crepeau, *Baseball: America's Diamond Mind, 1919-1941* (Orlando, Florida: University Presses of Florida, 1980); Steven A. Riess, *Touching Base: Professional Baseball and American Culture in the Progressive Era* (Westport, Conn.: Greenwood Press, 1980); Lewis A. Erenberg, *Steppin' Out: New York Nightlife and the Transformation of American Culture, 1890-1930* (Westport, Conn.: Greenwood Press, 1981); Robert Hughes, *The Shock of the New* (New York: Knopf, 1981); T.

Jackson Lears, *No Place of Grace: Antimodernism and the Transformation of American Culture, 1880-1920* (New York: Pantheon, 1981); and
essays in the special double issue of the *Michigan Quarterly Review* 19
(Fall 1980/Winter 1981) devoted to "The Automobile and American
Culture."

Helpful bibliographical and review essays in and around the fields
of the history of technology and material and popular culture can be found
in Harold Skramstad, "American Things: A Neglected Material Culture,"
American Studies International 10 (Spring 1972): 11-22; Linda Funk
Place, Joanna Schneider Zangrando, James W. Lea, and John Lovell,
"The Object as Subject: The Role of Museums and Material Culture
Collections in American Studies," *American Quarterly* 26 (August 1974):
281-94; Carl W. Condit, "Architectural History in the United States: A
Bibliographical Essay," *American Studies International* 16 (Autumn
1977): 5-24; James J. Flink, "The Car Culture Revisited: Some Comments
on the Recent Historiography of Automotive History," *Michigan Quar-
terly Review* 19-20 (Fall 1980/Winter 1981): 772-81; David A. Hounshell,
"On the Discipline of the History of American Technology," *Journal of
American History* 67 (March 1981): 854-64; Darwin H. Stapleton and
David A. Hounshell, "The Discipline of the History of American Technology: An Exchange," *Journal of American History* 68 (March 1982): 897-
902; David E. Kyvig and Myron A. Marty, *Nearby History: Exploring the
Past Around You* (Nashville, Tenn.: American Association for State and
Local History, 1982); Thomas J. Schlereth, *Material Culture Studies in
America: An Anthology* (Nashville, Tenn.: American Association of State
and Local History, 1982); and the essays on such subjects as animation, the
automobile, sports, stage entertainment, architecture, circus and outdoor
entertainments, food, and games and toys included in M. Thomas Inge,
ed., *Handbook of American Popular Culture*, vols. 1-3 (Westport, Conn.:
Greenwood Press, 1978, 1980, 1981). Journals that regularly publish helpful articles, books reviews or review essays include *American Anthropologist, American Quarterly, American Studies, Clio, Isis, Journal of American Culture, Journal of Cultural Geography, Journal of Popular Culture,
Journal of Regional Cultures, and Reviews in American History*

Print Literature and Advertising

Bibliographic references and survey histories which should be
consulted about the newspaper and magazine press of the period include
Edwin Emery and Michael Emery, *The Press and America: An Interpretive History of the Mass Media* (Urbana: University of Illinois Press,

1978); Anthony Smith, *The Newspaper: An International History* (New York: Thames and Hudson, 1980); Eleanor Blum, *Basic Books in the Mass Media* (Urbana: University of Illinois Press, 1980); John Schact, *A Bibliography for the Study of Magazines* (Urbana: University of Illinois Press, 1979); Joseph McKern, "The History of American Journalism: A Bibliographical Essay," *American Studies International* 15 (Autumn 1976): 17-34; Jennifer Tebbe, "Print and American Culture," *American Quarterly* 32 (Bibliography Issue 1980): 259-79; and Dorothy Schmidt, "Magazines," and Richard A. Schwarzlose, "Newspapers," in Inge, ed., *Handbook of American Popular Culture* 3 (1981): 137-62; 231-64. Also useful are the book reviews and annotated sections on recent articles and books in *Journalism Quarterly* and *Journalism History*. Bibliographies and articles on women, minority and ethnic magazines, and newspapers can frequently be found in the above journals.

Hazel Dicken Garcia and John D. Stevens' *Communication History* (Beverly Hills: Sage, 1980) is a recent attempt to rethink issues of studying the mass media over time. The chapters dealing with old and new approaches to writing the history of communications are especially useful for thinking about the role of print media between the wars. Also see Marion Marzolf, "American Studies — Ideas for Media Historians," *Journalism History* 5 (Spring 1978), and Jean Ward, "Interdisciplinary Research and Journalism Historians," *ibid.* And the essays by James Murphy, John D. Stevens, Marion Marzolf, Sally Griffith, and James Boylan in this volume are welcome additions to what is a relatively small body of literature on the press between the wars.

Several recent works that offer interesting insights into the social tensions or suggest new approaches to thinking about the value conflicts of the period are Paul L. Murphy, *The Meaning of Freedom of Speech: First Amendment Freedom from Wilson to FDR* (Westport, Conn.: Greenwood Press, 1972); Catherine L. Covert, "A View of the Press in the Twenties," *Journalism History* 2 (Autumn 1975): 66-67; 92-96; and "'Jumbled, Disparate, and Trivial': Problems in the Use of Newspapers as Historical Evidence," *The Maryland Historian* 12 (Spring 1981): 47-60; Terry Hynes, "Media Manipulation and Political Campaigns: Bruce Barton and the Presidential Elections of the Jazz Age," *Journalism History* 4 (Autumn 1977): 93-98; Michael Schudson, *Discovering the News: A Social History of American Newspapers* (New York: Basic Books, 1978); Graham J. White, *FDR and the Press* (Chicago: University of Chicago Press, 1979); John D. Stevens, "The Black Press Looks at 1920's Journalism," *Journalism History* 7 (Autumn-Winter, 1980): 109-13; and John B. Brazil, "Murder Trials, Murder, and Twenties America," *American Quarterly* 33 (Summer 1981): 163-84.

In respect to themes developed in this volume some issues dealt
with by Michael Schudson, Catherine L. Covert, and John B. Brazil are
especially relevant. Schudson, in the chapter from *Discovering the News,*
entitled "Objectivity Becomes Ideology: Journalism after World War I,"
examines the profession and 1920s and 1930s culture in relation to the
birth of the public relations field and to larger issues of the growth of
twentieth-century democracy and a corporate economy. He argues that
journalists'confrontation with relativism and the lack of central values in a
"modern" society must be examined in attempting to understand the
articulation of the ideal of objectivity as a professional value by the 1930s.
How and why newspaper editors and journalists institutionally distinguished between the political column or human interest story as subjective
strategies and the "news story" as an objective treatment of facts not as
"aspects of the world, but consensually validated statments about it"
requires further analysis.

Catherine L. Covert's article, "Jumbled, Disparate, and Trivial,"
on using the newspaper as a historical document tells us a great deal about
both the problems and challenges the newspaper offers as a cultural
artifact of the 1920s. Through a discussion of her research in progress on
the "mode of transmission of Freudian thought through the American
press of the 1920s," she offers some suggestions about the public's intense
response to Freud during the twenties. She sees the culture torn between
"old ideas about autonomy and responsibility, and the new liberating
explanations of behavior; a society looking to science for good, but despis-
ing its sale to the highest bidder, valuing emotion and sensations but
shrinking from too much of it at close-hand." In explaining how the
newspaper can be studied in its role of introducing and successively "ignoring," "modifying," and "reinterpreting" aspects of Freudian thought she
suggests a way to analyze more completely the life of the minds of a variety
of twenties Americans.

A third essay which re-examines events of the twenties by looking
at the newspaper as a source is John R. Brazil's discussion of the coverage
of murders and murder trials. He raises questions about the "newspaper-
reading public's fixation with criminality" in relation to confusion about
individualism, "a deeply American theory of behavior." By comparing
"the formulaic language of sensational journalism" with the "causal language" of social science (Williams, Dewey), the "wish-fulfilling language"
of popular western and detective novels and the "questioning language" of
serious fiction (Fitzgerald and Dreiser), Brazil shows members of twenties
America struggling to examine the same assumptions about individualism
as Covert depicts. However, his focus on a variety of cultural forms

available to and read by often distinctly different social groups suggests another way of thinking about the splits and connections between elite and non-elite audiences. Finally, Sally Griffith's essay in this volume offers an illuminating but seldom-used approach to the analysis of the tension between traditional values and the new culture of consumption. She examines the visual consumption position and the news, editorial, and advertising content of one small-town newspaper.

A field much neglected until recently in relation to understanding the growth of mass consumer society in the twentieth century is American advertising and public relations. Insightful studies date back to Frank Presbrey's important text, *The History and Development of Advertising* (New York: Doubleday, 1929) and include several works published during the 1950s and early 1960s: David Potter, *People of Plenty: Economic Abundance and the American Character* (Chicago: University of Chicago Press, 1954); James P. Wood, *The Story of Advertising* (New York: Ronald, 1958); Daniel Boorstin, *The Image: A Guide to Pseudo-Events in America* (New York: Atheneum, 1961); Otis Pease, *Responses of American Advertising, 1920-1940* (New Haven: Yale University Press, 1958). More recent works include Donald Meyer, *The Positive Thinkers: A Study of the American Quest for Health, Wealth, and Personal Power from Mary Baker Eddy to Norman Vincent Peale* (Garden City, N.Y.: Anchor, 1966); an essay by Merle Curti, "The Changing Concept of 'Human Nature' in the Literature of American Advertising," *Business History Review* 41 (Winter 1967): 335-57; Daniel Boorstin, *The Americans: The Democratic Experience* (New York: Vintage, 1973); Stuart Ewen, *Captains of Consciousness: Advertising and the Social Roots of the Consumer Culture* (New York: McGraw Hill, 1976); and Don S. Kirshner, "Publicity Properly Applied: The Selling of Expertise, 1900-1929," *American Studies* 19 (Spring 1978): 65-78.

Further, just in the last few years there is evidence that more attention is being paid to the intellectual and social history of American advertising and public relations. T. Jackson Lears, in two unpublished papers, "From Salvation to Self-Realization: Advertising and the Therapeutic Roots of the Consumer Culture, 1880-1930" (presented at the American Historical Association Annual Meeting, Washington, D.C., December 30, 1980) and "The Humbug and the Suckers: Problems and Prospects in the Historiography of American Advertising" (presented at the Popular Culture Association Annual Meeting, Louisville, Kentucky, April 16, 1982), which represent the beginnings of research on a book about the history of American advertising, argues for the need to explore the subject in relation to a "network of institutional, religious, and psychological changes." In particular he focuses on a "therapeutic ethos stressing self-realization in this world" articulated by liberal ministers, psychologists, and other "therapeutic ideologues" as well as by advertisers. He rejects assertions that advertising executives deliberately and self-consciously promoted the development of a modern character or personality which fit the needs of an expanding capitalist economy. Rather, he argues that business elites' motives regarding the "therapeutic ethos" conflicted in ways similar to the rest of the population. "As much as any other social group, national advertisers helped to popularize a pseudo-religion of health and an anxious self-absorption among the American population. But many would have been dismayed if they had known it." A useful bibliographical essay on advertising is Elizabeth Williamson's "Advertising," in Inge, ed., *Handbook of American Popular Culture* 3: 3-29. Richard S. Tedlow, in *Keeping the Corporate Image: Public Relations and Business, 1900-1950* (Greenwich, Conn.: JAI, 1979), discusses advertising as well as public relations. He places major emphasis on the growing role of persuasion as technique of social control in the 1920s and the different ways of using it chosen by public relations experts.

Leo P. Ribuffo's article, "Jesus Christ as Business Statesman: Bruce Barton and the Selling of Corporate Capitalism," *American Quarterly* 33 (Summer 1981): 206-31 is a well-drawn case study of one important advertising figure's liberal Protestant religious beliefs and a concomitant faith in the positive role of modern advertising's creation of new consumer desires and use of emotional techniques of persuasion. It is also representative of recent analyses of single important books or magazine writings of both popular and serious authors of the interwar period. Ribuffo looks at the content, marketing, and reception by a variety of audiences of Barton's 1925 best-seller *The Man Nobody Knows*. Other interesting studies that shed light on the roles of texts as economic commodities and cultural agents and of authors as "popularizers" of the ideologies of experts within intellectual communities include Ann Douglas, "Studs Lonigan and the Failure of History in Mass Society: A Study in Claustrophobia," *American Quarterly* 29 (Winter 1977): 485-505; Gail Thain Parker, *"How To Win Friends and Influence People:* Dale Carnegie and the Problem of Sincerity," *American Quarterly* 29 (Winter 1977): 506-18; Robert B. Westbrook, "Tribune of the Technostructure: The Popular Economics of Stuart Chase," *American Quarterly* (Fall 1980): 387-408; Peter Gregg Slater, "The Negative Secularism of The Modern Temper: Joseph Wood Krutch," *American Quarterly* 33 (Summer 1981): 185-205; Richard Wrightman Fox, "Epitaph for Middletown: Robert S. Lynd and the Analyses of Consumer Cultures," in *The Culture of Consumption in America*, ed. R.

W. Fox and T. Jackson Lears (New York: Pantheon, 1982); and Gregory W. Bush, "Face in the Crowd: Gerald Stanley Lee and the Engineering of American Attitudes," a paper presented at the Popular Culture Association Annual Meeting, Louisville, Kentucky, April 16, 1982. In this volume Michael Schudson's chapter challenging the causal role traditionally assigned to advertising in relationship to such social behavior as women smoking is an important contribution to advertising literature.

The most interesting recent examination of a fiction best-seller is Elizabeth Fox-Genovese's article, "Scarlett O'Hara: The Southern Lady as New Woman," *American Quarterly* 33 (Fall 1981): 391-411. She argues that Margaret Mitchell's *Gone With The Wind* spoke to the bourgeois cultural order of the 1920s, an order compelled to undergo change by the forces of personal questioning of identification and of challenges to the existing social structure presented by the various cultural forms of immigrant groups and the emerging southern black. "Its very status as a novel, straddling the worlds of elite and mass culture, captured the dilemma of a bourgeois society that struggled to preserve its own values against internal rebellion and to engage the allegiance of a broad and heterogeneous popular base. Not unlike the new languages of radio, film, and advertising, it appeared to offer Americans an image of themselves at once specific enough to invite identification and general enough to encompass national diversity" (p. 411).

Finally, scholars studying popular print fiction and nonfiction of the interwar years should begin with a reading of several classics: Frank Luthur Mott, *Golden Multitudes* (New York: Macmillan, 1947); Leo Lowenthal, *Popular Culture and Society* (Englewood Cliffs, N.J.: Prentice-Hall, 1961); Norman Jacobs, *Culture for the Millions* (Princeton, N.J.: Princeton University Press, 1961); James D. Hart, *The Popular Book: A History of American Literary Taste* (Berkeley: University of California Press, 1963); Theodore P. Greene, *America's Heroes: The Changing Model of Success in America* (New York: Oxford University Press, 1970); and John C. Cawelti, *Adventure, Mystery, Romance* (Chicago: University of Chicago Press, 1976). Popular entertainment literature is adequately surveyed in essays on such genres as detective and mystery novels, pulps, comic books, gothic novels, and science fiction in Thomas Inge, ed., *Handbook of American Popular Culture*. Also, of great interest, although not specifically addressing itself to issues of the interwar period is Janice Radway, "The Utopian Impulse in Popular Literature: Gothic Romances and 'Feminist' Protest," *American Quarterly* 33 (Summer 1981): 140-62. Radway offers an interesting new interpretation of the function of popular literature as "conservator of social values," but also with each form's "particular conservatism" appearing "to be a response to specific material changes posing a threat to the social structure's legitimizing belief system" (p. 161).

Photography, Film, and Radio

While a plethora of books and articles has been published in the last twenty years on the role of photographs and films as cultural artifacts, few of these works are successful at close historical and cultural analysis of visual or aural products of the interwar years. Often, the photographic and electric media of the period are dealt with in chapters of larger (and often excellent) synthetic works. Biographies of photographers, directors, film stars, or radio personalities have also been written, although often using only narrative and descriptive approaches to discussions of their subjects' lives and work. More recently, studies of such genres as westerns, detective, science fiction, gangster, comedy, and horror films have appeared. While these studies often provide interesting general insights into photography, film, or radio as reflections of the cultural values of Americans in the past, they seldom provide validation of these insights through close analysis of the content, form, and technological, organizational, and occupational norms surrounding the production, distribution, and diffusion of the artifacts themselves. Because of a failure to take popular culture seriously in the past, there is a dearth of a social and cultural history of visual and aural mass media in the interwar years. A very real secondary problem, however, is the difficulty of access to mass media artifacts. Much has been destroyed, the photographs, films, and radio programs themselves as well as the supporting printed business and government records and personal papers. Nevertheless, historians have begun to take popular culture and mass media much more seriously (as this volume indicates with the bringing together of journalism historians and intellectual historians). They are uncovering the documentary evidence and employing new analytical approaches, including sociological, anthropological, structural, semiotic, and other literary/linguistic and "new" social, cultural, and intellectual history forms.

Significant synthetic historical surveys of photography, film, and radio or works that focus on an analysis of perception and techniques of languages, technology, and criticism, but also consider twenties and thirties artifacts within their historical and cultural contexts are Susan Sontag, *On Photography* (New York: Farrar, Straus, and Giroux, 1977); Beaumont Newhall, *The History of Photography* (New York: Dover, 1964); John Berger, *Ways of Seeing* (Baltimore: Penguin, 1977); Raymond Fielding, *The American Newsreel 1911-1967* (Norman: University of Oklahoma Press, 1972); Erik Barnouw, *Documentary: A History of the Non-Fiction Film* (New York: Oxford University Press, 1974); Michael Wood, *America in the Movies* (New York: Basic Books, 1975); Robert Sklar, *Movie-Made America: A Cultural History of American Movies* (New York: Vintage, 1976); Garth Jowett, *Film: The Democratic Art* (Boston: Little, Brown, 1976); Louis D. Gianetti, *Understanding Movies* (Englewood Cliffs, N.J.: Prentice-Hall, 1982); and James Monaco, *How to Read A Film: The Art, Technology, Language, History, and Theory of Film and Media* (New York: Oxford University Press, 1981); Pierre Sorlin, *The Film and History: Restaging the Past* (New York: Barnes & Noble, 1981); Erik Barnouw, *A Tower in Babel: A History of Broadcasting in the United States to 1933* (New York: Oxford University Press, 1966), and *The Golden Web: A History of Broadcasting in the United States 1933-1953* (New York: Oxford University Press, 1968). Essays that survey photography, film and radio secondary sources are David C. Culbert's "Historians and the Visual Analysis of Television News," in *The Network News: Issues in Content Research,* ed. William Adams and Fay Schreibman (Washington, D.C.: George Washington University, 1978): 140-153, and his "Note on Government Paper Records/ Bibliographic Guide for Film and Video Studies," in *Scholars' Guide to Washington, D.C.: Film and Video Collections,* ed. Bonnie G. Rowan (Washington, D.C.: Smithsonian Institution Press, 1980): 235-61. On photography alone, excellent essays are Marsha Peters and Bernard Mergen "'Doing the Rest': The Use of Photographs in American Studies," *American Quarterly* 29 (Bibliography Issue, 1977): 280-305 and Thomas J. Schlereth, "Mirrors of the Past: Historical Photography and American History," in *Artifacts and the American Past* (Nashville, Tenn.: American Association for State and Local History, 1980), pp. 11-47. On film, incisive and inclusive essays are provided by several authors in John E. O'Connor, ed., *Film and the Humanities* (New York: The Rockefeller Fund, 1977); John E. O'Connor, "Teaching Film and American Culture: A Survey of Texts," *American Quarterly* 31 (Winter 1976): 718-23; Peter C. Rollins, "Film, Television, and American Studies: Questions, Activities, and Guides," *American Quarterly* 31 (Winter 1979): 724-50; Robert H. Armow, "Film," in *Handbook of American Popular Culture,* ed. M. Thomas Inge, pp. 121-50; and "Beyond Visual Aids: American Film As American Culture," *American Quarterly* 32 (Bibliography Issue 1980): 280-300. On radio, useful essays are Nicholas A. Sharp, "Radio," in *Handbook of American Popular Culture,* ed. M. Thomas Inge, 225-50; and J. Fred MacDonald, Michael T. Marsden, and Christopher D. Geist, "Radio and Television Studies and American Culture,"

American Quarterly 32 (Bibliography Issue 1980): 301-17. Essays on new
books on general radio programming and areas such as comedy, soap
operas and news that raise questions about the directions of new research
are Philip T. Rosen, "The Marvel of Radio," *American Quarterly* 31 (Fall
1979): 572-81 and Alan Havig, "Radio and American Life," *Reviews in
American History* 8 (September 1980): 403-407. An important general
essay on media theory is Michael R. Real, "Media Theory: Contributions
to an Understanding of Mass Communications," *American Quarterly* 32
(Bibliography Issue 1980): 238-58.

    Significant journals useful to those doing research on the interwar
period are *Afterimage, Cineaste, Film Quarterly, Film and History, History
of Photography, Image, Journal of Popular Film and Television, Journal
of University Film Association of American Film, Quarterly Review of
Film Studies, Photograph* and *Post Script: Essays in Film and the
Humanities.*

    Recent works that suggest new methodological directions for
research in photography, film, and radio have been written in different
fields of history and in American Studies. In the area of photography
Reese Jenkins' *Images and Enterprises: Technology and the American
Photographic Industry, 1839-1925* (Baltimore: Johns Hopkins University
Press, 1975) is a work solidly grounded within the field of the history of
science and technology. Its insights into the relationship between the
photographic industry and American society and culture are fully supported by the use of corporate archives, personal papers, and government
documents. While limited in the kind of statements that he is willing to
make about either the impact of the industry and its products in American
society or how the American political and social system shaped the technology and its uses, Jenkins' study is invaluable for future scholars who
wish to explore its role as a mass market product in the transition from
Victorian to modern life for middle-class Americans able to afford a
"Kodak."

    Neil Harris, in "Iconography and Intellectual History: The Half-
Tone Effect," in *New Directions in American Intellectual History*, pp.
196-211, goes beyond Jenkins' more narrow focus on commercial, industrial, and technological history to urge that the study of iconography, or
"pictorial description" be placed within both Jenkins' contexts and that of
the history of "taste, opinion, and artistic style." In encouraging intellectual and journalism historians to examine the "coming of the half-tone
engraving process" because it "possesses great significance to the study of
American thought and behavior during the late nineteenth and early
twentieth centuries," Harris' article also points to the need for looking at

the successful and unsuccessful uses within the print medium of pictorial strategies of illustration and the photograph in relation to changing twentieth-century mentality. *"Harper's* itself had begun to use the half-tone by the late 1880's, and steady improvements meant the easier repro-duction of oil paintings and wash drawings, to say nothing of the photo-graphs. True iconography, then, was capable of provoking outbursts on the general thrust of modernity and stimulating its discontents" (pp. 196, 197, 205).

Surely the richest interdisciplinary examination of photographs of the 1930s is William Stott's *Documentary Expression and Thirties America* (New York: Oxford University Press, 1973). He combines photo-graphic techniques, literary analysis, cultural history, and mass communi-cation theory to examine documentary photography, nonfiction, report-age, and the "documentary motive" in popular radio, advertising, and picture magazines. Most significant is his analysis of the cultural tension in his analysis of the documentary photographs in print publications, a revelation of the "contradictions" of a world that "can be improved and yet must be celebrated as it is." For a further view of documentary photog-raphy in the thirties see F. Jack Hurley, *Portrait of a Decade: Roy Stryker and the Development of Documentary Photography in the Thirties* (Baton Rouge, La.: Louisiana State University Press, 1972). A discussion of the decline of the "documentary look" at the close of the 1930s, can be found in Stott's "Hard Times and Happy Days: Picturing People in the 1930s" (Paper delivered at the Lowell Conference on Industrial History: The Arts and Industrialism, University of Lowell, Lowell, Mass., May 1, 1982).

Finally, books such as Michael Lesy's *Real Life: Louisville in the Twenties* (New York: Pantheon, 1976); Barbara Norfleet's *Wedding* (New York: Simon and Schuster, 1979) and her *Champion Pig: Great Moments in Everyday Life* (Boston: David R. Godine, 1979) are important contribu-tions to the study of photography in general and during the interwar period because they supply us with "pictures" of the lives of ordinary Americans — at work, at home, at play, in trouble, and participating in community celebrations and ceremonies. These texts abound in photographs and lack elaborative analysis or supportive documentation in appropriate govern-ment, business, or private records. Nonetheless, these studies must be duplicated with serious analysis as accompaniment. Perhaps Lesy's study of Louisville is the most disconcerting in its presentation of the original and retouched creations taken for commercial differs greatly from the matter-of-fact, human-centered, seasonally paced farm-town culture that had preceded it" (p. vii). Further studies are needed that look at industry photographs of "reality" and analyze content, techniques, and forms of twenties and thirties everyday American "snapshots" of events and people. This record of everyday life is too precious to be lost. I "In Selling Light: General Electric and the Urban Landscape, 1910-1930" (presented at the American Studies Association Annual Meeting, Memphis, Tennessee, October 1981), Davide E. Nye provides an important analysis of the photographs taken for public relations and advertising purposes and preserved in the General Electric collectionas "a disciplined expresion of corporate interests." They are "records of perceptions" which "illustrate photography's use as a means of ideological representation." Also see John R. Stilgoe, "The Urban Power House and the Electric Version" (paper delivered at the Lowell conference, April 30, 1982).

In the area of film there are two texts that are synthetic surveys of the history of women in films: Marjorie Rosen, *Popcorn Venus: Women, Movies, and the American Dream* (New York: Avon, 1973), and Molly Haskell, *From Reverence to Rape: The Treatment of Women in the Movies* (New York: Holt, Rinehart and Winston, 1974). Both are rich in their analyses of women's changing roles, especially in their chapters on the twenties and thirties. There are also several articles which have appeared looking at specific films and aspects of women's portrayal in relation to the tensions within the culture. The most interesting of these are June Sochen, "The New Women and Twenties America: Way Down East," in *American History/American Film*, ed. John E. O'Connor and Martin A. Jackson (New York: Ungar, 1979), pp. 1-16; Kay Sloan, "Sex Warfare in the Silent Cinema: Comedies and Melodramas of Women Suffragism," *American Quarterly* 33 (Fall 1981): 412-36; and Mary P. Ryan, "The Projection of a New Womanhood: The Movie Moderns in the 1920's" in *Our American Sisters*, pp. 500-18.

Two books which discuss the black experience in American films, both doing an excellent job on issues of racism and Hollywood in the interwar period are Daniel J. Leab, *From "Sambo" to "Superspade": The Black Experience in Motion Pictures* (Boston: Houghton Mifflin, 1975), and Thomas Cripps, *Slow Fade to Black: The Negro in American Film, 1900-1942* (New York: Oxford University Press, 1977). In *The Hollywood Indian: Stereotypes of Native American Indians in Films* (Trenton: New Jersey State Museum, 1980) John E. O'Connor discusses several specific films of the twenties and thirties which dealt with relationships between Indian and white culture. Jack Temple Kirby also offers some fascinating insights into a culture's view of a geographical region and its people in *Movie-Made Dixie: The South in the American Imagination* (Baton Rouge: Louisiana State University Press, 1978). In *Pursuits of Happiness: The Hollywood Comedy of Remarriage* (Cambridge, Mass.: Harvard

University Press, 1981), Stanley Cavell provides a brilliant analysis of the screwball comedy, a genre extremely popular with thirties audiences. Jeffrey Morton Paine takes the broader view of American culture in *The Simplification of American Life: Hollywood Films of the 1930s* (New York: Arno Press, 1977), and Richard Schickel offers a controversial and bleak interpretation of cultural "myths" in Walt Disney's animated cartoons in *The Disney Version* (New York: Simon and Schuster, 1968).

Finally, a recent anthology and monography should be mentioned. John E. O'Connor and Martin Jackson's previously cited text, *American History/American Film,* devotes nearly half of its essays to films of the twenties and thirties. The anthology represents the first effort to bring together a number of essays on film written by historians. Larry May's *Screening Out the Past: The Birth of Mass Culture and the Motion Picture Industry* (New York: Oxford University Press, 1980) is interesting because of its efforts to defend the idea that the movie industry was one of the major forces in the transition from a Victorian to a mass consumer culture between the 1890s and 1930s. While May examines only very few films, the insights offered into "the mutual interaction" which existed between Hollywood producers and their middle class audiences, both concerned with "devising personal solutions to the major alterations in work, sexual roles, and consumption" (p. xv) are exceptionally useful. Mark Fackler's essay in this text further explores some of the issues of the movies in changing rules of behavior.

Several studies on radio should be mentioned. First, Philip T. Rosen's *The Modern Stentors: Radio Broadcasters and the Federal Government, 1920-1934* (Westport, Conn.: Greenwood Press, 1980) argues that the federal goverment, especially in the guise of Herbert Hoover, stepped into a chaotic situation among competitor stations and institutions feuding for control of the air waves to establish and ensure a stabilized environment for the growth of the radio industry. Historians will probably debate with Rosen over whether the regulations Hoover engineered were the best policies for meeting the public's needs. However, grounding his narrative with research in voluminous primary documents from industry and government, Rosen draws scholars' attention to the possibilties for future research connecting cultural and economic history on radio in its early years.

Second, recent books whose primary focus on radio broadcasters and producers and specific radio programs are J. Fred MacDonald's *Don't Touch That Dial! Radio Programming in American Life From 1920 to 1960* (Chicago: Nelson-Hall, 1979) and Arthur Frank Wertheim, *Radio Comedy* (New York: Oxford University Press, 1979). As its title indicates,

MacDonald offers a broad historical overview of radio, arguing that programs were "products" of their respective periods and overwhelmingly influenced by the commercial goals of advertising. Joan Shelley Rubin makes a simlar argument in her chapter in this volume. Wertheim adopts an interdisciplinary approach in analyzing specific comedians' styles and program narratives. He argues that radio served a conservative function, especially during the Depression era. Daniel J. Czitrom offers further support for this assertion in his essay, "The Ethereal Hearth: American Radio from Wireless Through Broadcasting, 1892-1940," in *Media and the American Mind: From Morse to McLuhan* (Chapel Hill: University of North Carolina Press, 1982). The essay explores the changing responses of the public and government and industry to radio during its first forty years. Czitrom contrasts the public's initial fascination with their shift, at the close of the 1920s, to a more passive reception of a medium defined by the content of its messages. Of particular interest to Czitrom are the demands which advertising interests placed on radio programming to "present an aura of constant newness" and yet adopt older popular cultural forms such as the vaudeville format of the variety shows or the minstrel tradition in comedy programs.

Finally, David Culbert's *News For Everyman: Radio and Foreign Affairs in Thirties America* (Westport, Conn.: Greenwood Press, 1976) offers some of the most original research in archival sources: both recorded programs and written scripts and documentation in the private and public papers of the news commentators. Culbert is concerned with the role radio — as an aural medium — played in creating an interest in information about events in the rest of the world among mass media consumers. He sees radio commentators and their programs playing a far more important role than that print medium in influencing the average person's foreign affairs perspectives and offers comparative analysis of the reportage of newspaper journalists and editors with the radio commentators. (He does not consider news reels.) Scholars have quarreled with his conclusion that "when discussing public opinion and foreign policy in the 1930s we must think in terms of radio, not newspapers. The images and examples must come from an electronic medium or we do great violence to the past" (p. 11). However, until further close examinations of the content, form, production, and personalities of thirties mass media follow, his argument remains a strong one. The articles by Catherine Covert, Richard Schwarzlose, and Joan Shelley Rubin in this text are important because they take up the task of explaining how mass media creators and audiences interacted with the barrage of print, oral, aural, and visual modes of communication presented to them during the interwar period. In "And Counseling for Every

Family: The Psychological Profession's Radio Campaign, 1930-1950"
(paper presented at the Popular Culture Association Annual Meeting,
Louisville, Kentucky, April 1982), Sonya Michel disucsses the psychology
profession's efforts to use the medium through techniques ranging from
simple issuance of press releases to production of their own programming.
However, while focusing on the profession's efforts with radio, she is
sensitive to their attempts to coordinate radio programming with newspaper and magazine coverage and to the difficulty of attributing to any one
medium the power of influencing audience response. Further, Michel's
study is rich in its discussion of specific kinds of radio programming
developed by the psychological professions in the thirties and forties.

Index

245